The logic of writing and the organization of society

JACK GOODY

 CAMBRIDGE
UNIVERSITY PRESS

Published by the Press Syndicate of the University of Cambridge
The Pitt Building, Trumpington Street, Cambridge CB2 1RP
40 West 20th Street, New York, NY 10011–4211, USA
10 Stamford Road, Oakleigh, Victoria 3166, Australia

First published 1986
Reprinted 1988, 1989, 1992, 1996

Printed in Great Britain at the Athenaeum Press Ltd, Newcastle upon Tyne

British Library cataloguing in publication data
Goody. Jack
The logic of writing and the organization
of society. – (Studies in Literacy,
Family, Culture and the State)
1. Social structure 2. Written communication
3. Communication – Social aspects
I. Title II. Series
306   GN479

Library of Congress cataloguing in publication data
Goody. Jack.
The logic of writing and the organization of society.
(Studies in Literacy, Family, Culture, and the State)
Bibliography.
Includes index.
1. Writing – History. 2. Writing – Social aspects.
3. Social evolution. 4. Civilization, Ancient.
5. Africa, West – Civilization. I. Title. II. Series.
Z40.G66 1986   303.4   86–9717

ISBN 0 521 32745 8 hard covers
ISBN 0 521 33962 6 paperback

Transferred to digital reprinting 2001
Printed in the United States of America

Contents

Studies in Literacy, Family, Culture and the State: an introduction

The books in this series are the result of a journey that began in Western and Mediterranean Europe, then took a more academic turn to West Africa and to western India. Vicariously it reached backward in time and outward in space, buoyed up by a conviction in the unity of the social sciences, the value of which lay not so much in a generalized theory and a set of abstract, high-level concepts but in providing an incentive to tackle intellectual problems of the human situation, past and present, without being constrained to one field and one method.

The different fields that we call anthropology, sociology and history, are all aspects of the wider enquiry into human interaction that in more specialist contexts gets broken down into economics, politics, demography and religious studies. Each major field concentrates upon a certain set of societies ('simple' or 'complex', present or past, particular or general) and utilizes different methods and sources of information (fieldwork observations or written documents, deductive or inductive procedures). But substantive problems are best dealt with not by utilizing one method or confining the discourse to one field, but by trying to pierce the heavy curtains of instituted and institutionalized boundaries and by drawing upon as wide a range of resources as are available.

There are three threads running through the various studies. One is methodological. Among the reasons I originally undertook fieldwork in West Africa was the wish to lay out more clearly for myself some features of western society, for example, in the contrast between the written and the oral. Once there, I became deeply involved, personally and academically, in West Africa and have remained so ever since. Having carried out field research, I wanted to try to assess the conclusions more widely by looking at similar situations in other parts of the world, sometimes by way of informal comparison but also on a more systematic level (for instance, in *Production and Reproduction*, 1977, and in various demographic papers). For 'crucial experiments' through intensive fieldwork, and even the critical comparisons of neighbouring or regional peoples advocated by many anthropologists, are not in themselves always adequate, although I have made use of all these procedures at different times and for different ends. The result of this methodological quest was obviously to lead from ethnography back to earlier interests in comparative sociology (or social anthropology) and comparative history. Indeed if one is concerned with problems and topics rather than boundary-maintaining fields of study, such an interlocking of interests is essential, even if the results fall well short of a 'unified social science'.

The second thread has to do with the content of these studies. While there are many detailed differences in human societies that require very specific explanations (and I have attempted to look at some of these in two neighbouring communities in West Africa in my book *Death, Property and Ancestors*, Stanford, 1962), there are other more widespread features (similarities as well as differences) that call for some more general hypotheses. On one level these features relate to the assumptions that people make about the differences between, and the similarities within, oral and literate, simple and advanced, cold and hot societies. On another level they have to do with the ways people win a livelihood. The first set of problems were central to my study of the implications of changes in the means and modes of communication (*The Domestication of the Savage Mind*, 1977, and the present volume), the second to the analysis of aspects of domestic and political life in the context of changes in the means and modes of production and of destruction (*Technology, Tradition and the State in Africa*, 1971, *Production and Reproduction*, 1977).

The hypotheses suggested inevitably need refining and further testing. Any empirical situation involves a variety of factors other than those I have considered. But to understand the general flow of human history one has to start with some theoretical perspective and from some specific point of departure. In looking at family and marriage in West Africa, I first studied particular differences and similarities between two small ethnic sub-groups of the LoDagaa, then turned to look at some regional differences (*Comparative Studies in Kinship*, Kegan Paul and Stanford University Press, 1969), finally at certain general features of difference between Africa and the major societies of Eurasia (e.g. *Bridewealth and Dowry*, with S. J. Tambiah, 1973). Struck by certain inconsistencies between my model and early European systems of marriage and the family (the story of the last two hundred years raises other questions), I was led to examine the historical role of the Christian church in promoting and to some extent establishing new norms of domestic life (*The Development of Marriage and the Family in Europe*, 1983). That study in turn raised other questions, firstly about transformations over the last two hundred years, usually approached from the standpoint of the present (and always from that of Western Europe) but which need to be looked at comparatively and from the past, secondly about the possible implications of other temple cultures for marriage and the family as well as the role of charity more generally. But these are other problems for other enquiries and enquirers, which will benefit from improved data, concepts and methods in comparative social research, combining intensive observation, extensive surveys and documentary study.

Cambridge   JACK GOODY
February 1986

Preface

This book attempts to spell out some of the general differences between the social organization of societies without and with writing and the process of transition from one to the other. It is a ludicrously wide topic, but one that calls for some preliminary treatment as well as a few opening comments. Of necessity I have confined my attention largely to two such situations, one with writing, one mainly without: the Ancient Near East, that is, where writing emerged, and contemporary West Africa, where its uses have proliferated over the last fifty years. Different systems of writing have, of course, different implications in different societies at different times. But there are also important features that a number of these particular contexts have in common and it is to these I have wanted to draw attention.

I am not concerned simply with differences for difference sake. In the first place I am trying to provide a more satisfactory explanation, for myself and for the reader, of certain widely used concepts, sociological and anthropological, historical and common-sense, that have been used to describe the major differences or transitions in the history of human societies. This attempt leads me to shift part of the emphasis put on the means and modes of production in explaining human history to the means and modes of communication. At the same time, I find it necessary to challenge certain notions about the uniqueness of the West as far as the explanation for the emergence of the 'modern' world is concerned, since I see some of the pre-conditions more widely distributed than many current theories allow. But these aims, especially the last, do not always hold the centre of the stage, since I am dealing with aspects of an 'earlier' adoption of writing rather than with later developments in literacy.

The present form of this study came about largely as the result of my having been invited to give four lectures at the University of Chicago in October, 1984, to honour L. A. Fallers and his work. Significantly, his research spanned not only the 'simple' East African state of the Busoga as it adjusted to colonial rule, but the much more complex Turkish nation, the Islamic heirs of Asiatic nomads as well as of the plant, trade, population, government, and to some extent the traditions of the Byzantine empire centred on Constantinople. This shift of research from Africa to the Middle East did not come about by asking that only too frequently heard anthropological question 'Where shall I go next?', but by posing the same query with an intellectual rather than a territorial reference. Fallers' interests in the writings of Max Weber as well as the contemporary setting in which he worked – the emergence of the new nations of Africa – and his own reactions to these events pushed him towards a comparison of the nature of and the transition between simple and complex state formations. He moved towards an enquiry into the features and factors behind this dynamic contrast, a contrast that is certainly neither binary nor linear but represents a process with significant breaking points which one must be able to specify if any plausible reasons are to be teased out for social change, for the decline as well as the rise of states, empires and nations.

It was because I knew him to be concerned with such problems, and I use the verb with Quakerish implications, that when I was at the Center for Advanced Studies in Stanford in 1960 and he was preparing to participate in that significant collective move with Geertz and Schneider from Berkeley to Chicago, I sent him, for comment, an article, written by Ian Watt and myself, brashly entitled 'The consequences of literacy'. His reply was encouraging. At that time we had been working together on plans to publish a new *Journal of Social Anthropology* (see Stocking 1979), but since this proposal was very much in the air he suggested the piece should be sent to that important and already established journal, *Comparative Studies in History and Society*.

I followed up aspects of this article in a number of subsequent publications. An edited work, *Literacy in Traditional Societies* (1968), collected articles on the ethnography of writing from a number of societies from different parts of the world. A volume called *The Domestication of the Savage Mind* (1977) considered some of the implications of the graphic representation of language for cognitive processes, especially the partially decontextualized use of language in formal contexts, the list, the table (that is, paired lists forming rows as well as columns), the matrix (a more complex table), together with the development of more precise notions of contradiction, of forms of 'logic' (in the specialized sense), including the syllogism and of other types of argument and of proof (Goody 1977, Yoffee 1979).

The second aim of my enquiry into the implications of writing has been to consider the interface between the oral and the written, not only for cultures but for registers and performance within written cultures. This interface I have discussed in a number of recent essays, mainly on 'literacy' or 'art' forms, which I am presently trying to put together into a book (though it will always be depressingly incomplete).

The third aim, forming the present study, has to do with the long-term effects of writing on the organization of society. Let me try to clarify this goal. One part of the enterprise is to take certain features that sociologists and others have seen as important in the analysis of social institutions – for example, the particularistic–universalistic dichotomy or polarity used by Talcott Parsons as one of his pattern-variables (and derived essentially from Max Weber) – in order to see how far we can explain differences in their incidence in terms of developments in human communication. It is the same with discussions of legal systems. In all of this my own interests are close to those of Fallers, who was not worried about crossing the boundaries between anthropology and sociology, between synchrony and diachrony, between European and other cultures, because he was more concerned with proposing solutions to intellectual problems than with disciplinary or geographical boundaries.

Much of the material I use on the differences and transition between societies without, and societies with, writing comes from work, my own and that of others, on West Africa. The rest comes from the earliest literate cultures of the Ancient Near East; despite the thinness of my knowledge these are of obvious importance because we are dealing with the first developments in the uses of writing, with the beginning of a written tradition that, in a broad sense, fed into Greece and Europe. And in dealing with law I have discussed briefly the development of the use of writing in Europe during the Middle Ages as another transitional period.

The problems involved in any such effort are many and open to misunderstanding, more especially as the irony of the title of the 'domestication' study has not always been appreciated. For present purposes I examine these problems under the three headings of causal implications, categories and evidence.

My anthropological colleagues are used to analyzing a particular context, one they have either observed in the field, heard about from others ('informants' as they are sometimes barbarously called), or read about in books and documents. The analysis involves an unravelling of the threads that make up this human situation, and seeing how the various factors interact in the particular socio-cultural setting. My historical and archaeological colleagues are more used to tracing situations over time and establishing, among other things, chronological sequences of development, some of which, like the transition from hunting and gathering to farming, tend to repeat themselves under a variety of conditions. A third form of enquiry consists in taking a particular thread (or even a topic) and following its changing path through time and space. This is what I have tried to do and it is a form of enquiry with a respectable lineage. One might mention here, in the field of communication, Eisenstein's work on the implications of printing (1979) or Turkle's on the effect of computers on the 'human spirit' (1984), or, in the field of agriculture, White's work on the plough (1940) and on medieval technology more generally (1962).

These are broad types of enquiry loosely linked to particular academic disciplines. They do not exhaust the range of possibilities, which would include enquiries like that of Thomas (1978; 1983) on aspects of the changing consciousness at the time of the Renaissance, or like the admirable socio-historical account of medieval life in Homans' *English Villagers of the Thirteenth Century* (1942). But for the present the tripartite categorization will do.

At various times I have attempted all three forms of enquiry.

Each has its costs and gains. One obvious cost of enquiring into the possible implications of the plough is that some readers will regard the approach as one of single-factor determinism. On the other hand an enquiry into the total factorial or causal network in a field situation makes it difficult for the author to avoid being seen as a convinced proponent of a structural or functional approach. A historical study is often viewed as part of a wider perspective of evolutionary development, sometimes even characterized as unilineal. But tempting as these characterizations are, they need to be avoided.

In taking writing and the written tradition as my topic, for example, I do not imply for one moment that these are the only factors involves in any specific situation, only that they are significant ones. In these enquiries one would like to be able to assess the relevance of different elements and to produce a path-diagram that weighted, in some more or less precise way, the factors involved. Unless of course one is content to leave the analysis at the functional level of showing that everything influences everything else, or at the structural level of indicating abstract homologies or underlying principles. But that more exacting mode of assessing the contributing factors, so widely used in economics because of the numerical nature of much of the data, is hardly possible, at least at present and possibly in prospect, for many of the situations with which the softer social sciences are dealing. As a consequence, choosing a topic to investigate means not only that one runs the danger of inflating its importance but, worse, of being seen as believing that human affairs are determined by a single factor. Some writers even appear to assume that what is meant by 'causal relations' are those determined in just this way – that is, situations that have one cause, everywhere, all the time.

I do not accept such a view of socio-cultural analysis, nor the oppositional nature of social theory and practice that it embodies. To some extent, however, misunderstandings arise from the different kinds of enquiry to which we have called attention. The point is clearly put by Cole and Keyssar in a recent paper:

There is also agreement that the general causal impact of literate knowledge is not unidirectional from technology to activity. Activities provide greater and lesser opportunities for particular literate technologies to be effective. As recorded in Goody (1977), or Schmandt-Besserat (1978), the interplay of socio-economic and literate/technological forces represents a classical case of dialectical interacting systems that are always incipiently in a process of change. (1982: 4)

That some readers should interpret the argument as unidirectional while others recognize the two-way, multi-factored influences may be due to the difficulties of written as distinct from oral communication, rather than to a failure to understand. But there is also the question of a willingness to suspend not one's disbelief but one's 'beliefs', one's ideological commitments, one's predetermined categories of the understanding. It is to try and avoid some of these misunderstandings that I have chosen for the title a form of words suggested to me by Marshall Sahlins, 'The logic of writing . . . '.

That was not the only positive result of my visit to Chicago. R. T. Smith was an excellent host and I had useful comments from B. Cohen, T. Turner, E. Shils and others as well. Earlier I had reason to be grateful to J. Flanagan for reading various chapters. Carolyn Wyndham and Antonia Lovelace did the word-processing and helped with references. John Baines and Keith Hart have been of very great help with the manuscript as a whole while John Dunn and A. L. Epstein have read particular chapters. I have to thank the University of Cambridge for giving me the early retirement needed to finish the manuscript and St John's College for providing a room and the proper atmosphere in which to continue working. In the Spring of 1985 I gave the lectures in altered form at Le Collège de France (thanks to an invitation initiated by Françoise Héritier-Augé) where the warm social and intellectual climate of a Parisian spring stimulated me to return to the task of revision; the effort of preparing the course for a different audience helped me reformulate parts of the argument, as did working with my translators Anne-Marie Roussel and Anne de Sales. I am also most grateful to Patricia Williams, to Anne Nesteroff of Armand Colin, and to Michael Black of Cambridge University Press.

I have a final caveat. Although I have divided the topics of the chapters along the lines of the frequently accepted sub-systems of society – that is, religion, economy, politics and law – a number of the themes and features crop up under each of these headings, which are in any case overlapping. This duplication is inevitable as

I am trying to pull out a number of general factors rather than go into a detailed examination of particular situations, partly because in some cases this latter has been undertaken in other writings. Anthropologists will no doubt be irritated by this lack of field data in my presentation, historians by the absence of specific accounts, sociologists by the paucity of references to published social theory. They will all, from the standpoint of their particular domains, be justified in their comments. Worse still I have omitted a treatment of a number of topics such as ritual action, kinship and education, my excuse being that I have tried or am presently trying to deal with these topics in other contexts.

But enough of this preface; let us get down to the arguments themselves. I begin in the first chapter by dealing with the influence of writing on religion because this raises most of the major issues at stake. I first consider how far the presence of writing has affected the notion and the study of religious phenomena. Here, as I think with law, the written book leads us to different ideas of what religion is, ideas that also relate to substantial matters of form and content. Form, because of the fixing of a boundary to 'belief' as well as to practice, which brings out questions to do with the nature of belief, truth and of conversion. Content, because of the tendency of writing to over-generalize norms. In both ways religion acquires an increased measure of autonomy in relation to other aspects of the social system. But the emergence of religion as one of the 'great organizations' (not simply as a partially differentiated aspect of, say, intra-familial interaction) implies autonomy at another level: the autonomy of the church as an organization. It is the partial autonomy of these organizations that requires us to qualify Durkheim's attempt, in *The Elementary Forms of the Religious Life*, to use the term 'church' in an all-encompassing way (as other anthropologists have done with law), as well as to modify those social theories, of many different inspirations, that assume religion, even in its ecclesiastical form, to reflect the dominant themes of the rest of the socio-cultural system in any tight structural or functional way. The 'great organizations' with their literate tradition acquire a certain independence of their own, promoted by their custodianship of the books as well as their interest in earthly continuity and other-worldly salvation.

1

The word of God

In the beginning, we are taught, was the word. And it was, of course, the word of God, God who created the world, or the word of his prophets, then of his son who saved the world. That word was not only spoken but was written down in a book, the Holy Book, the Bible, the Testament. What difference does it make when the word, as in Judaism, Islam and Christianity, is written in a book (or an array of books) rather than being just the word of mouth, the product of the spoken tongue? Are there any general ways in which oral and literate cultures tend to differ in their religious beliefs and practices? How do systems of worship depend upon specific modes of communication? And, over time, how far do traditions of intellectual activity depend upon the earlier presence of a religion of the Book?

These are questions of a highly general kind but they are ones that are touched upon by many scholars, thought about by some, pushed aside by others and about which various assumptions are tacitly made. I want to try and give voice to these largely silent thoughts, taking as my starting point a broad contrast between certain features of African and Eurasian religions, including in the latter not only the religions of the Middle East focussing on a single book but also those that significantly depend upon writing, especially alphabetic writing, for the transmission of myth, doctrine and ritual. However, these forms taken by the Eastern religions are often more eclectic than the Mediterranean ones, modifying the tendency to an exclusive commitment of the congregation if not always of the priests. While the question of this and other differences is an important one, I am here dealing with general trends.

Let me begin by saying that at the most general level there is much in common between the two; that is, in Africa the Eurasian observer would easily identify an area of belief and practice that he would designate as religious, ceremonial or ritual, irrespective of the question of his acceptance of those beliefs. For example, he would pick out the rituals centred upon the human and the cosmic cycles. The first comprises the rites of birth, marriage and death (as well as those marking various intermediary phases, pregnancy, initiation, divorce, retirement, etc.); the second includes the rituals of the annual cycle, which in most agricultural societies are celebrated at the beginning and end of the productive season. Then there are the occasional performances, often held when misfortune strikes, in the form of sickness or death, drought or floods, events whose very irregularity requires the act of divination to elicit the agencies or forces involved, whether human or not.

In studying those rites that mark phases in the human cycle, we are by definition concerned with the entry and exit of males and females into this world and the next. The mysteries of birth and death are central to religious experience. For it remains true, at least until recent, secularised times, that all human societies have some concept of the other world and of the movement of the soul (and sometimes the body) between the two. Consequently all religions are dealing with the two worlds and their inhabitants, largely humans in the one case and 'superhuman agencies', even forces, in the other, with some kind of High God being in most instances the creator of this world although inhabiting the other. Questions of life and death, the conduct of gods and men – these are the domain of religions everywhere.

While much is held in common, the very general differences between the religions of Africa and Eurasia are worth exploring in the light of their association with oral and literate cultures. This is not only a matter of synchronic contrast. The fact that the word is written in one case and not in the other is important, diachronically, to help account for the characteristic diffusing of the so-called world religions (which in Africa's case are Islam, Christianity and Judaism) by conversion and by absorption, a diffusion that was accompanied by the gradual decline, or should one say incorporation or adjustment, of the local religions.

In the West we inevitably take as models, in courses on comparative religion for example, those that have written texts on myth, doctrine and ritual. These are the world religions, sometimes called the ethical religions. I shall suggest that there is an intrinsic connection between the features of these religions which these epithets imply and the literate mode itself, the means by which religious beliefs and behaviour are formulated, communicated and transmitted, at least in part. But first to Africa.

In that continent the only religions of the book were those from the Middle East and the important areas of their distribution were north of the Sahara. Historically Egypt provides us with one of the first written religions, a priestly temple cult in which the teaching and even use of writing came to be largely concentrated in priestly hands; as in Mesopotamia writing was critical both to religion and to the priesthood. Geographically that religion was mainly confined within the political boundaries, and it may be significant that it was only with alphabetic writing that some religions decisively broke through their national frontiers to become religions of conversion. In Africa parts of Ethiopia, like adjacent Yemen and Arabia, were influenced by Judaism at an early stage, and later by Christianity and Islam. The Carthaginians brought from Phoenicia a set of Semitic cults and beliefs which subsequently gave way to Jewish practices along the Mediterranean littoral; indeed it has been suggested that an important element of the Jewish diaspora into Europe consisted of converted Phoenicians from North Africa.[1] Later the same area also became the home of the Donatist Church and for a brief period Christianity extended throughout the whole of North Africa from the Maghreb to Ethiopia, embracing the Copts of Egypt and the Christian kingdoms of the Sudan. Finally it was precisely this area of Christendom that later became dominated by an expanding Islam (leaving behind small pockets of Jews and Christians) which spread across the Sahara both in the west and in the east, as well as right down the East African coast as far as Madagascar. Aside from those in Ancient Egypt, these religions were associated with alphabetic writing, which was more widely distributed within and more easily adopted without; they were therefore more likely to be 'world' than 'national' religions. Indeed one could say that these alphabetic religions spread literacy and equally that literacy spread these religions. And it was the spread not only of a particular religion but of 'the idea of a religion'.

The concept of 'a'/'the' religion

Let me first explain what I do not mean by this remark. I don't mean the idea of religion. As we have seen, one doesn't have to be much of a comparativist to recognise aspects of practice and belief in all societies that centre around notions of life and death, of the other world, of spiritual beings and of divination, propitiation and sequences of rites. But in African languages I find no equivalent for the western word 'religion' (or indeed 'ritual'), and more import-antly the actors do not appear to look upon religious beliefs and practices in the same way that we, whether Muslim, Jew, Hindu, Buddhist, Christian or atheist, do – that is, as a distinct set. This dif-ference is suggested in the way we define an African religion, not only by its characteristics as a sect or church (*pace* Durkheim, who applied the term even to the simplest societies) but as Kikuyu religion or Asante religion. In other words we define a religion in terms of the practices and beliefs of a particular group of terri-torially bounded individuals – a tribe or a kingdom. Indeed one can argue that it was not until the competition from Islam or Christianity that the idea of an Asante religion, as distinct from the more inclusive concept of an Asante way of life, began to take shape, first in the mind of the observer and then in that of the actor. This sugges-tion is given some support by the fact that when an attempt was made to define such religious systems in a comprehensive way, leaving on one side the 'ethnic' designations, European scholars then turned to labels such as paganism, animism, heathenism, that describe religions in terms of an opposition to the hegemonic written forms.

Boundaries

The reason for this state of affairs is fairly obvious. Literate religions have some kind of autonomous boundary. Practitioners are com-mitted to one alone and may be defined by their attachment to a

Holy Book, their recognition of a Credo, as well as by their practice of certain rituals, prayers, modes of propitiation. I do not claim that it is always easy to tell who is a Muslim, a Jew, a Christian, a Buddhist, a Hindu; the boundary is often far from clear. But there exists some concept equivalent to that of the *Dharmashastra*, the way. Hence some are in and others are out – and not purely on a spatial or territorial basis, though propinquity is often an important factor. Contrast the situation in societies without writing. You cannot practice Asante religion unless you are an Asante; and what is Asante religion now may be very different from Asante religion one hundred years ago. Literate religions on the other hand, at least alphabetically literate ones, are generally religions of conversion, not simply religions of birth. You can spread them, like jam. And you can persuade or force people to give up one set of beliefs and practices and take up another set, which is called by the name of a particular sect or church. In fact the written word, the use of a new method of communication, may itself sometimes provide its own incentive for conversion, irrespective of the specific content of the Book; for those religions are not only seen as 'higher' because their priests are literate and can read as well as hear God's word, but they may provide their congregation with the possibility of becoming literate themselves. What I am claiming here, in effect, is that only literate religions can be religions of conversion in the strict sense, as distinct from the shift to a new Cargo Cult, medicine shrine or anti-witchcraft movement.

Despite this difference, local beliefs and practices tend to be visualised, both by actors and observers, as in some sense alternatives to 'boundary-maintaining' systems of religion such as Islam or Christianity. At the district court of Lawra in northern Ghana in the nineteen fifties all those appearing before the colonial Commissioner were offered the alternative of swearing to the truth of their statements on the Bible, the Qur'ān or on a local shrine, designated 'fetish' by one and all. Thus in the courtroom, a local, LoDagaa cult was placed on an equivocal par with the world religions and inevitably suffered by contrast if only because its oaths employed sticks or stones – an idol instead of an icon or the written word. In this context, at least, the written word of God was seen, again by one and all, as being more effective than the purely oral one, or even than the visual shrine or the envisioned idea, because of the evident performative force of that channel of communication and the hierarchical status of its practitioners.

Change

Although I argue that in oral cultures conversion, in the usual sense of the word, is impossible, I do not mean that changes in the religious system, as distinct from changes in religious adherence, do not occur: quite the opposite. The label 'Asante religion' may conceal considerable shifts from one decade to the next, even though this ethnic way of labelling, of talking about things, appears to assume a continuity, a homeostasis, an assumption that also underlies many scholarly discussions of non-literate religions. But my point runs counter to any such assumption about the static nature of the religious systems of the simpler, non-literate societies as contrasted with those of the dynamic, changing, modern world. The contrast may well hold true for technology, for economics and for other related spheres of social action. But for religion it must be challenged. In the first place, the world religions of which I have spoken all have their Holy Book or Scriptures – the Torah, the Bible and the Qur'ān. Such works are sacred repositories of the word of God, which in themselves remain unchanging, eternal, inspired by the divine and not by man alone. While the liturgy of the Catholic Church may change over time, and while the techniques of prayer may differ as between the Qadariyya and the Tijaniyya in Maghrebian Islam, between Orthodox and Reformed synagogues, or between Calvinist and Lutheran churches, while interpretations vary, the word itself remains as it always was. (Though every reading is different, it is a misleading exaggeration of the literary critic to say that the text exists only in communication.) And it has been the prime duty of copyists, of Islamic calligraphers, of printers to the King or Queen (such as Cambridge University Press) to preserve the text in precisely the same canonical form by producing 'authorized' versions. A single misprint (and it happened) of Judas for Jesus gives rise to a scandal. It is true that Eastern religions do not focus upon one major sacred book in the same way, but they do possess a body of scriptures that are handed down in a precise form and are hence 'canonised'. Not long ago (1977) in an Indian village I heard my Brahmin neighbour reciting each day his daily prayers, in Sanskrit, from the Rgveda, reputedly composed more than 3000 years ago. In Indonesia I attended a public reading and exegesis of an ancient Buddhist text; the exact words were preserved, translated into low Balinese by the puppeteer and at the same time given a broader interpretation. One can find the same Sanskrit mantras recited or read as far away as China, Tibet and Japan, in different contexts it is true but using the same texts over an enormous area of time and space. Writing is surely critical in the fact that Hinduism (even taking into account the variety of local cults and local manifestations) exists in recognizably similar forms throughout the subcontinent, whereas in Africa or New Guinea local variance in religious belief and ritual action is enormous.

It is usually the rituals, myths, beliefs and practices of the simpler societies that we consider (and certainly treat) as static, as persisting unchanged over the generations, handed down in a fixed (at least underlying) form from one to another. The evidence for this assumption has never been presented in an adequate way, if only because unwritten cultures leave little trace of the oral past. But the advent of the tape-recorder fixes the flow of speech, the words of a recitation, on magnetic tape, and the results tend to show the inventiveness of African cultures in religious matters, including ritual and myth. Indeed the great variation in neighbouring groups itself compels us towards such a conclusion. Those who have dealt with what has been called the cultic aspects of religions are satisfied that the evidence on the migration of 'medicine shrines' between ethnic groups and political units shows that this adoption and adaptation of beliefs and practices is not a new phenomenon. In West Africa the Asantehene (the paramount chief) monitored such imports from outside, motivated by political considerations rather than by any attachment to religious orthodoxy; others have sought, successfully, to profit by them. Some uniformity is undoubtedly established, some variation held in check, by a centralized political system. But shrines did circulate in pre-colonial times and however they arrived, brought in new ideas, new prohibitions, new taboos, and were never simply 'more of the same'. By so doing they often modified in significant ways the classificatory systems of the community into which they penetrated by introducing new evaluations of experience, sometimes having far-reaching effects on the political, moral and cosmological order. Such was the case with the migration of the Kungkpenbie shrine of Birifu to the outskirts of Kumasi, and with the advent of Little God to the LoDagaa (Goody 1975). In the first instance the mud sculptures of Birifu became widely diffused throughout Asante; and in 1950, when I was first in the area, a Kumasi brass band made its appearance at the funeral of Chief Gandaa, who was the custodian of the parent shrine. This penetration of material culture from one society to another is indicative of other cultural transfers, and while the rhythm of the movement of shrines undoubtedly increased with the establishment of the colonial regime, such mobility was certainly present in earlier times. The Little God movement represented a rather different shift of perspective, being in part a synthesizing cult. But the potential for such a synthesis has been present at least since the advent of Islam, and even before that contradictions in the notion of a Creator God (here yesterday, gone today) made his reappearance at the human level, albeit temporary, an ever-present possibility.

Obsolescence

I have argued elsewhere (Goody 1957) that in certain areas of religious activity, those connected with affliction and fertility, with specific, concrete, human ends, there is a partial contradiction between what is offered and what is received, what is given and what is taken. There are times when the cult fails to deliver the cargo, to provide the hoped-for relief, so that the individuals or groups concerned are led to seek other means of satisfaction. Hence African systems of belief are open-ended in a meaningful way, encouraging the search, the quest, the journey after, yes, the truth (if I can translate in this way the LoDagaa concept of *yilmiong*, the proper way, the proper speech). You may regard this statement as indicating an overly pragmatic view of religious activity; but I am not trying to account for the whole of its scope, only to explore the reasons why African religions are more 'flexible' than many theories would allow, subject to change and absorption rather than to rejection and conversion.

The same seems to me to be true of myth, those formal recitations partially abstracted from the flow of ritual action. And here I have to extend the pragmatic explanation offered above and argue for an intellectual search (though the dichotomy is less compelling than the words suggest). Let me turn to the data I present in support of my contention that myth is more flexible than many theories allow. A number of years ago I recorded the long Bagre recitation among the LoDagaa of northern Ghana (Goody 1972). At that time I thought I had a standardized oral form that was deliberately taught and varied little over time and space. Since 1950 the use of the portable, battery-operated tape-recorder enabled us to capture many other versions over the years, some from the same settlement and others from neighbouring ones. The differences are many and profound, especially in the more speculative, 'mythical', Black Bagre. But variations occur at a number of other levels. Individuals will even correct versions of the formal, opening invocation of some twenty lines as if it were fixed, yet that short, repeated section turns out to have almost as many variants as speakers, a stark contrast to the fixity of the Lord's Prayer or the College Grace, both embodied in a written text and read or learnt 'by heart'.

Flexibility, then, is a characteristic of African religious beliefs and practices, rendering them open to internal change as well as to external imports. That is the history of Asante and its cults, many of them coming from the north. For truth involved a search, not only inside by means of divination but outside too. To find the real truth about the British intentions at the time of their invasion in 1874, the Asante court sent representatives to the Dente shrine of Kete Krachi, well outside their effective dominion. They also enquired in the Gonja town of Salaga about getting the advice of learned Muslims from Kano in Hausaland whose knowledge was seen to derive from the study of the Holy Book. The search meant taking independent advice outside the political unit, thereby drawing within itself the work of religious practitioners from other countries, from other regions.

In the literate churches, the dogma and services are rigid (that is, dogmatic, ritualistic, orthodox) by comparison; the creed is recited word for word, the Tables of the Lord learnt by heart, the ritual repeated in a verbatim fashion. If change takes place, it often takes the form of a break-away movement (the verb 'break away' is used for sects that separate from the mother church); the process is deliberately reformist, even revolutionary, rather than the process of incorporation that tends to mark the oral situation.

Incorporation or conversion

When you have boundaries, markers of the kind involved in religions of the Book, then you get not only break-away sects but break-away individuals, individuals who are apostates or converts. Conversion is a function of the boundaries the written word creates, or rather defines.

I take as an example the advent of the White Fathers to the north-west of the Northern Territories of the Gold Coast (now Ghana) in the early 1930s. Care of the sick, combined with prayers for the crops that were fortunately quickly deluged by rain, both benefits being among those conferred by local deities and their shrines, led first to a minority, then to mass adherence to the Catholic Church. Such rapid attachment to a successful new shrine was well within the scope of local practice, and new shrines as we have seen often brought new taboos. But in the present case the results were more dramatic and at the same time unanticipated. For in the longer term the acceptance of Christian beliefs and practices meant, not simply a supplement bringing limited modifications to the existing religious system, but the rejection of all else. It meant conversion, the cross-ing of a boundary, the exchange of one total set for another of a different, literate type. Eclecticism was no longer the order of the day. Orthodoxy took over. Truth took on a different meaning for there was a new measuring stick, the written word.

Universalism and particularism

Let me now turn to examine some related features of the moral system. The written religions are often known as world religions in contrast to local ones; in his book *Primitive Culture* (1871) Tylor referred to them as ethical in contrast to non-ethical cults. The two features are inter-related because literate religions tend to be associated with more than one place, more than one time, more than one people. This means that their prescriptions for behaviour are inevitably placed in a wider framework than one is likely to find with a purely local cult. In other words they are marked by the feature that Weber and later Parsons spoke of as universalism, which is contrasted with the particularism of local religions.

In his introduction (1947) to the translation of Part I of *Wirtschaft und Gesellschaft* ('Economic and Social Organization'), Parsons referred to Weber's idea of a process of rationalization outside the economic sphere, rationality being concerned with reasoning and calculation but being also "a receptive attitude towards new solutions of problems by contrast to traditionalism" (1947: 28). This process is characterized, among other things, by the devotion to a task for its own sake without ulterior motives (that is by the notion of 'a calling'), a readiness to fit into functionally specialized roles and by the willingness to be governed by 'universalistic standards' (1947: 28). This universalism is related in turn to the presence of a rational–legal state as well as of a universalistic legal system, an argument developed in his work on political sociology. But the idea is also very evident in his sociology of religion where he analyses the special orientation of Western society, an attitude he sees as distinctive of 'ascetic Protestantism' and as having five main components (Parsons 1947: 71–2). First, there is the transcendental orientation. Secondly, this orientation is directed towards the Kingdom of God on Earth; it is this-worldly. Thirdly, it is 'rational'. Fourthly, it is marked by ethical universalism, that is, "the insistence on treatment of all men by the same generalized, impersonal standards" (1947: 72). Parsons noted that while this notion is common to all branches of Christianity, it has a special importance in connection with the 'active ascetic attitude' of Protestantism. And fifthly, it encourages role specialization.

Whether or not we look upon the suggested relation between the rise of capitalism and the growth of 'ascetic Protestantism' as a matter of a unique empirical association or of 'elective affinity', the features that we are dealing with seem much more widely distributed in the religions of the book and in literate societies more generally than is here suggested. The overall point has been strongly argued for Islam, for Buddhism, as well as for Hinduism, a fact that must lead us to challenge Weber's stimulating thesis. In this context

I would like to suggest that one component of universalism, especially of ethical universalism, is characteristic not only of Christianity but of all the major world religions and is directly related to their use of writing. For literate religions influence the normative structure of a social system towards universalism in two outstanding ways. First, in so far as the religion comes from the 'outside' in some sense, by the process of conversion and expansion, its norms are necessarily applied to more than one group or society. Secondly, written formulations encourage the decontextualization or generalization of norms. The second of these processes works in the following way. In written codes there is a tendency to present a single 'abstract' formula which overlays, and to some extent replaces, the more contextualized norms of oral societies. I mean by contextualized that in simpler societies norms against violence, for example, tend to be related to particular conditions, such as segmentary structures. In those societies without central government the response to a killing varies according to the social distance of the parties involved so that, as Evans-Pritchard convincingly showed (1940), a limited reaction takes place between members of proximal segments, while more aggressive measures are employed against more distant groups or individuals. Killing within the 'tent' may be dealt with by exile, by leaving the punishment in God's hands, by taking no violent action, while killing between clans may lead to a continuing feud, where an individual's obligation (the responsibility of 'the redeemer') is to avenge the blood of his brother or sister (Daube 1947; Black-Michaud 1975). This is true of acephalous societies which privilege segmentary processes. State systems inevitably tend to apply state-wide norms, at least in critical spheres such as the control of force. If religion is linked at any level to the polity, then a centralized government will tend to have a similar effect on some elements of worship, as we see in Asante. But written codes carry this process of generalization, of consolidation, a stage further. First, when the codes (more especially the alphabetic ones since they are more easily adopted) are associated with religion, they often extend outside the bounds of any particular state to embrace the whole community of the faithful. Secondly, in their very nature written statements of the law, of norms, of rules, have had to be abstracted from particular situations in order to be addressed to a universal audience out there, rather than delivered face-to-face to a specific group of people at a particular time and place. The communicative context has changed dramatically both as regards the emitter and as regards the receivers, with consequent implications for the nature of the message. In written communication a universal injunction 'thou shalt not kill' tends to replace the more particular phraseology of 'thou shalt not kill other Jews', or, perhaps, 'thou shalt not kill except under the orders of leader, party or of nation'.

Cognitive contradictions in the general and the specific

Both these polar types of normative structure, the segmentary (or particularistic) and the universalistic, give rise to contradictions at the cognitive level. Let me begin by elucidating the first of these. In attempting to 'explain' homicide rituals in non-literate, non-centralized, societies, I have pointed out how even justified killings (that is, honourable slayings, those carried out in defence of the family or of the village) have a negative side; for they run up against widespread humanitarian feelings, that is, feelings of humanity, about the shedding of blood and the taking of human life (Goody 1962: 115–21). The destruction or expenditure of resources in the environment, whether human, animal, plant or mineral, is qualified not only by the particular demands of husbandry but by the more general desire to preserve what God or Chance has provided. It is easy to see how husbandry works to emphasize conservation as well as growth. With cereals in particular, a portion of the crop has to be set aside as seed corn for the following year; the killing of the corn spirit – the scything of the stalks, the binding of the sheaves, the flaying of the ears – must be accompanied by its resurrection, a theme which Frazer so dramatically traced from Classical sources in the Osiris myth of Ancient Egypt as well as in other Near Eastern religions. With domestic animals, a limited and selective culling is even more essential if the people are to be fed and the flock is to be maintained, much less increased. It might be argued that the widespread existence of 'sacrifice' as a formal method of slaughtering livestock to the gods is linked to the ambivalence, psychological as well as social, involved in the dual process of first raising and then butchering animals for human consumption; that is, in the process of having to tend and cherish what one subsequently does to death and cooks. Is the problem mitigated by handing the living animal over to the gods, or by getting the servants of the gods to wield the knife and kill in their name? For in this way the hand that tends the lamb is not the one that sheds its blood, while the 'true' recipients, the perceived recipients, are gods not men. With written religions, this type of sacrifice tends to disappear in the long run, offerings to the gods taking different forms, partly through a process of 'rationalization', of querying contradictions, by literate specialists, partly because gifts are now channelled to the support of those very literate specialists and their works (Goody 1983). Both Christianity and Hinduism have largely set aside the offering of animals to the gods, and, for some of the religious hierarchy, their killing and consumption as well. Is the centrality of the image of the shepherd and flock to Christian teaching and that of the cowherd and the cows also related, in a different way, to the problem of killing and at the same time conserving?

This ambivalence towards the shedding of blood emerges most clearly when human life itself is at stake. Human groups are enjoined to kill under one set of circumstances but to preserve life under another; the practice connected with the taking of human life (that is, the rituals to which a homicide is subjected) are often of the kind that make explicit, and therefore perhaps act out, the problems inherent to intra-specific killing; these problems are such that even an honourable killing in war or feud requires expiation before humanity completely forgives its perpetrator – or the perpetrator entirely exonerates himself for the shedding of blood.

The same kind of structural ambivalence towards the slaughter of animals and plants exists even in those societies which on the surface seem purely predatory, that is, societies where a person's livelihood is obtained by hunting and gathering. For the husbandry of animals in the wild is almost as important as for animals in the house, even if it involves care at a distance; so too is the preservation of bushes and plants in order that they may once again produce fruit in the following year. Wanton destruction is contrary to the interests of human kind. As ethnographic support for this statement, I refer to an incident, not from a hunting society but from the LoDagaa, who are typical hoe agriculturalists in northern Ghana. One evening I was vainly attempting to reduce the number of flying insects that clustered around my lamp as I was writing down my field notes. "Don't you know those are God's creatures?" my assistant protested, perhaps implying that as we did to them, so He would do to us, the kind of attitude that Shakespeare so vividly expressed in King Lear, "As flies to wanton boys are we to the gods. They kill us for their sport." Some time later I found him destroying what I considered to be a harmless lizard because, as he explained, it carried the danger of leprosy, the association between that disease and the animal resting upon the colours of its skin. In reprimanding me earlier, my friend was not, I think, influenced by Christianity, Islam or any other of the so-called 'ethical' religions: his view derived from a more general idea of the interconnectedness of the world of living things. The problems arising from the protection of some species and the destruction of others (sometimes for more easily identifiable reasons than the transmission of leprosy, such as personal danger or the provision of food) is, I suggest, given a more formal statement in the doctrines and practices of totemism, where one species is associated with and preserved by a particular group, whereas for the rest of the tribe it is an acceptable prey. Totemism of this kind (and there are other kinds and other aspects to them all) is especially important in hunting and gathering societies, where man's dependence on nature in the wild is total. One problem of oral societies, then, is that this kind of universalistic concern tends to get understated because of the embeddedness of speech and action in a specific context, and hence it appears largely in the form of an 'implicit contradiction'. The situation in societies with writing suffers from the opposite pressure on the normative system. For if I substitute 'thou shalt not kill' for 'thou shalt not kill other Jews', I am not only extending the range over which my moral norms apply, I am making them less applicable to actual contexts. In other words it becomes difficult, perhaps impossible, for any individual or group to live up to this kind of universalistic moral or ethical injunction. For at one level, written religions are clearly working on a more explicitly abstract (or generalized) base than those of purely oral societies (even centralized ones). And the overt recognition of this discrepancy, made explicit by and through writing, may give rise to dissent groups, for example, those constituted by pacifists or vegetarians. For them the contradictions have to be resolved by taking up positions that are at once 'extreme', but nevertheless 'logical' within the framework of universalism, totally rejecting the killing of men and animals as well as the consumption of their flesh.

This process of generalization may, indeed virtually must, lead to some tension between the universalistic formulae of the church and the more particularistic demands of the polity – whether at the state, familial or individual level. Such tension may eventuate in conflicting normative and jural injunctions which become of especial interest for the development of social systems when they are embodied in specific texts and in specific organizations, resulting in the classic opposition of church and state. While warriors and priests, Kshatriyas and Brahmins, complement one another, their roles and norms bring them into a measure of conflict arising out of this fundamental pattern. Differentiation is not simply a matter of complementarity and reciprocity, but also of the opposition, conflict and even domination that mark the relationships of 'great organizations' in complex, literate, societies.

Specialization: priests and intellectuals

This argument points to a further element in the contrast between religion in literate and oral societies, namely the specialization of roles and of organizations. In the first place, one form of specialization clearly occurs in those religious organizations which have an establishment of learned men, especially when these practitioners in some sense control knowledge derived from the book, at least from the religious Book. I do not suggest that a priesthood, as a distinct body, is not to be found in oral societies without writing. Something approaching such a body was present in the religious systems of Asante and Dahomey in West Africa, especially in the latter society where initiates were taken off to a separate establishment for a period of training, away from the general life of society, a further development of the kind of 'instruction' that occurs in numerous rituals of entry or initiation. With writing a new situation arises since the priest has privileged access to the sacred texts (whether in the singular or plural) of which he is the custodian and prime interpreter. As a mediator he has a unique link to God, whose Word only he is often able to read. In the beginning was the Book, but it was the priest who read and explained it. Hence religions of the Book are often associated with restrictions on the uses and extent of literacy. In the extreme case the priests are the one category of persons able to read at all; in other words the division between literate–illiterate corresponds to that between priest and laity. Such was the position at those various stages of Indian history when literacy was restricted to Brahmins (Das 1930; Ingalls 1959). This was virtually the position in early medieval Europe, following the decline of lay literacy with the fall of Rome. In England *clericus* became identified with *literatus* and that with a knowledge of Latin (Clanchy 1979: 177). Such a knowledge brought great privileges; at a later stage the 'benefit of clergy' meant that the ability to recite the 'neck-verse' in court could save a person from being hanged, a forceful stimulus to minimal literacy (p. 185). Most religions (including more recent Hinduism) do not carry the separation that far, even though the languages of written religions are often not simply archaic but dead or foreign. With the alphabet the skills of literacy become more easily available to others outside the scribal or priestly company itself. On the other hand, under Christianity, Islam and Judaism teaching (at least the promotion of advanced literate skills) continued to be dominated by religious specialists until the advent of modern secular education, a position that it was obviously in their interests to preserve in order to maintain their role as gate-keepers of ideas; even when the techniques were more widely diffused, the ideological content remained largely under their control. Right down to the present, the religious supervision of schools has a fundamental socio-political significance in many parts of the world, as we see from recent events in France or in Northern Ireland.

The effective control of the means of literate communication, at least the means of reproducing not only the texts (in the *scriptorium*) but its readers (in the Hindu *parsallah*, the Muslim *madrasa*, or in the *collegium*) gave the church or temple immense power over the literati whom they have charged themselves with producing. This power has nowadays been largely assumed by the state, but the kind of separation between the priest and the teacher, between the religious orders and written accomplishment that occurred in Greece, and to a lesser extent in China, has been a rare feature of literate civilizations.

Endowment and alienation

If the teaching of the skills of reading and writing is an intrinsic part of religions of the Book, its specialists inevitably acquire control of the input and output of a considerable segment of available written knowledge. But in addition they need the means to maintain the schools in which this instruction is given. Such maintenance requires not just a building, a temple, but personnel (teachers and pupils) who have to be supported not by daily offerings alone, but by more substantial, more permanent endowments. Of especial importance were endowments in land, large quantities of which fell under the control of literate churches – in Western Europe one-third of the cultivable land, roughly the same in medieval Ceylon and in parts of southern India, considerable amounts in Nepal and Tibet and substantial quantities under Islam, as much as one-third again in Ancient Egypt. Indeed, literacy is not only one of the ends but the means too, being critically involved in the process of acquisition itself since the making of written wills and deeds often accomplishes, indeed legitimises, the alienation of property from family or lineage to church. As I note in discussing law, there seems to be a close association between literacy and variable inheritance.

Such endowments create the problem of what Weber described as 'the paradox of all asceticism'. It is a contradiction that gives rise to opposition both within and without the church. An example of such internal dissent from the dominant trend is found among the forest-dwelling ascetic monks in medieval Sri Lanka. Their emphasis was on the contemplative existence at a time when life at some of the large Buddhist monasteries tended to be 'comfortable' if not 'luxurious' (Gunawardana 1979: 350; Carrithers 1983). Though their numbers were small, their worldview and style of life gave them prestige and influence among the laity, and this in turn endowed them with the authority needed to play a major role during the period of reform in the twelfth century that followed foreign domination (at the end of the tenth), political interference and the confiscation of property of the *sangha*, the community of Buddhist monks (at the beginning of the twelfth). The ideological tension inherent in the accumulation of corporate property by an ascetic sect led to the formation of a dissident trend which represented a source of ideology and personnel that could be called upon for movements of reform. Not that the tension was permanently resolved but the *sangha* was given a new life and a new beginning. As I have argued in the case of the opposition to luxurious consumption in China and elsewhere (Goody 1982), the continuing importance of such dissident trends becomes greater when dissent, like scepticism, is crystallized in writing to become a part of a continuing tradition, a handing down, of a philosophical, critical or radical kind.

The twin bureaucracies

The growth of the church as a bureaucratic institution, in the simple-minded sense of having an office with written records, opened up another area of conflict of interest between Church and State. Such developments are of course not confined to literate societies; a certain dualism of secular and religious power is a feature of many simple state systems. Nevertheless the development of bureaucracy, the control over minds and skills, the accumulation of landed property, that literacy permits or encourages, widens the gap between the interests of the church and state. They are united in some common concerns, for example, over the activities of the dispossessed, at least where these threaten established hierarchies in the lay or clerical fields, although the church often displayed a greater concern with charity which formed a corner-stone of its ideology and a justification for the accumulation of property, partly intended for redistribution. But they may also compete for power, even political power, leading to the domination of one by the other. This process may work both ways. Religious literates often think that, ideally, God's reign should come to pass on earth and the priesthood should administer His estate, an idea embodied in the medieval papacy, in the Caliphate of Islam and in the Shiite ideology of contemporary Iran. On the other side, secular rulers like Atatürk work hard to diminish the role of religion in the wider political arena.

The situation of the twin bureaucracies arises out of the fact of their partially independent endowments and the organizational requirements of the accounting system by which the funds are administered. These aspects I will discuss in greater detail when examining the relation of writing to the economy. But here I want to deal with the role of literate activity itself in contributing to the structural economy by creating a written tradition in the domain of religion.

Organizational and structural autonomy

The question of organizational complexity and the nature of literate activity is closely related to the increased autonomy of religious systems. A written religion, with a propertied church, can no longer be regarded as a reflection of or as homologous with other aspects of the social system, as part of a superstructure ordered in any straightforward way by the infrastructure of the political economy. Indeed such a contention (like the opposite, idealist, pole) implies a vast oversimplification of the state of affairs even in oral culture, but in those with writing, there is ample evidence of an increase in autonomy, in independence. Once the Holy Word has been written down in book form and institutionalized in a church, it becomes a profoundly conserving force, or better a force for continuity – its own continuity, not necessarily the state's, despite changes in the polity or economy. Of course a written religion (even in the form of a church) is never a purely conservative (as distinct from a conserving) element in society, even when the charisma has been routinized; for the early words of the prophets, the high aims of the founders, have been encapsulated in words and may represent powerful potentialities for change. Subsequent appeals of 'back to the book' are frequently made by revolutionaries who organize and legitimise their activities by returning to what was once a new, reforming creed. Even in ordinary times the normative implications of the text often provide a yardstick for the difference between reality and potentiality, between what is and what should be, between existence and Utopia. In this way it supplies a measure of our discontent. In northern Nigeria in the early nineteenth century, Muslim reformers turned back to the Qur'ān, declaring that now was the time to cleanse the world and restore it to health in accordance with the word of God. Among contemporary fundamentalist sects in Iran, the Sudan and elsewhere, a return to the earlier provisions of the Book meant among other things veils for women and the loss of hands for thieves. The many 'heretical' movements in medieval Europe, culminating in the Protestant Reformation, looked back for inspiration to the original, unadulterated Word. While these movements display some similarities with the Cargo Cults of Melanesia, they also manifest significant differences associated with the nature of written communication.

These differences relate to other features of societies with and without writing. In the latter there is a relatively close accommodation between religion and other aspects of the social system. As far as morality and ethics are concerned, the notions of goodness and evil are more closely attached to specific social situations. As with myths and oral traditions generally, these values tend to alter with the changes in the rest of the system and so, at one level, provide a kind of ever-adapting charter for social action – an adjusting, even homeostatic, normative and ideological schema. I refer here to the central, hardly-to-be-differentiated, role of religion and ritual in social life, not to the particular forms which, as I have suggested, are subject to creative transformation – hence the degree of variation in time and space. Once literacy enters into interpersonal communication, then good and evil tend (though not immediately) to be written down and systematized as a code of law or ethics. Ideals embodied in a text rather than a context are no longer attached to present concerns in the same tight way; an old eschatology may persist or a new one be created which conflicts, by accident or design, by interest or essence, with other aspects of the socio-cultural tradition. In other words, religion can become a relatively distinct element in the social matrix, both manifesting and creating a greater complexity of beliefs and practices. For example, while Hindus may recognize spirit cults, Hinduism does not. Christianity more deliberately excludes magic, but to many Christians alternative beliefs in astrology have been as much a part of their worldview as alternative medicine to many a hospital patient. Over the long term the 'adaptation' of religion to society takes on a different shape when we move from oral to written communication. The religious word acquires a physical embodiment of its own and shifts from being a more or less integral part of the culture into having a more or less distinct, sometimes determining, later diminishing, role with a larger measure of structural autonomy; if I may use current terms in a specialized sense, there is a shift from worldview to ideology, if we see the latter, like Gellner (1978), as being essentially partial, oppositional. We can see this in a small way with systems of divination. The adoption of Islamic modes of divination in Madagascar and West Africa (Hébert 1961, 1965; Goody 1968a: 25–6) changed the conceptual apparatus of the borrowing society in one limited but significant way, providing a link with fragments of the symbolic system of another, literate civilization.

The relatively close accommodation between religion and other aspects of the social system in oral societies (though once again contradictions are by no means entirely absent) may give way in written religions to a considerable lack of fit, indeed to a situation where religion, far from 'reflecting' the social system, may in fact influence it in a variety of significant ways. There can be little doubt, I think, that in contemporary Africa, as in St Augustine's England, New Spain in the sixteenth century (Bernand and Gruzinski 1985) or in seventeenth-century Scotland (Goody 1983: 216–19), the Christian church has changed the laws of marriage in very significant ways. Some of these changes were advantageous to the church in the short run as indeed all were in the medium term. This fact alone should prompt us to modify the notion of the neat functional or structural interdependence of religion and society and to recognize that writing, the presence of the text of the word in addition to its utterance, favours a partly independent role for ideology, giving it a measure of 'structural autonomy' which it doesn't possess in oral societies.

The Great and Little Traditions: spirit cults and world religions

The existence of an orthodoxy is an invitation to seek alternatives. The major world religions clearly vary in their tolerance of heterodox beliefs, cultic practices and magical procedures that do not stem from the body of their orthodoxy. At least in practice they make different kinds of accommodation, depending upon creed

("Thou shalt have no other gods . . . "), upon political demands and upon the ability to enforce jurisdictional claims – that is, upon their control of courts, property and propaganda. The Middle Eastern churches, Judaism, Christianity and Islam, were certainly more insistent on their unique claim to spiritual truths than the Eastern religions of Hinduism and Buddhism. Nevertheless even in the East one finds a continuing opposition between literate religions on the one hand and the local spirit cults on the other. The literate religion is universalistic in its framework. It has to be if only because its influence is not limited to a particular time and place. On the other hand the spirit cults are associated with local practices, local pools or groves, and take more account of local phenomena, the micro-climates of the spirit. In this way the two sets of beliefs and practices tend to supplement one another in actuality although the literate religion claims dominance, often attempts to exclude the local cults from serious theological or intellectual consideration, and defines them away as 'magic', as 'folk', as deviations from the right path.

In his discussion of spirit cults in Thailand, Tambiah examines the interaction between "grand literary Buddhism and village religion" (1970: 367). He notes that as far as India is concerned, there have been two anthropological approaches to the relationship between literary text and field observation. One derives from the Chicago school of Redfield and his associates, an approach that is especially clear in Marriott's essay "Little communities in an indigenous civilization" (1955); with this one can associate the work of Srinivas on the process of Sanskritization (1956). In contrast lie the ideas of Dumont and his collaborator, Pocock, concerning pre-Hinduism and the historical past of the literary religious culture (1957; 1959). Tambiah criticized Marriott's discussion on the grounds that the Great Tradition did not stand in opposition to that of the village, therefore the processes of universalization and 'parochialization' cannot be understood in terms of the two Traditions, Great and Little. The Great Tradition already existed within the village itself in the shape of written texts.

Dumont and Pocock employ an alternative version of the two levels, on the one hand the traditional higher Sanskritic civilization which is essentially literary and demonstrates the unity of India, and on the other the lower or popular level of culture and religion which emphasizes diversity. Tambiah criticizes these authors in turn for replacing one dichotomy by another; religion in the villages includes written texts that come from the past, and form part of the learning and ritual incantations of village officiants. However, for the villager, he argues, there is a unified field of vision. The so-called levels are in some way homogenous or homologous, since there are a number of 'complementary relationships' running between the two, namely the pure/impure distinction, the double link to the divine through priesthood (that is, a mediated relationship) and through possession (that is, directly), and thirdly the distinction in cults between male and female deities. At the same time, he claims, the general ideas of the written tradition are worked out locally, a notion that appears to resemble Marriott's concept of parochialization.

It should be noted that the complementarity involves hierarchy, which is also a hierarchy of evaluation; purity congregates at the upper pole, impurity at the lower. Priesthood is high, possession low; Hindu gods generally consist of sexual pairs, while the lower, local, deities are often female mother figures (Fuller 1984).

Tambiah regards the whole notion of two levels as being profoundly ahistorical since the texts themselves range over a wide time-span. The two levels are an artefact of the anthropologist whose observations take place over a limited time period, augmented by a library search to pull out the relevant literature. The trouble is, he remarks, that anthropologists have not been oriented towards the "collection and recording of ritual texts and literature used by rural specialists" (p. 372). In short, "anthropologists dealing with complex literate societies should pay greater attention to the role of the traditional networks of learning and transmission of knowledge" (p. 373). For certain kinds of literature have a referential base for the whole society, even for the unlettered masses, a point that Stock (1983) makes for medieval Europe. That implies a difference between the sociological and the historical perspective, neither of them being necessarily wrong. For the actor there is a unique perspective, a single field. But for the observer looking at the historical picture, there is an opposition between the literate and the non-literate, between Buddhist–Hindu practice and the local cults. The general run of this debate displays some similarities to that between Fortes (1936) and Malinowski (1938) on the subject of culture contact. Is there one field or two? Are there two cultures clashing or is there a single network of social relationships?[2]

Internally the problem is more clear cut, and can be seen to depend partly on the difference between the actor and observer, between what some have called emic and etic points of view. But while the actor operates in a single field that comprises both world-religion and local cult, that field is differentiated, not simply in historical terms but by, for example, the normative structure. This is clear from Obeyesekere's analysis of Buddhism in Sri Lanka (1963). Here we find a written specification of the five basic precepts which the Theravāda Buddhists are meant to follow and which are somewhat similar in role and content to the Ten Commandments in Judaism and Christianity. For example, there is to be no killing, no stealing, no adultery, no lying and no drinking. These prohibitions are phrased in a slightly fuller fashion in the original Pali text. But the critical point is that in an oral culture, the prohibitions would hardly be laid out and enumerated in this formal, organized way, possibly not be formulated at all since their announcement would tend to be contextualized to a much greater degree. Once written down they take on a universalistic stance, which means that they cannot be followed to the letter by anyone participating in social life in Sri Lanka or Thailand, except perhaps by monks, priests or saints, that is by religious specialists, by the 'perfect'. They have become generalized, normative statements of the kind that the written word promotes.

The gap between code and actuality may be filled by local alternatives, giving rise, in both Sinhalese and Thai Buddhism, to a basic contradiction, or perhaps tension, between the written tradition of the ascetic religion and the everyday social practice of merit-making combined with the rites of the 'magico-animists', the spirit cults. There is tension but there is also interpenetration. There are 6,000 monasteries in Sri Lanka inhabited by monks who instruct the ordinary people in the religious life (Ames 1964). Even hermit monks are sought by laymen for their learning, a process that lessens their religiosity and isolation but helps to pass on the ideals of the higher tradition to a wider population. These monasteries are linked to the class system; monastic education provides for the social advancement of its pupils, both those who stay within the walls and those who return to ordinary life. Much of the learning utilizes a dead language, Pali, preserved for religious purposes in a manner that resembles the use of Latin in medieval Europe. The literature itself often consists of elaborate ritual texts. For example, Buddhist monks have to follow 227 precepts in order to reach Nirvana. Scholasticism, 'learning', elaboration and precision are characteristics of the tradition, which emphasizes the contrast between literate purity and asceticism on the one hand, with every-day profanity and pollution on the other, a contrast that runs parallel to the distinction between the generality or universalism of written norms and the greater particularity of oral presentation. In these various ways the existence of writing is as critical to the discussions of the Great and Little Traditions in India as it is to those of High and Popular Culture in Europe and the Americas.

Writing and religion in Ancient Egypt

The cult of the dead

In order to trace some of the influences of written communication on a religious system I turn to one of the earliest of literate societies, that of Ancient Egypt. In the Old and Middle Kingdoms much use of writing and of graphic forms centred upon the cult of the dead. What has come down to use from this period are largely monu-mental texts concerned with religious display rather than adminis-trative texts which normally used less durable materials. The con-nection between developments in the two spheres are clear from the monuments, since most pictures included writing and much of the earliest writing consisted of pictures. The walls of tombs were elab-orately decorated with scenes of life on earth, a major source of knowledge for scholars of the ancient world. It is clear that com-munication was directed not towards living men but towards the dead and the gods, for these pictures are hidden from the eye of man, the opposite of monumental regal display. The exact import of the representations, whether they depict life after death or provide an environment for the living-dead, has been much argued, and there would seem to be little point in trying to select among alternatives when the evidence is scanty and the possibilities are not exclusive, except to note that one set of interpretations is sometimes allocated a 'moral' superiority over the other. Egyptian religion has sometimes been seen as gradually acquiring 'morality' and even 'rationality' as time goes on, and as tendencies towards monotheism predominate.

The line of argument is a recognizable part of the scholarly traditions of the West, having an obvious appeal to followers of monotheistic religions. While this point of view, which informs much of the treatment of religious beliefs in UNESCO's synthetic study, *The Beginnings of Civilisation*,[3] is unacceptable as such, some aspects of these features, such as the generalization of norms ('morality') and their formalization ('rationality'), can be seen as related to the presence of writing. All human societies of course have normative systems, which are more widely extended in centralized states than in tribal communities, but I have argued that setting them down in writing tends to lead to more inclusive and to more constructed statements.

The cult of the dead was important in the development of a written tradition from another standpoint. For it appears to have been out of the worship of the dead royalty that the great temples developed, with their priesthood and flourishing literacy supported by endowments made by the Pharaoh; but these are matters for later sections and later chapters.

Materials and texts

The role of writing in the more 'literary' side of Egyptian religious activity may be linked not only to the personal nature of cults of the dead and to its close relationship with pictorial art but also to the nature of the materials used. In Egypt papyrus was known from the First Dynasty (*c.* 3000–2800 BC) and its use, like the use of writing for administration more generally, seems to have encouraged cursive forms of script from the very beginning; in its earliest form the hieratic (cursive) script differs from hieroglyphic only to the extent that would follow from using a pen rather than a pointed tool (James 1979: 89, 93). While one of the first written examples of papyrus scroll (the earlier one being uninscribed) comes from the Fifth Dynasty (*c.* 2500–2350 BC) and consists of the fragmentary temple account books from Abusir (although those from Gebelein, upstream from Thebes, may be earlier), the nature of the materials perhaps encouraged more 'literary' (continuous) types of texts.[4]

Didactic works such as the Wisdom text known as the Instruction of Ptahhotep, a form of 'letters to a son', has also been thought to date from the Fifth Dynasty, although many now consider it a later work from the first First Intermediate Period or the Middle Kingdom. Similar books of instruction are found down to the Roman period (first century AD), containing injunctions of the kind, "Do not acquire wealth until you have a strong room." Pessimistic, prophetic and meditative literature is found from the Middle Kingdom (*c.* 2000 BC). Literary compositions like the pessimistic Wisdom texts were the products of intellectuals, and their dissemination may have encouraged (or expressed) some further questioning of the existing order (James 1979: 136). Hymns to the Sun-god also occur in the royal Pyramid Texts of the Fifth and Sixth Dynasties, probably deriving from liturgies. So-called 'magical' components are prominent in Egyptian literature; they include incantations, calendars of lucky and unlucky days, the interpretation of dreams, oracular consultations, and amulets containing written texts for protection. The recording of stories and accounts of travel occurs in the Middle Kingdom. On the other hand, letters, which later formed part of school instruction, are found dating from the Fifth (in the Abusir papyri) and Sixth Dynasties, one of these being from a military commander in charge of troops working in a quarry who protests at the cumbrous way in which they had to collect their clothing. In the New and the Old Kingdoms, letters were also written to dead relatives, as well as to the gods, imploring their aid (O'Connor 1983: 197–9).

The composition of the pantheon

The unification of the country, the invention of writing and possibly the reorganization of the pantheon on a national basis, all happened at the same period, leading to the adopting of the falcon Horus as the first great god of the Egyptian kingship. Other gods, including

Ptah of Memphis and in the Fourth Dynasty the Sun-god, Re, of Heliopolis, were worshipped as national gods (Hornung 1982). Some local gods were absorbed into the pantheon but while this was national, being accepted by the whole priesthood, it changed over the long term. It would therefore be wrong to see the pantheon as entirely fixed; deities like Astarte were incorporated, deities like Hathor spread to Byblos, but the rhythm of change seems quite different from that in West Africa in recent times (Schoske and Wildung 1984: 181; O'Connor 1983: 147). For we are dealing with a period of history stretching over 3,000 years, during which most major figures and their iconography seem to have persisted, even if their relationships changed. Such relative stability, at least from the New Kingdom, was ensured by the great temples of the state, devoted to the public cult on behalf of the king, a cult that largely excluded the general populus except on the occasion of major festivals.[5]

Despite the diversity of the pantheon, it seems likely that in every important sanctuary "a daily ritual was carried out which, already by the Old Kingdom, had achieved a remarkable degree of standardisation throughout the country" (James 1979: 139). This uniformity was partly due to the fact that the king was everywhere presented as the officiant.[6] But in addition the writing down of a ritual (for example, the bathing and clothing of king and deity, the offering of incense and food) meant that this text could serve as a model, and as a regulator, of other performances elsewhere, just as a written record meant that the past too could provide a model for behaviour of a precise kind (O'Connor 1983: 189, 242).

Conservation and revolution

One aspect of the conserving power of written religions is brought out in the history of Amenhotep IV (1364–1347 BC), later to be called Akhenaten, who came to favour the worship of the Aten, the solar-disc associated with imperial power, "mythically colourless and a more suitable manifestation of the king's immanent divinity", being an aspect of the cult of kingship (O'Connor 1983: 220–1). In doing so he diverted attention and tribute from Amen-Re, the great and already strongly defined Sun-god worshipped at Thebes. The priesthood opposed this change and the Pharaoh reacted by dispossessing the priests and proscribing Amen-Re and the older gods, going to the extent of erasing the name of Amen from reliefs and sacred monuments. "Even the word 'gods' where it appeared in an inscription was often hacked out, and the mortuary chapels, the tombs and the statues of the king's ancestors were violated without mercy, and because his father's name was compounded with that of Amen even that name had to be obliterated from the walls of the great buildings wherewith he had enriched Thebes" (Woolley 1963: 726; Hornung 1982: 249).[7] Under the impulse of religious change, of mystical creativity, forgetting could no longer be left to the passage of time alone; reinterpretation had now to be a matter of deliberate revolution, of the physical destruction of the word, a verbal equivalent of iconoclasm. It is not of course that writing prevented any change. In some spheres of knowledge a permanent record was a condition of future development. But in other spheres and to different degrees writing made change a question of deliberate reform rather than of continuous adaptation.

Of the earlier period of Dynastic Egypt Woolley remarks that Egyptian religion was very 'fluid' and 'confused' (1963: 717). In fact formalized schemes and a system of decorum predominated, although some invention continued. However in so far as confusion exists, here and elsewhere, it is perhaps the 'natural' condition of oral religion, if by that word one refers to the frequent absence of a formalized pantheon and to the continuous incorporation of changing practices as a result of the built-in obsolescence of much religious activity. Increased formality and greater conservatism enter into the picture when writing reduces the bubbling effervescence of supernatural discovery (or invention, depending on one's point of view) to a set of specified relationships among deities endowed with a more stable existence, partly by their incorporation in the text, partly by their fixed position in the schema and partly by their institutionalization in a temple whose literate priests, like those of Amen-Re, are reluctant to see their gods and their livelihood disappear; indeed it is their power over the means of communication that enables those priests to resist such threats.

The Akhenaten 'revolution' did not last and the old order and its priesthood once again established its sway in a strengthened form and the new artistic styles disappeared (Schoske and Wildung 1984: 186). On the popular level its monotheistic notions had not been at all successful, eliminating as they did some major festivals (O'Connor 1983: 221). Nevertheless the ideas embodied in the new cult had a more lasting effect on "the small body of thoughtful and more or less philosophic writers", the intellectuals no less. Some scholars have detected a continuing monotheistic trend in the religious expression of Ancient Egypt;[8] for once the new cult had been promoted in writing it was difficult to eliminate all trace, so its revival remained as an ever-present but distant possibility. Given literate expression, even dissent established its own tradition. One role of the intellectual was to develop and to preserve alternative views of the world (that is, ideologies), the accumulation and further diffusion of which were largely a function of the intervention of writing since it prevents scepticism and speculation from being totally absorbed in the dominant cultural ethos; that is to say, writing may provide even the opposition with a semi-permanent platform. In Ancient Egypt, for example, even in tombs one finds harpists' songs that deny the value of mortuary provision, claiming "no one has ever come back from there".

I do not see such developments as immediate or as inevitable. The trends emerge over the long-term within the framework of a written tradition. The literate Hittite culture of Anatolia provide a good example of the dynamic process. In setting up their newly literate kingdoms Hittite rulers not only took over earlier elements but were peculiarly ready to adopt high culture, including the gods, with which they were brought into contact (Woolley 1963: 729). Those to the east borrowed wholesale the mythological legends of Sumer, perhaps primarily as works of literature, while the Hurrians in Syria to the west adopted as their own the West Semitic deities. The pantheon, writes Woolley, was "strangely eclectic and confused", a fact which he attributes to the incorporation of local deities at the time of conquest and imperial expansion. However the process was not simply one of incorporation but of identification; the innumerable local Storm gods – each Hittite city had its own – were in time merged in the national Storm-god.

The formalization of a pantheon is often connected with the formation of the state, with the incorporation or identification of local gods within a wider national framework. Indeed the expansion of the relations between states means that identification between deities (such as Allah and the local High God) takes place not only within but outside the community as well. But the call for 'rationalization', for formalization, has a much greater force in literate cultures where the very fact of making lists of deities, on tablets or on monuments, creates a hierarchical order as well as identifying particular figures from different groups, sorting them out with reference to their specific roles and relationships and thereby laying out a pantheon of a much more uncompromising and unambiguous kind.

In this sense the effects of writing on the religions of the Ancient Near East can be seen as a preliminary to the further degree of framed enquiry that took place in alphabetic times when the system became more cursive, simpler and hence more widespread, permitting the easier elaboration and hence extension of commentaries on the text and similar treatises, what later became the products of the medieval 'scholastic', of the authors of the Hadith, of the commentators on the Torah, of the works of the Christian fathers. Asking how many angels could stand on the head of a pin was the kind of minute questioning (no doubt apocryphal), the attempted unravelling of ambiguities, that was encouraged by the medium they were using, a medium that over time promoted a partly decontextualized use of language and definition of subject, as well as a more abstracted debate.[9] From one standpoint, these enquiries represent conservative formalism, the comments on a canon, a ritualization of thought; but from another angle the process was potentially capable of raising questions and producing commentaries by the 'educated' elite. In Egypt we do not find the emergence of a 'canonical' religious literature, accompanied by exegesis, in the form we know it from the Judaic or Christian tradition; but the copying and glossing of important texts did occur, representing a similar kind of writing-dependent process.

The organization of the priesthood

The organization of the Egyptian priesthood was based not only on the royal cult, on the maintenance of temples, but also on their role, at least in the later period, as teachers of scribes and as custodians of old texts. These positions were in turn supported by the ownership of land, constantly donated by kings, to whose status these gifts were indispensable and, in the first millennium, by individuals. At one time the temple lands amounted to as much as a third of the country's cultivable resources so that ecclesiastical landlordism provided a sound economic base for the elaboration of magico-religious activities (O'Connor 1983: 202).[10] With the defeat of the Hyksos invaders and the subsequent adoption of their military weapons and tactics, the Pharaohs extended their dominion from the Nile valley to the banks of the Euphrates. The gods of Egypt became the gods of the conquered lands which contributed annually to the treasuries of the temple. Although it is possible to overemphasize the degree of separation of temple and palace, in the late Twentieth Dynasty (1200–1085 BC) the Pharaoh became no more than a cipher in the power struggle between priests and military.

It goes without saying that the take-over of state by church, or vice versa, is only possible when a clear separation of powers, functions and organization already exists. The 'priest-king' of the Frazerian account of the history of religions had both political and religious domains under his control; indeed the domains were scarcely to be distinguished. The separation of the roles of 'priest' and 'king', of religious and political officiants, meant it was also possible, under certain conditions, for one party to take upon himself the functions of the other. But the domination of the one by the other becomes a continuing possibility with the emergence of two distinct organizations, especially when both are buttressed by significant incomes from taxes, tribute or land-ownership, and by significant control of force, whether military, spiritual or ideological. Inevitably the state, with its control of physical force, is the more likely to come out on top. But examples of the domination of the church are to be found in the take-over of the Tibetan state by the religious orders as well as in the power of the Holy Roman Empire and later the Papal states of Italy. The frequently discussed opposition between church and state is a function of this differentiation, linked to an elaboration of the means of communication, of the ways in which knowledge can be stored. Even though writing was chiefly used for lay, governmental purposes in the Ancient Near

East, it was often taught in temples, which (as with the abbeys and monasteries of medieval Europe) might serve as libraries of the written word as well as schools. As a result temples acted not only as centres of instruction but as centres of scholastic activity (Oppenheim 1964: 243), which demanded increasing specialization as over time the language of written knowledge inevitably diverged more and more from that of ordinary speech, even if it had once corresponded phonologically or semantically; as in other areas the incorporation of knowledge in a system of writing that endured over a long period led to the need for deliberate reforms because it froze the process of constant adaptation (Baines 1983: 584).

The far-reaching importance of writing for the priesthood and for cult practice is seen in the internal organization of religious activity, especially in the part played by temple schools and in the role of priests as scribes and record-keepers.[11] All this is abundantly evident in the titles they are given in the Onomasticon of Amenope, an encyclopaedic listing (albeit incomplete in preserved copies) of all categories of persons and objects existing in the universe. Following entry 113, "chief of the record-keepers of the House of the Sea", we come to a new section of priestly persons, listed by Gardiner as:

114. the royal scribe and lector-priest as (?) Horus;
115. scribe of the House of Life, skilled in his profession (the House of Life designating those temple scriptoria in which religious and learned works were composed and copied);
116. lector-priest of the royal couch;
117. Chief priest of Amun in Thebes;
118. Greatest of the Seers of Re-Atum (the title of the high-priest of Heliopolis);
119. Greatest of Artificers of Him who is South of His Wall (i.e. of Ptah, the title of the high-priest of Memphis);
120. Semite-priest, Perfect of face (i.e. of Ptah, the second title of the high-priest of Memphis);
121. overseer of the Granaries of Upper and Lower Egypt;
122. King's butler in the Palace;
123. chamberlain of the Palace;
124. great steward of the Lord of the Two Lands;
125. scribe of the placing of offerings for all the gods;
126. major priests (literally, god's servants);

127. god's fathers;
128. (subordinate) priests (literally 'pure' or 'clean' ones);
129. lector-priest;
130. temple scribe (for general purposes including accounts);
131. scribe of the god's book;
These entries are followed by 132. porter; 133. elder of the portal; 134. hour-watcher (astronomer); 135. bringer of offerings; 136. bearer of the wine-jar stand (after Gardiner 1947: 1, 35*–63*).

The lector-priest, whose name signifies "he who carries the ritual-book", is often depicted in temples and tombs as reading from a papyrus roll, though sometimes he is simply prominent in the ceremonies. His principal qualification was a knowledge of ritualistic usage, which was no longer only a matter of experience and memory within the grasp of each and every participant; that is to say, ritual was no longer mainly accessible directly in the societal memory store (by which I mean nothing more mystical than the memories of old men), but indirectly in books. This role of priests in the funerary cult is well expressed in an inscription of the Old Kingdom, referring to their help when passing by the tomb: "Beloved of the King and of Anubis is the lector-priest who shall perform for me the things beneficial to a blessed spirit according to that secret writing of the lector-priest's craft" (Gardiner 1947: 1, 55*). These temple priests, readers of incantations and prayers, were referred to by the Hebrews as the 'sorcerers of Egypt', and are also described as magic practitioners (Baines 1983: 585); one's own priests are often the magicians of strangers. But in any case, as Gardiner's discussion shows, writing was essential for the proper performance of temple ritual and even for some forms of personal rite as far back as the Old Kingdom, the earliest period when continuous texts were in use.

Writing and religion in other early civilizations

There are of course great differences among societies in what aspects of a religious system are written down and what continue to be communicated only through the spoken channel. The portions committed to writing represent different segments of the totality, as with the royal divinations in early China. In different societies writing is used for very different purposes. In Crete, on the one hand, almost no surviving text relates to religious activities; all is administrative lists (Chadwick 1976). Among the Hittites, on the other hand, the rich archives of Bogazköy offer up many details of cult, shedding light on a temple organization that was supported by contributions from the king, the palace and the municipality. Strict rules were specified for physical and ritual cleanliness, punishments for the breach of which were of great severity, including death itself. Here as elsewhere the forms of divination were influenced by literacy, not surprisingly since divination usually involves the manipulation of objects sometimes marked with graphic signs. For example, the examination of the liver of a sacrificed sheep, haruspication, was learnt from the Mesopotamians; at Alalakh, as in Etruria, we find a clay model of a liver mapped out diagrammatically to bring out the significance of its markings.

The results of making written reports of specific events, of recording experience for future use, had particularly interesting results in regard to Mesopotamian omens. Notes were made of unusual acts of animals and unusual happenings in the sky with the result, according to Oppenheim, that "divination moved from the realm of folklore to the level of scientific activity" (1964: 210). "The subsequent systematization of such collections represent high scholarly achievement." The way this happened is of considerable interest for any examination of the implications of literacy. "Once in the hands of scholar-scribes these compendiums [of omens] grew more and more complex and arcane. The preservation of this written text became important to the copyist, and this concern increased the philological difficulties, since a discrepancy developed between the scribe's language and that of the text he copied. Explanatory glosses and commented texts became necessary as divination moved completely into the domain of scholarship" (Oppenheim 1978: 642).

Akkadian divination was highly regarded throughout the area, the texts being copied in many places and the practices spreading to the East and West even after the disappearance of Mesopotamian civilization. In certain forms of divination, the gods are asked to 'write' their messages on the entrails of sacrificial animals. The recording of such practices, their interpretation and results led to a scholarly form of written divination that appears to have existed side by side with folk versions. It was the royal art of astrology for which Mesopotamia was famed. The bulk of the texts come from the library of Assurbanipal and from these one can discern a 'canonical' series of some 70 tablets dealing with the heavenly bodies (Oppenheim 1964: 225). In the fifth and third centuries BC we find horoscopes mentioning "the date of birth, followed by an astronomical report", concluding with a prediction about the child's future.

This involvement with omens "engendered speculations that reflect concern with theological problems and led not only to refinement of the methods of interpreting omens but also to constant changes in techniques of divination" (Oppenheim 1964: 226). While overtly sceptical reactions were rare, they do exist, sometimes displaying a distrust of the professional honesty of the diviners but also doubts of a wider, more inclusive, kind about the system itself (Oppenheim 1964: 227). Such scepticism is not unusual in oral societies but when predictions are written down it is more difficult to escape the intellectual consequences of their non-fulfilment. New forms of divination may entail more complex, more 'objective', more 'scientific' interests in the heavens, leading to the development of astrology and astronomy. At the same time the accumulation of scepticism in writing leads to the establishment of a critical tradition that rejects 'magic' side by side with a more orally based one that accepts it. While such developments were undoubtedly extended by classical Greece (Lloyd 1979), in medieval Europe (Stock 1983) and in the Renaissance (Thomas 1978), the germs of the process were already to be found in the written tradition of Mesopotamia.

Another aspect of what one might call the reflexive potentialities of writing can be dimly discerned in Mesopotamian texts. Oppenheim referred to "Lists of deities, organized in several ways, or lists that enumerate the sacred animals of certain gods, and other scribal attempts to speculate about the gods and their relationships – in short what may be termed *theology*" (1964: 180, my italics). He saw this as reflecting the scholarship rather than religiosity of the Mesopotamians but the fact that a distinction can be made at all is important, not only in itself but also because the construction and contemplation of the text constitutes a reflection on the religious life, an invitation not simply to consolidate but to elaborate, an embryonic form of the process that Stock (1983) explores for the European Middle Ages. Various writers on 'primitive religion' have pointed to the relative absence of dogma and theology, especially Robertson Smith in his major work, *The Religion of the Semites* (1889). One could put the same problem in a different way and at the same time suggest a possible mechanism; the construction of the text, which is in any case something other than the transcription of discourse, can lead to its contemplation, to the development of thoughts about thoughts, to a metaphysic that may require its own metalanguage.

However, writing could also freeze aspects of religion as we see with regard both to ritual and myth in Mesopotamia. As in Egypt, performance became dominated by the text. This shift of ritual to the written register, for performance "by priests and priestly technicians in the sanctuary", is also a feature of Mesopotamia where the texts "prescribe, often in considerable detail, the individual acts of a ritual, the prayers and formulae to be recited (given either in full or cited by incipit), and the offerings and the sacrificial apparatus required" (Oppenheim 1964: 178). Of a particular sequence of rituals from Assur, Oppenheim comments that they belong to the "stream of tradition", going back to much earlier prototypes and using Sumerian prayers, that is, prayers in another language. With different emphasis and intent, no doubt, but the application of an unchanging formula of this kind to a wide set of very different circumstances over a long period of time is difficult to visualize in an oral culture although perfectly at home in a written one.

There is a specific comment I want to make on the fixity of the text. To write down a prayer is to fix it in a particular way so that it becomes essential to repeat, for example, the Lord's Prayer in the exact words in which it had been written, even if we scarcely understand them, rather than invent our own variation that may be more appropriate to the times and the occasion (Goody 1986). There is an interesting example of this in Mesopotamia. "Just as the acts and offerings of the prayer are fixed, with little variation and few departures from the small number of existing patterns, so the wording of the prayer exhibits a limited number of invocations, demands and complaints, and expressions of thanksgiving" (Oppenheim 1964: 175). This "repetitious diction" in prayer results from a standardizing of the verbal offerings to the god with a limited regard for the occasion. It is a standardization over time that leads to an increased divergence from ordinary language (as in "hallowed be thy name") and even to a lack of understanding. In this way the ritual text may become mumbo-jumbo to the populace, requiring a specialist body of interpreters to 'translate' (in one of several possible ways) the words addressed to the deity. At the same time there is a tendency of such texts to simplify complex procedures, placing emphasis on repetition, verbatim repetition, for which end the Book is highly instrumental.

Writing affected myth in an even more direct manner. The form in which we have the Mesopotamian myths is certainly not that of oral recitation. In their written versions the stories "represent the most obvious and cherished topics for the literary creativeness of a civilization . . . These literary formulations", writes Oppenheim, "are . . . the work of Sumerian court poets and of Old Babylonian scribes imitating them, bent on exploiting the artistic possibilities of a new literary language" (1964: 177), with all its 'archaic' and learned artificialities. We are clearly dealing, as so often with what are presented as the products of oral culture, with a distinctive literary treatment.

In Phoenicia the dramatic myths of the agricultural rites that emerge in the written texts (cult texts rather than literary, mythical ones) show similarities with the beliefs and practices of the early Hebrews as well as with those of Mesopotamia. The Hebrews, despite their 'nomadic' past, were always associated with the literate cultures of cities, and right from its effective beginning in the Mosaic creed, the religion was imprinted with the presence of writing in the shape of the Twelve Tables. The Bible does not represent the writing down of an oral religion so much as the creation of a literate one. That is not to deny that the 'mythological' parts of Genesis did not have oral forerunners, nor that the genealogies of Numbers and the prohibitions of Leviticus are not in certain respects comparable to those found in non-literate cultures. Comparisons with tribal society are certainly relevant, and the suggestions, implicit and explicit, made by Evans-Pritchard (e.g. 1956),

Schapera (e.g. 1955), Malamat (e.g. 1973), Flanagan (e.g. 1981) and others in this regard have cast useful light on Ancient Israel. But it is also clear that the uses and consequences of literacy were many and important: the freezing of the genealogies, the ordering of the Ten Commandments and the enumeration of the Hebrew tribes (Num. 1:1ff.), the detailing of the methods of constructing the temple, the collecting of proverbs and the listing of the Levitical taboos, all these were strongly affected by the use of writing.

When the Levites were established in their priestly role, Moses is bidden by the Lord,

Speak unto the children of Israel, and take of every one of them a rod according to the house of their fathers, of all their princes according to the house of their fathers twelve rods: write thou every man's name upon his rod. And thou shalt lay them up in the tabernacle of the congregation before the testimony, where I will meet with you. And it shall come to pass, that the man's rod, whom I shall choose, shall blossom: and I will make to cease from me the murmurings of the children of Israel, whereby they murmur against you. (Num. 17:2–5)

A similar use of writing on sticks or cards for divinatory purposes is found among the Chinese in contemporary Taiwan as well as in the more frivolous forms of the Christmas cracker and the fortune-telling machine. It has its Biblical counterpart in a type of ordeal that utilizes a procedure common in Muslim areas today (see Goody 1968: 230). In testing a woman accused of adultery ('the trial of jealousy'), the priest laid a curse upon her. "And the priest shall write these curses in a book, and he shall blot them out with the bitter water: and he shall cause the woman to drink the bitter water that causeth the curse; and the water that causeth the curse shall enter into her, and become bitter" (Num. 5:23–4). After this the priest takes her offering and burns a handful upon the altar as an offering to God. But the ordeal itself rests upon the internalizing of the written word by the accused for which there are early Egyptian and other parallels (Baines 1983: 588–9). Writing bites deep, even into divination, ordeals, magical procedures of many kinds.

The insistence upon taking lists of those belonging to the community, in other words upon the construction of a census, is a striking feature of early Hebrew society. "And the Lord spake unto Moses in the wilderness of Sinai, . . . saying, Take ye the sum of all the congregation of the children of Israel, after their families, by the house of their fathers, with the number of their names, every male by their polls; from twenty years old and upward, all that are able to go forth to war in Israel; thou and Aaron shall number them by their armies" (Num. 1:1–4). There follows a list of the tribes with their representatives who "declared their pedigrees after their families, by the house of their fathers, according to the number of their names, from twenty years old and upward, by their polls" (1:18). In this way the different 'tribes' are numbered for military purposes and their tents located in a particular spatial arrangement around the tabernacle.

Moses himself is said by the compilers of the Torah to have recorded laws and legal decisions in writing (Exod. 24:3–7; Deut. 31:24–6), as well as to have made memoranda connected with the journeys of the Israelites. He "wrote all the words of the Lord" and read the book of the covenant to his people; when he "had made an end of writing", he told them to put the "book of the laws . . . in the side of the ark of the covenant". He appointed literate officials (šōṭerîm) to keep track of decisions and order affairs more generally (Deut. 1:15; cf. Exod. 18:21–2). While others could 'handle the pen of the writer' or 'staff' of office (Judg. 5:14), a Kenite family descended from Caleb long continued to be noted as specialists (1 Chron. 2:55). From the time of Moses to that of David we possess an unbroken list of those who guarded the ark that had with it the Torah or basic 'state' documents (Deut. 31:24–6). From David to Josiah, beginning with the period of a definite, centralised government (Flanagan 1979), we are given the names of the state scribe, a high officer ranking above the Chronicler (maẓkîr) who kept the many state records (2 Sam. 8:16; 1 Kings 4:3). The Chief Scribe was a royal adviser; others were employed on military or census duties (2 Kings 25:19; Jer. 52:25), and the senior ones amongst them had their own rooms in the palace or temple (Jer. 36:10, 12–21). But until the Exile the scribal profession itself seems to have been largely separate from the priesthood, which had its own secretaries and scribes.

Ritual and writing

There remains one other point concerning ritual rather than religion that will be taken up in later chapters; that is the question of the use of writing for recording changes of individual status in the life cycle – birth, marriage, death, etc. Oral societies usually make an open and public announcement that a change of this kind has occurred – I speak here of organizational rather than structural changes. The public manifestation may include a procession, dance, beer drink, ceremony, or other communal activity. Of course, the communication of the news of such a change is by no means the only function of rites of passage; the rite affects the change, and the formality of tradition is important in itself. In contemporary England many people who are not otherwise 'practising Christians' want to get married in church, although the ceremony can be carried out in a registry office and the announcement made through the columns of a newspaper. Alternative, 'non-ceremonial', means of contracting a union are available in contemporary literate societies; 'witnesses' are still required, although the function of these persons has changed considerably. It is significant that with the growth of literacy the rites of passage associated with birth, marriage and death have become largely private affairs whereas in oral societies they are public. I was a long time among the LoDagaa before overcoming a certain sense of shame at barging in on the funerals of other people's dead; indeed I do not think I ever got over this feeling. Yet in the LoDagaa terms I was accumulating grace. One day I was walking along a path some way from Birifu, after being out on a hunting expedition, when I met a somewhat uninhibited character who demanded to know who I was. I told him where I had come from. "Yes, we've heard of you." Then, after using a rather extravagant form of praise, he continued, "You're the one that attends every funeral around here."

Publication, which is an important aspect of these occasions, takes a variety of forms and of aspects in written cultures – for royalty the messages inscribed in stone, for land-owners the inscriptions on boundary stones, and in Rome the display of notices of changes in an individual's status, changes in laws and changes in the law-makers. These forms of display, in the context of the changing nature of urban society, may lead to a certain decay of ceremony except on a minimal scale. While it would be dangerous to assert that the loose category of ritual behaviour is any less prevalent in contemporary literate societies, it is certainly the case that ceremony is less intrinsic to the many changes in the life-cycle of birth, marriage and death. But this change was a slow one. In earlier times the writings undertaken at marriage and death, for example, were not intended to publicize the event but rather as a conveyance of property and other rights. Only relatively recently have the occasions themselves regularly taken a written form with the recording of life-cycle events in church registers during the later European Middle Ages. The earlier use for quasi-contractual purposes will be examined later in connection with the effects of writing on law.

A number of the points made about the influence of writing on religion will come up again in other contexts. Other substantive matters have been omitted. For the sake of completeness (a distinctly written formula for the production of knowledge), I should have considered the shape of literate rituals and the construction of a ritual text, the reproduction of the Book (scriptoria, calligraphy and the role of exact repetition), as well as the training of the readers – in other words, the early school itself. These facets are linked to the growth of the temple complex, the huge abbeys of Western Europe, the mosques of the Middle East, the temples of Hinduism, the monasteries of Buddhism, which have played so important a part in Eurasia, Indonesia and in northern Africa on the levels of aesthetics and learning as well as of social organization, providing in many cases hospitals and hotels as well as centres of scholarship and commerce.[12] These are matters that require more extended treatment than could possibly be given here.

I would have wanted also to give a fuller discussion of some of the implications of writing for the content of religions. I have referred specifically to the 'ascetic' element, manifested not only inside the church but outside in the person of dissenting individuals and groups of certain kinds, those who reject food, sex or other pleasures in opposition to the major trends in civil society. It is a subject I have touched upon earlier (in *Cooking, Cuisine and Class*, 1982) and to which I shall return in the context of economic and political action.

Not unconnected with this development is the general move from sacrifice in the literal sense to 'sacrifice' in the metaphorical one, a path that a number of written religions have chosen to follow. And perhaps in more complicated ways, relating to obsolescence and record-keeping, to theodicy and the problem of evil, is the increasing pre-eminence of a High God.[13] But these again are paths down which I cannot now tread and which would require more time, more erudition and perhaps more speculation than I am at present able to offer.

2

The word of mammon

In this chapter I want to deal initially with the part played by economic activities in the origin of the first complete writing systems, those found in the Ancient Near East. Recent research has insisted on two aspects: the early role of writing in exchange (effectively commerce) and the role of writing in the management of the economic affairs of the temple and the palace. Once introduced, however, it affected other areas of the economy.

The nature of that domain has been considered under four heads by economic anthropologists (Nash 1968): (1) technology and the division of labour; (2) the structure of productive units; (3) the system and media of exchange; (4) the control of wealth and capital. This is not the place to discuss the influence of writing on developments in technology and its application, since it would lead into a search for those inventions that were promoted not only by the use of graphics but by the whole literate tradition. Of course literacy had an influence on inventions and on the division of labour that resulted from their application. But in itself writing constitutes an important technology requiring a category of highly trained specialist which has to be maintained at the expense of the community. Some of these specialists were priests and some administrators, who employed writing in the running of the temple and palace respectively. Given the importance of the temple in relation both to writing and the economy, the effects of writing on its economy demand some prior treatment. While one cannot separate these spheres in any definite way, and while the characteristic features of their written communications overlap, I shall go on to discuss the palace economy (taking up the theme of the twin bureaucracies), then mercantile activities and individual transactions, as I think these may have been affected by changes in the means of communication. My implicit contrast remains with Black Africa (though this was not entirely non-literate), and in a final section I will make this explicit in discussing some modern developments.

The central problem concerning the contribution of writing to the economy has to do with its role in 'development' in the very broadest sense, that is, in promoting new technologies (and the associated division of labour), in extending the possibilities of management on the one hand and of commerce and production on the other, in transforming methods of capital accumulation, and finally in changing the nature of individual transactions of an economic kind. The problem has been considered in two different ways. If we take recent moves to expand the economies of countries of the Third World, a certain rate of literacy is often seen as necessary to radical change, partly from the limited standpoint of being able to read the instructions on the seed packet, partly because of the increased autonomy (even with regard to the seed packet) of the autodidact, partly through a fuller participation in the wider socio-political system. Another line of argument stresses the need for access to an existing written tradition in order to be able to contribute and adapt as well as to accept and imitate, not only in the economic field but also in those other aspects of political, legal and religious activities, both internally and externally, that writing promotes and which, in their elementary forms, are the subject of this book.

There is yet another, more basic, level at which writing intervenes and which seems to have been particularly critical in its early development. Most obvious is its use for book-keeping of various kinds, to which I will return. But there is also the related question of the link between different systems of circulation, of money on the one hand and of the written word on the other. Many pre-established notions of the distinctions between societies, or, more dynamically, notions of the development from one form to another, take a particular view of the socio-cultural context of money and of types of market exchange, of free wage labour and of the productive processes with which it is associated. A consideration of the role of writing may lead us not to abandon but at least to qualify some of the radical contrasts that lie behind many discussions of the 'rise of the West' and of the Ancient Economy, just as it should about the nature of the pre-industrial economies of their successor states, what Parsons called the 'intermediate, oriental societies' of China, India and the Near East. That is a question that remains implicit in our discussion. First, we need to outline what writing may achieve, facilitate or accompany, the nature of the association in any particular case being a matter for specific determination rather than for general assumption.

In looking at the effects of writing on social life it would have been reasonable to begin with the economy rather than religion, not because of any idea of a universal economic determinism, but because so many scholars of the Ancient World have claimed this domain to be the one in which writing first emerged. Note that there is little or no evidence to suggest that the economy was linked in any very direct way with the systems of proto-writing that developed in other parts of the world, such as those most prominent in North and Central America; there one of the most general developments was for mnemonic and calendrical ends, although in the centralized states graphics were used for a variety of royal purposes, mainly on a monumental level. However, with the full writing systems of the Near East the case is different. It has even been argued that Mesopotamian cuneiform "was not a deliberate invention, but the incidental by-product of a strong sense of private property" (Piggott 1950: 180, after Speiser). In this form the claim need not be taken too seriously, for the allocation of property rights to individuals was no invention of the Bronze Age (Renger 1979: 249), and they are strongly held in many simpler economies. In some non-literate societies such rights are indicated by graphic marks of ownership on pots and livestock, giving rise, some suggest, to semiotic codes of limited scope. Certainly they are embryonic forms of writing often associated with specific claims to property. Seals, which play a rather similar role, have long been recognized as important in the development of writing (Schmandt-Besserat 1978; Hawkins 1979: 133). Almost all our knowledge of the third-millennium Harappa script of north India and Pakistan comes from these seals and stamped signs sometimes found on pots both in the Indus valley and in Mesopotamia, between which important trading relations existed. They appear to have served mainly as a means of identifying property in exchange, although other uses must have been made of this device.

Marks of an identifying kind were widely used in the early cities of the Ancient Near East. Currency silver, which was central to the economy of Mesopotamia, was given a hall-mark to guarantee its quality (*gin*, 'normal', is the stamp) as a sign both of exactness and of legitimacy (Oppenheim 1978: 664); the control of quality and the standardization of weights and measures used in exchange was an important aspect of authority then as now. Above all this supervision was a matter for the temples who sought to assuage the afflictions of the poor, trying also to control rates of interest (Oppenheim 1964: 107). But this particular use of graphic signs did not require a full writing system, bearing a close resemblance in this respect to the widespread types of ownership marks found on livestock and pots, the latter being employed at times, like the signature on a painting, to indicate the creator as well as the owner. The same is true of the clay tokens ('calculi') of different shapes which appeared widely in the Near East around 8500 BC. These tokens were not of course graphic, although some bore incised or punched markings, but they seem to have served as representations of transactions carried out either by merchants or in the centralized economy of state or temple, probably in both (see Schmandt-Besserat 1980, etc.). Whatever their earlier role, they were later linked with economic activities that subsequently became embodied in writing itself – that is, in graphic representations of language.

Given the apparent link between earlier sign systems and later writing in the economy of Mesopotamia, where the bulk and quality of the evidence is great, I will reverse the procedure of the previous chapter and consider first of all those features of the Ancient Near Eastern economy that seem to have been affected by writing, dealing implicitly rather than explicitly, with the contrast with oral cultures, though to this contrast I will return at the end.

The origin of writing and the ancient economy

Accounts of Mesopotamia insist on the extent to which the economy was dependent upon writing and writing dependent upon the economy. "Based on intensive cereal agriculture and large-scale

breeding of small livestock, all in the hands of a centralized power,
[this civilization] was quickly caught up in a widespread economy
which made necessary the meticulous control of infinite movements, infinitely complicated, of the goods produced and circulated. It was to accomplish this task that writing developed; indeed
for several centuries, this was virtually its only use" (Bottéro 1982a:
28). The sequence of development is put in even more precise terms
by Amiet:

From that time, the capitals of the two adjacent regions played a decisive
part: Uruk in Sumer and Susa at the foot of the Zagros mountains which
saw the emergence of the first states worthy of the name, firstly with a break
from the prehistoric tradition symbolised by painted pottery, then by the
elaboration of a system of accountancy which had become essential to the
management of their vast riches. This book-keeping led naturally to the
creation of a system of writing, still primitive, partially pictographic but
mainly abstract, which later became known as cuneiform and was adopted
and adapted by the greater part of the Ancient East. This writing is found in
Uruk at the end of the period of that name, around 3300 BC when their
neighbours, of the same culture, only practised numerical accounting.
Writing and book-keeping were established by a priestly administration
that patronised an art resolutely realist in opposition to the stylized works
of the prehistoric period. (1982: 19)

It is true that some writers have taken a seemingly different view.
Woolley maintained that in Mesopotamia "Writing was a temple
invention and therefore first practised by the priests" (1963: 467).
However, this statement points in the same general direction since
the writing they invented and practised was used primarily for the
conduct of economic affairs. For early writing in Mesopotamia was
employed for book-keeping rather than recording myths and
rituals. The books were primarily the accounts of temple stores
(p. 510), so that while writing was practised by priests and temple
administrators, and possibly a temple invention in its complete
form, its origin was hardly religious in the ordinary sense of the
word but emerged from the nature of the economy of early
Mesopotamian society. The records of day-to-day activities in
Mesopotamia "originated in the realm of an elaborate bureaucracy
that handled with technical skill and methodological consistency the
affairs of temple administrations of southern Babylonia" (Oppenheim 1964: 23). Such records also come to us from royal palaces and
later on from private legal transactions, sales, rentals and loans, as

well as marriage contracts, adoptions, wills and so on. Temples, Adams points out (1966: 126), were "crucial centres for innovation in such specialized administrative skills as writing and the keeping of accounts", partially perhaps in return for the agricultural surplus they absorbed in the god's service. As early as late Protoliterate times knowledge of the application of writing for keeping accounts would have strengthened "the managerial functions of temples" as well as encouraging among its practitioners "a sense of detachment from and superiority to the day-to-day concerns of secular life". Thus writing represents not only a method of communication at a distance, but a means of distancing oneself from communication.

How did such a system develop? In the 1930s the German expeditions to Uruk, at the heart of Sumerian society, found the earliest examples of writing to be tablets of accounts (Falkenstein 1936: 43; Green 1981); there were also a number of lists constructed for economic purposes as well as lexicons for 'school texts' (e.g. VAT 9130 from Fara), a very striking phenomenon of the Meso-potamian tradition but one that is not our prime focus of interest here. These tablets of accounts appear to be linked with the earlier use of tokens in the Near East and, later, with a kind of invoicing device found distributed between Elam in the south-east and Syria in the north-west.

The facts about the tokens and the envelopes appear to be as follows. Clay tokens, modelled into a range of shapes, mostly geo-metric, are found in archaeological deposits in the Ancient Near East dating from around 8500 BC, roughly contemporary with the beginnings of agriculture. With the emergence of cities, about 3500 BC, the tokens underwent a radical change, indicated by the proliferation of markings on their surfaces. And about 3500–3200 BC we find the first clay envelopes which are used as con-tainers for the tokens.[1] These round hollow objects about the size of tennis balls, which have to be distinguished from the ovoid 'bullae' used as sealings to hold the strings of bundles of merchandise, were first discovered in the proto-Elamite levels at Susa. It was Oppen-heim's recognition of a much later, second millennium, envelope as a recording system based on tokens forming a complement to written book-keeping in the palace of Nuzi that set the stage for further developments (Schmandt-Besserat 1980: 360). For the movements of a herd belonging to the Palace could be recorded by moving the relevant tokens from one container (i.e. field) to another. The examples from Susa were then identified by Amiet (1966) as "pièces de comptabilité", with the tokens representing goods and commodities.[2] He further suggested that they might have been used as bills of lading accompanying shipments of merchandise from centres of production in the country to the administrative centres in the town, in the same general way that letters of contract were later used by the Assyrian merchants trading between Assur and Kanish in Anatolia.

The sequence of developments is most clearly illustrated at Susa. In the second half of the fourth millennium, transactions (numbers only, according to Le Brun and Vallat, 1978) were symbolized by tokens, and those representing a single transaction were enclosed in a ball of clay "au montant du contrat" (p. 30); on the surface of this envelope one or two cylinder seals were then rolled to seal the document. In case of dispute the envelope could be opened, but being broken it was then of no further use. So a second stage consisted in marking the contents on the surface either by imprinting the shape of the tokens themselves in the clay or by some inscribed copy. It was now no longer necessary to open the envelope. Indeed the tokens themselves now became superfluous, giving way to the so-called "numerical tablets" – "impressed tablets" for Schmandt-Besserat (1981b) since she takes a broader view of the meaning of the tokens. In fact at Susa these tablets are found in the same level as envelopes and tokens but they are replaced in level 18 by incised proto-Elamite pictographic signs,[3] which in the mid-third millennium give way to the cuneiform writing of their neighbours in Mesopotamia.

Some authors see the envelopes, and the later developments of writing, as linked to the temple administration, recording gifts given to or taxes levied by that body. Indeed Schmandt-Besserat would associate the appearance of envelopes in the fourth millennium with the time when "the priesthood was invested with the power of enforcing the delivery of goods by sanctions" (1980: 381), although the earlier tokens were scattered throughout the Fertile Crescent and may have been connected with trading activities. She sees the invention of the envelopes as being stimulated by the need to confer an official character on certain transactions by the means of seals, since all those found in the major administrative centres were so marked. Others however see the finds of envelopes and tokens as representing the archives of traders (Le Brun and Vallat 1978), containing records of private contracts, especially loan agreements; certainly in later times we find land sales, house sales and farming leases which constitute 'private' rather than 'public' transactions. The point is crucial, first, for those like Polanyi, some Marxist historians and most anthropologists who see the economy of the Ancient World as organized centrally by state or temple, whether considering this to be an example of Oriental despotism, state-capitalism or a redistributive system, and, secondly, for those like Woolley and other scholars of the Ancient Near East who lay greater stress on the actions of groups of merchants working on their own account but contributing taxes, dues and gifts to the 'great organizations' of state and temple. It is a question to which I return after looking at the evidence from a later period, but meanwhile the role of tokens with regard to writing raises another significant issue, although less directly linked to the economy.

It is claimed by Schmandt-Besserat that not only were the tokens connected to writing by means of the clay envelopes that later became the writing tablets, but that the tokens themselves were the prototypes of specific 'pictographic' cuneiform signs. This contention would set aside once and for all the idea that writing developed from yet earlier systems of pictograms (that is, pictures of objects as distinct from signs for words). Undoubtedly many Sumerian signs have figurative components, as do many Chinese characters. But that there is no general move from concrete to abstract is clear from the 'abstract' nature of many of these early signs, especially number signs. As Boas argued many years ago (1927), the same is true of 'primitive art' and design in general, an idea that is confirmed by a moment's serious thought about contemporary oral cultures. Indeed it may be the very fact that we required a large number of signs in a logographic system that encourages some degree of pictorial representation for mnemonic purposes, just as the identification of some of the myriads of stars in the sky is helped by representing particular clusters as The Big Dipper, Orion's Belt, and so on. I make this point partly in order to modify the notion of a general shift from concrete to abstract such as lies at the basis of some formulations of cultural differences or developments; the shift has to be related to domain-specific activities and associated with particular mechanisms, and there are some aspects, of visual representation for example, that have moved in the opposite direction (see Baines 1985).

However, there is one element in these developments that does lead to abstraction and generalization. Tokens represent the content of transactions in an abstract way, when we compare these operations not only to straight barter, to transfers in kind, but also to the forms of 'money' represented by certain types of exchange item, such as silver in Mesopotamia and bars of salt in West Africa. Of course few if any human societies are limited simply to swapping one object for another at the same moment in time; some transfers involve delays, others some functional generalization of goods as media, whether these be raffia mats or bolts of cloth. But the systematic use of tokens marks a first move towards an economy based on a generalized media of exchange that we may refer to as money. The use of that term raises problems of definition, connected with the degree of its generalized use over the range of possible or potential transactions. But if tokens were so closely connected with writing, then both must be seen as facilitating the use of more generalized media of exchange, a point we will take up again in discussing 'letters of credit' and 'units of account'.

This is not of course to suggest that tokens were media of exchange; it seems certain that in the later period they were used in book-keeping either for mercantile or organizational purposes. Nor do I suggest for one moment that in oral cultures people do not employ arbitrary representations of exchange. Among the LoDagaa of West Africa, one interesting use occurs in gambling. As in many other parts of the world, one gambled not only for 'tokens' and even 'money', but also for other items over which one had a claim, eiven one's wife. Cowry shells, which constitute a medium of exchange of some generality, are used not only as the means of gambling but also as the bet itself, like taking the penny you have tossed as a reward for success. But as elsewhere a certain formation of the shells may stand in a purely arbitrary way for something else, for one's wife, for the rights to make the first move in a game or in divination (when the gods are more deliberately guiding the fall of the dice) for the need to make a sacrifice. The use of these forms of abstract representation are intrisic to the human condition. Nevertheless, while I do not see the use of tokens in the ninth millennium as marking the beginning of 'counting', nor even of record-keeping at the simplest level, it does, like writing, mark a point in the further separation of number from object that is essential for the development not only of 'money' but of mathematics, the roots of which are often seen as lying in the third millennium, with the beginning of writing (Friberg 1978–9).

There is another way in which graphic representation lends itself to accounting, not through numbers alone – which, being a self-defining system, can develop separately – but through words. For writing encourages a non-syntactical use of language that renders it especially adapted to the purposes of accounting that are so characteristic of Aegean Linear B. Even in Egypt, where the uses for religious purposes and for monumental display were so important at an early stage, Baines sees 'administration' (i.e. 'accounting') as having "primacy in the origin of writing" (1983: 575), that is to say, the kind of administration that characterizes the complex, bureaucratic state. This 'non-textual' (what I have referred to elsewhere as 'non-syntactical' or 'decontextualized' in terms of sentence structure) use of writing embodied in lists of various kinds affected other areas of communication but it dominated administrative uses, probably resulting "in a vast proliferation in the amount done, allowing improved central control of economic activity, as well as a more precisely monitored distribution of royal largesse".

These non-syntactical forms involved in record-keeping had a feedback effect on other uses of language and possibly on language itself, for the use of lists, categorical and conceptual as well as administrative, was important, especially for schools (Goody 1977). The point is given some support in Ancient Egypt where Baines notes that, while almost from the beginning writing served the two purposes of administration and monumental display, for nearly half a millennium there is no evidence of "continuous texts". The "original restriction of writing to tables, marks of ownership and captions" continued to exert its influence, even on spoken forms. In an interesting story from a later period (c. 1200 BC), a cowherd 'lists' what he is carrying as 'Emmer: 3 sacks; Barley: 2 sacks, etc.'; on this Baines comments, "People may not really . . . talk like this, but the influence of tabular presentation on written material involving numbers is profound" (1983: 575). Book-keeping and lists developed a different kind of language, introducing extensive formulae and omitting verbs, as Veenhof has remarked in the case of Mesopotamia (1972: 346). If I were in practice telling someone what I was carrying, I would construct simple sentences rather than formulae: "Well, there are three sacks of emmer, and then there are two of barley", etc. Speech is not normally telegraphic. What we have developing here is a written language adapted to book-keeping for the administration of temple and palace as well as for commercial exchange and interpersonal transfers.

Writing and the temple economy

Endowment and income

It was not only the central administration in Egypt that benefitted from literacy; as in Mesopotamia the church did so too. In the early period the only large body of documents comes from mortuary temples of the Fifth Dynasty kings (c. 2500–2350 BC) and this includes examples of "minute record keeping"; religious foundations near the royal residence were "relatively wealthy and tightly run, and had the resources for and interest in elaborate documents" (Baines 1983: 585).

As we have seen in Chapter 1, the dichotomy of temple and palace, as distinct socio-cultural institutions each with their own interests, marks both of the great written cultures of the Ancient East.[4] For the Old Kingdom in Egypt, Goedicke has explained how the great temples did not develop initially out of local cults, for the latter lacked both economic substance and a professional priesthood.[5] Rather, in the case of the cult of Horus, these seem to have developed *pari passu* with the expansion of the state (1979: 116); the priesthood at Heliopolis had been active since the Third Dynasty but it had no economic independence, being so much a part of the political structure. Rather the "economic and administrative function of the cult-temple evolved from the funerary responsibilities of the crown" (p. 120), since extended care, especially in the form of the daily food offerings, came to require administrative prep-

arations and these in turn required economic resources in the shape
of the royal funerary foundations which Goedicke compares with
the Islamic *waqf*, the religious corporations later to be so prominent
in precisely this same region.

When the largesse required to appease the gods is no longer
supplied by daily gifts but by permanent endowments, the result is
a greater measure of independence for the priestly administrators.
I do not suggest this holds universally, but if we think of the present
day one does not have to be committed to a notion of the primacy
of the economic domain to see that it is 'natural' (i.e. likely) that
schools, colleges and sects will strive to be independent of the daily,
monthly or annual begging bowl.

In Egypt the endowments flowed largely from the crown and are
often recorded in writing. On the Palermo Stone, which is probably
a late copy of the annals compiled in the Fifth Dynasty and going
back to the First, for almost every year royal donations are listed or
endowments mentioned, and these consisted of landed property as
well as offerings, mainly to deities supported for political reasons as
well as for piety.

An inscription recording a gift of this kind stipulates that "its
entire produce [or estate] is a god's offering, exempted like god's
land" (pp. 127–8) – in other words, freed from state taxes. This
exemption, detailed in a decree of King Neferkare, seems to apply
not to one cult alone but to all "priests". These priests do not seem
to have been full-time personnel but pluralists. Nevertheless we are
in the presence of a professional elite that relies not only on daily
offerings (the bowl of rice, the widow's mite) but on the product of
an endowment consisting of the basic agricultural resource – that is,
land.

For this purpose the endowment has to be land under a certain
type of productive system. The land a West African ruler could provide would not be much of a gift unless he could supply the labour
as well and even then the benefits would be minimal. You cannot
create endowments out of most forms of shifting cultivation – only
offerings are possible, although these may accumulate. Under these
conditions the entailment of the religious cults with other aspects of
society is great and the relative independence, the structural
autonomy, of church from state, is small.

Independence means that the ruler may have deliberately to seek the support of the church, which is not always automatically given. Goedicke suggests that the concessions made by Neferkare to the priesthood may have been offered in return for their support of his slightly dubious claim to the throne by fraternal succession (p. 129). However this may be, these concessions led to the priests becoming increasingly independent as a result of their holdings of 'god's land', although the fact that priests might be allocated a plurality of such tenures in different parts of the country qualified their personal independence, while their independence from the state was limited by the fact that many served as its high officials. Over time the separation between institutions and their personnel, as between state and church, increased. This independence was fostered by later kings who had to make further endowments to gain their political support. It was this complex system of a church and a priesthood endowed with lands that required a complicated system of record-keeping, although of course the state made similar demands probably at an earlier date.

The relationship between church and state fluctuated over time. In Mesopotamia there was more distinct separation, at least at times, than in Egypt. After the Old Babylonian period there is a shrinking of the economic growth and hence the political importance of the temple following the rise of palace organization headed by the king (Oppenheim 1964: 187). Hammurabi, who brought much of Mesopotamia under his sway, attempted to bolster economic support for the crown by subordinating the temple households to the direct control of the palace administration, a process that has been described as secularization (Renger 1979: 252; Harris 1961: 117–20).[6] While the church demands and receives support because of its good works to gods and men, its accumulated resources provide a constant temptation for the palace and for the ruling class generally, whether its treasures are to be taken for private gain, public development or simply to reduce its power. Nevertheless the temple remained one of the two "great organizations", together with the palace, consuming the best products of the fields and the herds which were sent to the temple to be used as food for the image, as income or rations for the administrators and workers, and, thirdly, to be stored for future use or converted into export crops and exchanged for raw materials.

As we have seen, the resources at the temple's command came

from various sources: gifts from worshippers, the allocation of tax resources and contributions of labour. Much came from the king whose responsibility the temples were (Larsen 1976: 119). One Old Assyrian text makes use of the formula "For the sake of his life and the prosperity of his city he built the temple" (p. 64). As elsewhere part of the wealth required came from the booty of war; even those highly predatory Europeans who invaded South America made some contribution to the building of churches as well as to the king's treasury.

From victorious Mesopotamian kings "the temple expected a share in the booty, especially precious votive gifts to be exhibited to the deity in the cella and the dedication of prisoners of war to increase the labour force of the temple" (Oppenheim 1964: 108). Kings were made to see that their duty lay in the building of "larger and more sumptuously decorated sanctuaries with higher temple towers . . . , an expression of thanks as well as a guarantee of future successes". Nevertheless the interests of palace and temple diverged on certain central issues, leading to clashes of interest. "While the temple strove for economic independence secured by agricultural holdings and sufficient manpower, the king also had to maintain and increase the fiscal base of support of the palace, i.e., of the state" (p. 109).

Accounts

The permanent endowment accumulated by the church, and received mainly from royal, that is, 'governmental', sources, carried a number of implications. Firstly, writing became critically important in the alienation of the property, particularly in the land, required by the great organizations. Secondly the acquisition of the basic means of production put the temple in the business of production and of organizing the production of others. Thirdly, the organization of production was associated with the organization of trade, although the latter might make its own independent contribution to the income and activities of the temple. Finally, the very complexity of the temple economy, the necessity of feeding and clothing its priesthood, meant keeping records of income and outgoings. In all these contexts the temple made use of writing, as extensively as the palace and the merchant, for it was carrying on similar activities. Since its activities were devoted to different ends, internal contradictions arose between ideology and practice, between heavenly and earthly accounts.

These themes can be better illuminated from later history where the examples are richer. The role of literate temples in a later economy is well brought out in the story of the Christian church of early medieval Europe. Despite an ideology dedicated to the abnegation of worldly wealth, it developed into a property-owning church with its ritual texts and formal records, documents which throw so much light on the general workings of the economy.[7] But I want to take another example, from medieval Sri Lanka, because it reminds us that until recent times the importance of the temple economy was crucial throughout much of Eurasia.

In his account of Buddhist monasteries in the early medieval period, Gunawardana (1979) points to the significance of the religious endowments beginning in the second century BC. While Buddhist monks had originally been devotees of the ascetic life and the first gifts were caves, the rise of clerics and monasteries required a more regular endowment and a more man-made habitat. Their total dependence on the fluctuating levels of gifts to supply food and clothing became impracticable and they needed a stable source of income so they could provide for themselves independently. Only rights in the basic means of production would do.

Offerings from the congregation continue to be of importance in most temple communities, in the form of both self-consuming items for the image, incense, flowers, burnt offerings, and more enduring consumer items for the priesthood, although money in the plate is a more flexible gift than goods in kind. Such offerings are outward signs of the participation of the faithful, a small gift being a visible expression of the hope for an immediate blessing in return. Endowments in perpetuity tend to come from those concerned with continuity over the longer span, from kings, nobility, those contemplating their fate in the other world, where the notion that one's future in the next is related to one's good deeds in this is of obvious benefit to the intermediaries between gods and men as well as to rich sinners.

In Sri Lanka the improved technology of agricultural production, especially the extension of irrigation that began around AD 100 and lasted for the following seven centuries, meant that kings and nobles had sufficient surplus to make the enormous endowments required both for the construction and the maintenance of temples and monasteries. These endowments took the form not only of rights over land, sometimes ownership, but also of rights to receive rent, taxes and irrigation dues as well as labour services, including the gifts of slaves themselves, even though this was against both the letter and the spirit of the *sangha*, the Buddhist community (pp. 121, 345).

An important aspect of the system of management of the properties and the labour resources (which were related to the endowments) was the tradition of accounting and of keeping records. In Gunawardana's words, "The interest evinced by the monastery in book-keeping and accounting was worthy of a business house" (1979: 125–6). The monastery maintained a register of resident monks of the kind also reported from northern India. In the Abhayagiri monastery the name and duties of all employees had to be recorded. According to the Mihintale Tablets, all receipts from estates, all payments made for the supply of food and for repairs, as well as the names of those entitled to allowances, were entered in the registers.

The monastery was run by a committee of management, as in the Hindu temples of South India, which in some cases included laymen since the rules of discipline embodied in the *Vinaya Piṭaka* directed monks to refrain from all profane activities including the acceptance, management and employment of material wealth. The existence of that endowment immediately drew attention to what Weber called "the paradox of all rational asceticism" which creates the wealth it rejects. "Temples and monasteries have everywhere become the very *loci* of all rational economies" (Weber 1947b: 332). In other words, the 'rationality' of writing, an economic 'rationality', is located at the heart of religious institutions concerned with the 'non-rational'.

From the entries in these registers the committee of management prepared a daily statement of accounts. This was duly signed and placed in a locked casket which was then sealed and put in a relic shrine. At the end of the month a further summary was prepared and at the end of each year the twelve monthly accounts were collected for the annual statement presented to the assembly of monks. One inscription proclaims that this should be done before the eighth day of the waning moon of the month of Vap (October/November), seven days before *Dīpāvāli*, the day on which Hindu merchants settled their annual accounts (Gunawardana 1979: 129).

The extraordinary development of book-keeping and auditing was connected not only with the collective, corporate nature of the *sangha*, a true corporation of joint consumers, but because it held property in common. This property it exploited in a variety of complicated ways that encouraged if it did not require some system of reckoning by means of written records. Each monk was entitled to a 'share' in the annual surplus, a practice reminiscent, as indeed is the whole system of accounts and auditing, of the 'dividends' formerly received by the Fellows of some Oxbridge Colleges, not to speak of the annual distribution of the corporations of modern business life. It is not surprising to hear that the loss of property later suffered by the monks as the result of foreign rule and political confiscation had "a detrimental effect upon the corporate existence" of the monastery (p. 328). It was a situation to be repeated in many subsequent cases of "the dissolution of the monasteries".

The internal working of the monastic community was based upon a type of *jajmānī* system that depended more on rents in kind than on transactions in money, although gold was used for the purchase of cloth and other commodities – that is, for the products of external commerce. Nevertheless it is quite clear that the Buddhist ethic was no hindrance to the accumulation of property, nor yet to the exercise of 'rational' economic judgement. Was the demolishing of a temple economy, the return of its capital and income for secular use, perhaps more critical than the demolishing of a specific economic ethic (which was circumvented as easily in Sri Lanka as in Islam and Christianity) for the development of the modern industrial economy? There is certainly little evidence that the 'failure' of South Asia to develop forms of western capitalism can be explained in terms of the limitations of a religious ethic, much less an Oriental mode of production. While influential factors in the development of sixteenth-century Europe certainly included changes in the modes of communication (see Eisenstein 1979 on printing) as well as

changes in the mode of production, the longer-term historical
perspective may also show that we have seriously over-estimated
the gap that existed between East and West at this time and that
there is both less and more to explain than we thought.

This analysis has suggested that Hocart's idea of the unity of
church and state in Sri Lanka (1950: 67) cannot be sustained, much
less the notion that the monastic organization was a 'department of
state'. As Gunawardana insists, the economic position of the
monastery and the prestige and authority of the *sangha* guaranteed
a large degree of autonomy. Symbiosis was antagonistic, modifying
any tendencies to despotic centralism (p. 350). Indeed in all temple
economies such independence must have been a check against the
monolithic accumulation of power and, most importantly, would
have encouraged feudal decentralization.

As we have seen, the dangers of the relative autonomy of church
and state are that each may interfere in the workings of the other,
with potentially disastrous results more especially for the 'weaker'
body. The late-tenth-century Cola invasion of the northern plains of
Sri Lanka placed the *sangha* in a difficult plight for it lost both
patronage and property. The restoration of the unity of the country
reversed the trend until the clerics themselves interfered in politics
and aroused the anger of Vikramabahu I by trying to stop him from
becoming king. On coming to the throne, he proceeded to confis-
cate monastic estates despite the efforts of some monks to defend
their possessions and their privileges by employing Tamil mercen-
aries (Gunawardana 1979: 349), thus setting in train a series of
irreversible events of long-enduring consequences down to the
present day.

Writing and the palace economy

The temple received much of its endowment from the palace, which
in turn collected revenues, organized primary production, participated in trade (at times more than others) and distributed its goods
within the royal household as well as without. The accounting of the
revenues had to make use of similar written procedures to those
found in the temple economy, but they were applied more widely to

the recording of booty as well as to the numbering of the population for purposes of taxation and control.

Taxation and census

Agricultural taxes in Mesopotamia were paid in kind and formed a percentage of the year's produce; theoretically this was 10%, but the system of tax-farming meant more was extorted, from between one-fifth and one-half of the yields. These contributions were dispatched by the tax collector to government depots, where the officials might call him to account for delays and kept a careful record of all income, which was then put into circulation as quickly as possible; "the animals might be sent to join the state herds: other perishable goods were sold or lent to merchants at regular rates of interest, or were handed over to government factories for manufacture" (Woolley 1963: 628).

Other taxes were levied on town goods and on people. A check upon the activities of collectors as well as a forecast of the budget was obtained by the registration of all tax-payers, that is to say, by the census. "A register of births was kept, so that a poll-tax could easily be applied; but for taxation in general the lists dealt with property as well as with persons" (Woolley 1963: 628). In Babylonia the names in such lists were divided into three categories: "First come the peasants, semi-serfs, subject to the *corvée* and to military service, owners of small plots of land or vineyard, of whom it is often remarked 'has no cattle'; the next in order are the middle class, amongst whom we find tradesmen, gardeners, herdsmen and grooms; last come the gentry, distinguished by the possession of chariots" (p. 629). Here we are vividly reminded of the intimate connection between writing, the census and taxation. Non-literate states collected the analogy of taxes by the kind of process that Polanyi called 'redistributive' (1957), that Pryor designated 'centric accumulation' (1977), and that Sahlins has described for Polynesian kingdoms (1958) and Herskovits for Dahomey (1938). But elaborate systems of taxation, the more precise forecasting of needs, resources and income, plus the resulting fear among the population of being numbered in the census – which represents the penetration of the state into the domestic life of its subjects and constitutes the means of raising taxes now and in the future – all this is critically dependent upon the use of writing (see also Postgate 1974).

Central administration

While the economy of Mesopotamia was at first largely a temple economy which later became secularized, in Egypt, following the suppression of the nomarchs or provincial governors, the economy was mainly controlled by the ruler although later on the priests sometimes proved more powerful than the king. During the New Kingdom, the great temples acquired enormous landed properties by royal gift, and the revenues from these lands provided for the maintenance of the priesthood and the observance of the service of the god. Such ecclesiastical landlordism on this scale was possible only under a system of intensive (and enforced) cultivation, which on the other hand was civil in origin. It was the fact that the church could operate as a productive corporation that made it here, as in medieval Europe and Tibet, a rival for the control of the political system. Its position did not depend upon the accumulation of resources alone. The temples were essential to the teaching of writing; by the Third Intermediate Period they largely controlled the training of the scribes and bureaucrats who ran the government machine.

For most of the historical period, then, the national economy of Egypt centred upon the Pharaoh. Much of the remaining two-thirds of the land not controlled by the temples was worked by serfs under the supervision of his appointed officials. However land was also allocated to individuals under a variety of arrangements and could be transferred either by will or by sale, both acts involving written documents. The tenants might hold other crown property for whose use they also paid an annual assessment recorded in the tax registers of the 'White House', the Treasury of Egypt. Taxes were paid in kind and stored in the royal and temple magazines. This was the archetypal 'central storage economy' exemplified in the Biblical story of Joseph's administration, and it was one that depended, at least on this scale, upon record-keeping.

As we have seen, this fact had interesting consequences, conceptually as well as practically. For all goods brought into the magazines – grain, cattle, wine, linen – were invoiced under generalized terms for 'dues', one of which also meant 'labour' or was derived from the same root. So goods tended to be placed on the same basis as the *corvée* used to build a pyramid or clean a canal (Woolley 1963: 624). In other words there was some movement towards a generalized, and to some extent abstract, unit of account in which goods could be measured, a transformation parallel to the development of relatively generalized modes and media of exchange. The movement was certainly incomplete in Egypt, where there were multiple and not altogether interchangeable units of account, especially when it came to labour and commodities, but it was a movement of the same kind that comes to light in the recent adoption of accounts among the Vai of West Africa (Goody, Cole and Scribner 1977) discussed later in this chapter.

While the early use of writing was often associated with religion, the priesthood was itself closely connected with both the polity and the economy. But the polity made its own demands. In Egypt the appearance of writing seems to be roughly contemporaneous with the creation of a single state and an overall pantheon. "Writing was, in effect, originally an instrument for the communication of orders", declared Leclant, "rather than for a registration of ideas. It is absolutely essential for organization and command" (Woolley 1963: 664), although the term 'command' hardly covers the whole field of information processing that was involved. Writing was critical in the civil administration of the early dynastic period, where the main administrative uses were closely linked with the economy. The most senior official was the Chancellor who was in charge of the Treasuries of Upper and Lower Egypt, that is, the White House and the Red House. His staff consisted of one or more 'assistants' and 'scribes' (sš). "Their functions . . . comprised not only the supervision of national revenue, which included by the end of the Second Dynasty, the organization of the biennial 'census of gold and of fields', but also the collection and distribution of various stores, such as oils and certain other products which were levied as taxes" (Edwards 1971: 38). The control of provisions figured prominently in the economic and administrative organization, as can be seen from the existence of various departments dealing with these matters; cereals were in the care of the 'Granaries'; supplies to

privileged persons including the temples and the court were distributed by the 'House of the Master of Largesse', a department
closely linked with the 'Mansion of Life' in the palace; vineyards
were under the control of the 'Food Office' and fats were kept in a
special storehouse called the 'House of Cattlefat'.

It is clear that such administrative tasks would be enormously
facilitated by writing; a bureaucracy of this scale would seem to be
difficult to manage without some form of externalized record-
keeping, at least of the kind that developed among the Incas by
means of the *quipu* (Murra 1980). But more elaborate transactions
in goods are made easier by the adoption of a written language,
especially in the sphere of the economy. Like others Gelb specifically links the origin of writing in Sumer to the needs of the public
economy. "With the rise in productivity of the country, resulting
from state-controlled canalization and irrigation systems, the
accumulated agricultural surplus made its way to the depots and
granaries of the cities, necessitating keeping accounts of goods coming to the cities, as well as of manufactured products leaving the
cities for the country" (1963: 62).[8] Nevertheless, while writing
subsequently played an important part in the administration of the
temple or palace economy, the origins themselves were perhaps
simpler. As we have seen, Sumerologists have been in general
agreement about the development of a fully fledged writing system
from earlier beginnings, possibly from tokens, starting perhaps with
the cylinder seals, then utilizing tags and labels attached to goods.

Both in Egypt and in Mesopotamia the economy of temple and
palace entailed a burgeoning of bureaucrats and bureaucracy, of
records and record-keepers. One document in the Ebla archives
from Syria lists a total of 11,700 men directly employed by the
dignitaries and the administration of the Acropolis, although the
number is hard to credit. Another works out the barley rations for
a quarter of a million persons, perhaps as an exercise. The advent of
King Sargon of Akkad (2334–2279) provides a more credible
example of the growth of administration, a shift from minimal
record-keeping to something much more extensive. Business and
administrative documents from this period have survived in some
numbers, and they seem to bear witness to the change of emphasis
from temple estate to the secular economy. Such documents are

marked by the bureaucratic formality (verging on formulae) of their contents.

The business tablets of the Agade period are mostly of a formal kind, lists and receipts, but legal documents are also present, depositions of witnesses, sales of fields, slaves, animals, and commodities, records of traffic, of lands and farmers, and of trade between cities. There exist also letters, characterized in this period by a peculiar exordium; they deal principally with the administration of estates and the assignment of leases, having only very occasionally references to matters of wider interest. (Gadd 1971: 450)

The real proliferation of the uses of writing occurred in the subsequent dynasty known as Ur III. Here the influence of writing spreads into every pocket of the economy, critical for trading operations, organizing workshop production in temple and state, collecting the agricultural 'surplus', defining the transfer and ownership of property. The nature of writing means that each activity is transformed in significant ways by its introduction.

Palace accounts

The book-keeping for the palace economy led to advances in accounting techniques. Already in the third millennium formulae are developed as ledger headings (Veenhof 1972: 345). The 'balancing of accounts' is a marked feature of the royal archives from Mari on the upper Euphrates dating from c. 1700. The registers of various distributions of food finish with a recapitulation of the quantity of comestibles issued during the course of the month (Birot 1960: 291). Some tablets are just summaries while others attempt to 'balance the account', that is, balance off income and outgoings,'sorties' and 'reçus'. Writing of a certain tablet, Birot notes that "the scribe was not content with aligning the figures of income and expenditure, but established a true balance" (p. 295). Once again it is a question of finding an abstract way of adding together apples and oranges. In the Old Babylonian period in Sippar this was done in the "crown bureau of wool accounts" by reducing wool and barley to silver, which acted as "a standard by which the value of commodities was determined" (Yoffee 1977: 4).

These tablets reveal the full complexity of the palace economy, showing it to be very different from that of an African kingdom, even one as centralized as Dahomey in West Africa. In the first place an elaborate system of tribute and taxation supported the royal household, maintaining *les repas du roi* by which the king kept not only himself and his household but his status and position as well. As in the temples of medieval Sri Lanka, income and outgoings were balanced and summarized to give monthly and annual totals. The same accounting was applied to metals; gold for example was issued to smiths but the court exercised "rigid control over the use of the precious metal given out to the goldsmiths" (Birot 1960: 315).

There was a proliferation of officialdom to control this central economy. These officials developed record-keeping of many different kinds and in ways that were far removed from the event-structured universe. For example, some tablets give a list of workers of the two sexes grouped by occupation (Birot 1960: 331). For both Mari and Terqa we have two lists of the same personnel, one being a statement of grain rations issued on a monthly basis to each individual, the other being a simple nominal roll. As in the temple economy, the palace 'household' developed elaborate ways of keeping track of transactions, balancing the books and auditing the accounts, activities which fed back into linguistic behaviour and into social life more generally (see also Dalley 1984).

Textile production

The palace was involved not only in accounting for its income and expenditure but more directly in production and trade. In the production of textiles it acted much like the temple and the merchants at different periods. The early economy of Mesopotamia was largely a temple economy rather than one based on individual craftsmen, although these did exist, and such centralization needed records of personnel and input/output. The use of ledgers and accounts was related to the organization of temple 'factories' (as Woolley calls them) or what others refer to as 'workshops', or 'workhouses', reserving the term factory for workshops where machines (that is, more complex machines) are run by hired rather than by servile labour.[9] These workshops produced cloth which as in many early state economies, in China, India, Peru and Africa, was an essential commodity for external as well as for internal consumption and exchange, being one of the first materials to be manufactured mechanically. As the activity expanded from purely domestic production into the export trade, it appears to have shifted from women's work to predominantly men's;[10] women spinners were still employed in Ebla and elsewhere, but their exclusion from weaving itself may be partly due to the introduction of the loom, which required more strength, as well as to the commercialization of production. Mesopotamian cloth was largely woollen whereas the basis of the cloth trade was linen in Egypt, cotton in India and silk in China.[11] In Mesopotamia woollen cloth became the main export commodity, produced by specialist workers belonging to guilds, in workshops owned by wealthy merchants, by temples and by the palace; most of the workers appear to have been slaves but others were free citizens, some of whom may have worked at home, taking the thread from the temple store and bringing back the finished cloth (as suggested by the temple receipts).

Detailed lists were kept of the individual workers, the amount of wool each received, the quantity, weight and quality of the cloth completed and the payments in kind made to them (for slaves this consisted only of rations); "note is taken of deaths, of absences or of substitutes employed in place of a sick employee . . . Not less businesslike was the stocktaking . . . ; the lists are immensely long and most detailed, giving measurements, weights and qualities and noting issues, generally against receipt – 'Gift of wool to the royal musicians at the great smithy; receipt of Maššaga' " (Woolley 1963: 593). And very similar employment ledgers and stock lists are found for other trades carried on in the temples of the Third Dynasty of Ur, though after 2000 BC individual workshops and civilian associations take over more of the production.

Trade

The role of the palace in trade has been at the centre of controversy about the economy of the Ancient Near East. As with the production of commodities and of agricultural produce, the extent of the control exercised by the palace, temple and merchants or farmers varied at different times. While large-scale trading in Ancient Egypt seems to have been mainly organized by the state,[12] the absence of timber, stone and metals in Mesopotamia meant that the region depended heavily for basic materials on foreign trade in which both private merchants and temple priests took part. For although the patron god of the city, represented by the priests, was the 'owner' of the land, large parts of the divine estate were let to individuals, some of whom traded in the produce they cultivated. Hence mercantile relations in Mesopotamia were often less dependent upon political relations than they were in Egypt, partly because of the absence of an over-arching government for most of its history. Although merchants had a freer hand, their internal and external dealings were partly regulated by the politico-legal system, to which codes such as that of Hammurabi made but a limited contribution (see Chapter 4). This is a question to which I will give more attention in the section on 'Writing and credit'. But, while private trade was undoubtedly an important feature of Mesopotamian economic life, there were times when the traders seem to have become "royal emissaries carrying precious gifts from one ruler to the other" (Oppenheim 1964: 93) and when they are expressly referred to as being on the 'payroll' of the palace.

Much trade in the Near East was carried on by corporate bodies, that is, by the state as well as by the temple. Documents from the archives of the Syrian state of Ebla dating from the period 2400–2250 BC show a central economy, where "the most systematic form of registration was reserved for consignments, or . . . despatches, of finished goods – the textiles produced in the city – and the arrivals of tribute, taxation and payments in gold and silver" (Matthiae 1980: 178). The nature of the records was 'essentially book-keeping, the aim of the administration being above all to transcribe the amount of the outgoings and incomings of goods' (pp. 178–9); book-keeping accounted for 70% of the texts in the archives, another 10% being historical and 20% literary, with many of the latter written in Sumerian rather than Old Canaanite or Eblaite (Pettinato 1981: 231).

Commercial and financial documents seem to have been kept in the Ebla archive for several generations. Of especial importance were those records having to do with the textile trade, which extended as far as Palestine in the south, to central Anatolia in the north and the Tigris Valley in the east, including the Mesopotamian city states of Mari, Assur and Kish. We find a large number of texts treating of the consignment of barley ration for the women workers in the spinning mills, workers who are specifically designated as not being slaves.

Writing and the mercantile economy

It is difficult, and unnecessary, to try and separate in a definitive fashion the activities of merchants, temple and palace in Mesopotamia, since all three clearly interacted with one another, particularly in the economic domain. However, certain uses of writing came to the fore in the realm of commerce and banking, especially in the two inter-related spheres of shareholding and credit.

Shareholding

I have already referred to the 'dividends' of religious corporations, but the holding of 'shares' in mercantile activity, by independent merchants as well as by the great organizations, was an important feature of Mesopotamian trade. Its extent and complexity again made writing a virtual necessity, not only in keeping track of merchandise but in maintaining a record of the enterprise, a record that was not simply a statement of accounts but a certificate of debts and of shares. For the terms on which money-holders invested and merchant-adventurers accepted varied to such an extent as to require some specific record. Moreover, once established, such 'shares' in the 'sack' (Larsen 1976: 96) could be bought and sold, yielding another complexity of rights and duties, claims and counter-claims, to be kept in mind, or, better, recorded. Some money-men advanced funds at a fixed rate of interest without running any personal risk. In other cases, the lender participated in the profits of the venture; sometimes he might sell "a share in the sea expedition", engaging in a kind of maritime insurance (Oppenheim 1954). Keeping track of such transactions was clearly helped by the existence of a means of communication that did not rely upon the memory of witnesses who were subject to the constraints of forget-fulness, mortality, or partisanship.

Many ancient historians have drawn attention to the similarity between these partnership arrangements and the *commenda* that are found in Europe from the tenth century onwards and that played so prominent a part in raising investment capital in the development of mercantile activity in late medieval and early modern Europe. Indeed there may well be a continuous connection between this financial institution in the Renaissance and in the Bronze Age, for European merchants seem to have learnt of the practice from the Near East (Lopez 1952: 267). The subject has great general signifi-cance for reconsidering the role of communication in the economy, but at this point I want only to indicate the striking support given to these suggestions by an economic historian writing about such partnerships in twelfth-century Genoa. The information comes from data "scribbled on three small scraps of paper . . . regarded as the earliest examples of medieval mercantile accounting. Although crude, they prove that partnership arrangements made it indis-pensable for the merchants to keep records, not only about accounts payable and receivable, but also about any elements that would enable them to determine profit or loss" (de Roover 1963: 52). We are dealing here with non-familial rather than familial partnerships, although writing may affect even the latter. It is critically important for the general theme that this institution depended upon writing, which was already available as a means of raising capital early in the second millennium.

Credit

Small as they were, Mesopotamian ships enabled goods to be trans-ported to an overseas market in direct exchange for other goods or valuables. The journey by land, on the other hand, could not cope with the transport of bulky goods, and valuables were risky to carry. The risks were mitigated by issuing what might be called 'letters of credit', a system facilitated by the existence of established agents on the trade-routes.

The traveller, starting with a consignment of grain, might sell it in some town on his road, receiving a signed tablet with the value expressed in copper possibly, or in silver, with which he could buy there or elsewhere something to the same value which he could sell at a profit farther along his journey. Again he might realise his promissory note not necessarily in the form of the actual goods mentioned therein, or even in actual goods at all, but in the form of another note guaranteeing the delivery of some commodity for which there was a demand farther north. A clever salesman could effect several operations, and make a profit on each, in the course of a single journey. Since there was no coined money he was not troubled with difficulties of foreign exchange at the various frontiers; his tablets, payable on demand by the agents to whom he was accredited, were the ancient equivalent of a paper currency based on commodity values. (Woolley 1963: 613–14)

The use of such written modes of credit clearly facilitated the profitable exchange of goods by decreasing risk and increasing the flexibility, and hence the complexity, of the transactions.

There is a tendency to put into writing a note of transactions already carried out and promises relating to future deliveries and payments; the popular I.O.U. is a kind of proto-cheque, an informal acknowledgement of debt – a written promise, legitimated by the signature, and sometimes in medieval Europe by a mark, in particular a cross, which is the sign of the cross, bringing supernatural sanctions into play. The signature is a pledge of faith; indeed, the signature is the moral person himself, or at least the legal person, *homo legens*. On the other hand blessings which resemble promises, in that they refer to the future but appeal to supernatural agencies and are hence subject to the will of others, tend to remain in the oral domain, except for the more generalized hopes expressed for the future of the dead on funerary architecture. Curses fell in between, for in Mesopotamia they were used in written form (though not at the earliest stages) to protect boundary stones, the monuments of royalty and in particular the sanctity of the dead and their habitations.

Merchants often worked for the king and the temple but also on their own account, especially during the Dynasty of Ur III when silver became increasingly used as a means of payment and a standard of value (Garelli 1969: 103). The point is subject to much argument, Polanyi claiming that silver was used only as 'money of account', with Veenhof asserting its role in exchange. However even in Old Babylonia both uses of silver were in evidence (Yoffee

1977: 16–17). Private traders, as we have seen, were present from the beginning. But the most extensive evidence of such activity comes from tablets found in Asia Minor consisting of the commercial and legal archives of Assyrian merchants working in Anatolia in the nineteenth century BC and handling the export of textiles and tin, while acting as intermediaries in the trade in rare metals in exchange for these commodities (Larsen 1967, 1976; Oppenheim 1964; Veenhof 1972). The merchants belonged to an organization called the *karum*, 'the quay', and by extension the market and its official buildings. Situated outside the town, this 'port' provided a centre of import–export, a bank, a chamber of commerce and of compensation. It was also a centre for collecting the taxes on trade as well as for judging disputes of a commercial kind. Such institutions existed in all the important towns of central Anatolia, the main one being at Kanish, which was in turn subordinate to the authorities of the town of Assur. The leading merchants of Assur "advanced capital, regulated prices, fixed rates of interest, controlled exports and the routes of caravans, activities in which one can never altogether separate their official from their private role" (Garelli 1969: 119). Public and private finances often appeared to overlap, even with the ruler of Assur, "qui fait plutôt figure de gros marchand que de roi".

The Assyrian capital of Assur has been described as a fortress functioning as "a transit town on the network of caravan roads" (Larsen 1976: 3); it was "a consumers' and producers' city which depended upon long distance trade to satisfy its need for food supplies". Equally tin was a scarce and essential commodity for the Hittites in Anatolia, being required in the manufacture of bronze and imported both from Iran (via Assur) and from Bohemia (Mellaart 1968). The trade with Kanish appears to have been carried on sometimes by partnerships of the kind found among seafaring merchants of Ur at roughly the same period, sometimes by family firms. Some of the correspondence shows the merchant to be located at Kanish, while his wife is in Assur where she might have a large degree of autonomy in organization and decision making. For example, a certain Lamassi sends sixteen textiles to her husband; since this number was too big for her to produce single-handed, she was presumably aided by daughters and slave-girls in a kind of home industry (Veenhof 1972: 113). Other textiles were produced by the great organizations, some in workshops but also by 'putting-out'. "In the great cities, the temples and palaces were the home of [the woollen] industry; but quantities of stuff were served out under bond to private establishments to be worked up and returned or paid for" (Johns 1904: 203). Therefore the lady merchant could buy another cloth, either locally made or imported from the south, paying higher prices when there was a scarcity due to a revolt or other circumstances (Veenhof 1972: 87, 98, 116). Whether or not she had her own separate trading account is not clear but she enjoyed much freedom of action, redeeming a slave girl, paying debts, and carrying out similar activities (p. 123). In one case an unhappy wife writes to her husband saying how she had to collect her own jewelry and give it to the City Hall as payment for some precious stone (Larsen 1976: 198–9), perhaps making temporary use of her dowry to support the joint enterprise.

Family participation was considerable. Children were sent back from the out-station to be educated (Larsen 1974: 471). Later some acted as agents, then became independent merchants on their own account (Larsen 1967: 173). The dissolution of the firm on the death of the father could lead to serious internal disputes (Larsen 1976: 97). "In this complex social and economic system, incorporating the family structure which to a large extent equals the economic structure, the investment-contracts which amount to long term partnerships, and a highly evolved pattern of representation and agency, we have the framework for the success of the Old Assyrian commercial expansion" (p. 102).

It is also the case that the trade, which we know about largely through its written records, was intimately dependent upon those records. Of these there were three kinds, two emanating from the colony, one from the capital. These were: (1) transport contracts, sent with the person taking back the money to purchase goods; (2) notifying messages, to tell the agent what was required; (3) the caravan accounts, detailing the expenses, taxes, purchase price and other details concerning the goods purchased. In addition, there were contracts for sale or promissory notes, as well as loan documents, some of which incorporate a fixed date, while others use the phrase "borrow money on interest" (p. 104). The whole trade was regulated by way of a series of highly standardized documents.

These documents illustrate very clearly the process of generalization involved in book-keeping of this kind, especially in the caravan accounts which attempt to render a balance sheet. One such text totals up the money/silver received, the goods purchased at Assur as well as other expenses, a list that included linen clothes, tin, donkeys and fodder, wages, tolls, etc. (Larsen 1967: 39–40).[13] Sometimes the expenses included lodgings, gifts to officials, possibly bribes, payments for crossing rivers. Some cloth was given to the harnessers of the donkeys of the caravan as 'working capital', so that they could make something for themselves (p. 150). Once again the separation of private and corporate funds was insisted upon, as was the case within the family (Veenhof 1972: 116). There was a distinct concept of a firm with its own accounts in which all these different items had to be reduced to one kind of valuation, one unit of account, so that a reckoning could be made of the profit and the loss. The identity of each item was temporarily swallowed up in a global account of the transaction in which a variety of entries were reduced to a common denominator.

The Assyrian merchants of Kanish were not a solitary example of the highly complex trade carried on by independent merchants. Similar features are to be found at roughly the same period in the overseas trade of Ur, which acted as a 'port of entry' for copper into Mesopotamia at the time of the Dynasty of Larsa. The trade was in the hands of a group of seafaring merchants "who worked hand in hand with enterprising capitalists in Ur to take garments to the island of Bahrain in order to buy large quantities of copper" (Oppenheim 1954: 6–7). The copper in fact came from elsewhere but the island served as a 'market centre'. On their return successful merchants offered gifts to the temple of the goddess Ningal. Contracts show them to have borrowed money as the 'capital for a partnership', though some of these specify that the lender refuses to share the losses, and therefore the profits, of the expedition; they want only the return of their capital plus interest. The Code of Hammurabi wanted the investing merchant to share the losses as well as the profits of the travelling merchant, but this responsibility was not always adopted in practice; however one contract does declare "together they will make profits and suffer losses".

The kinds of arrangement were many. "The complex legal relationship between the investing and the travelling merchant has created a number of loan types of which at least two are mentioned in the Code of Hammurabi" (pp. 9–10). Loans were made by women; one trader lent money to a partnership of which he was himself a member; in another case two partners take out a loan for five years. Once again the complexity is such, with the multiplicity of roles and individuals involved, the separation of till and pocket, the variability of prices, the range of expenses and the opportunities for profit, that book-keeping is practically a prerequisite, a prerequisite that had important consequences not only in terms of trade but of the conceptualization of a series of transactions and of the very nature of the items involved.

Writing and individual transactions

I turn, finally, to expand upon the part played by writing in individual transactions that affect the economy, a subject that is touched upon in the previous section on shareholding and credit.

The evidence of transfer

Even for the independent merchants, huge numbers of trading transactions were recorded. These written transactions included the transfer of rights in land, which was subject to loans and in some cases to sale, registered in the names of the parties involved. Without such a document, no claim by a professed lender was valid (Woolley 1963: 606–7). Indeed, the commitment to writing went so far, in the ideal terms of the Code of Hammurabi, as to prescribe the death penalty for buying or receiving on deposit property from a man's son or slave (that is, from someone other than the owner himself) without a written bond duly witnessed; 'that man is a thief'. In other words the written document served as evidence and guarantee of the legitimacy of a transaction. It provided protection for both parties in a manner reminiscent of medieval England, where one of the first forms of official record-keeping was instituted in 1194 to list loans made by Jews; the high literacy of the Jews was itself important for their role in the economy as proto-bankers (Clanchy 1979: 54) but they were also required to keep a note of transactions as a matter of protection for their clients and possibly for political control.

One of the reasons that writing was so useful in trade was its ability to store information over time and so to make 'memory' more reliable; confirmation of a transaction rested no longer on the longevity of 'eye' witnesses alone but on the retention of the document itself, often validated by means of signatures or marks, such as the colophon in the city state of Ebla (Pettinato 1981: 231–2), in addition to the witnesses themselves. Nor was certainty the only gain; by the use of writing the capacity of the memory store could be increased so that more transactions could be kept track of, and hence carried on, at any one time. Not a necessary result, and one from which the internal memory may suffer. But the external storage provided by the book offers a new, alternative, potentiality for human communication.

To make the point in a different way, members of oral cultures often observe minutely the movements of the planets, the times of the rising and the setting of the sun and of other heavenly bodies. But the advances in astronomy made by the major non-European civilizations depended to a considerable extent upon two types of technological device: first, instruments of measurement and observation that made use of graphic or geometrical formalization; and secondly, and more importantly, writing, with its ability to record (that is, to preserve) multiple, repeated observations of the events and thus to allow precise assessments of their similarities and differences, leading to further generalizations about their movements and to predictions of the future. The reliability of observations and their preservation were intrinsic to the development of astronomy as of other 'exact' sciences; that is what made them 'exact' and 'scientific' in the sense that regularities could be perceived and future events predicted. To an important degree, the basis of early science was 'book-keeping', the keeping of the books.

Title to land

Writing was used to record personal loans as well as commercial transactions but in no area was it of greater importance than in registering title to land. We have seen the prominent part that ecclesiastical landlordism played in Mesopotamia. Much of the territory of a city state lay in the hands of the patron god, with the human ruler acting as 'tenant farmer' and being the effective lord of the land. The land might be let on lease to private individuals, worked directly by the temple or rented out on the condition of providing service to that body. At times there was a conflict, as in Lagash, between the interests of the ruler (*ensi*) and those of the temple. In this version of the widespread conflict between church and state, between temple and palace, between priest and king, the secular arm was sometimes accused of making use of the lands of the religious for its own purposes. Always, remarks Woolley, "there was the tendency to substitute private ownership for that of the community or of the god" (1963: 626). Records were one way of preventing such sequestrations, although the allocation of lands to the temple, which presumably represented an alienation from some other owner, was often carried out by similar means.

As time went on royal claims were extended, especially in the period of Ur III; even before this records show the king of Kish purchasing large estates. Indeed contract tablets demonstrate that, in the second millennium, land generally was bought and sold more freely. It was also assigned to individuals as rewards for service or to assure loyalty; in Hammurabi's time the officers who recruited for the police and the army received tax-free holdings that were transmitted in the male line, providing that the original duties were carried out by the grantee's descendants, a practice that long continued in the Near East and Mediterranean in Graeco-Roman times, in Byzantium and right down to the Turkish empire.

The ownership and transfer of rights in land was central to the political economy and it was here especially that writing came into its own in a variety of ways, some of which I have already noted. First, the transactions in land could be registered for future reference to provide evidence of title; one Old Babylonian contract tablet from Uruk (*c.* 1750 BC) is a deed of sale recording the purchase of a plot of land by two brothers for one-sixth of an ounce of silver and including the oath sworn by the parties as well as the names of seven witnesses (British Museum catalogue 1963, no. 6).[14] Under the Kassite kings of Babylon, such title deeds were sometimes incorporated in boundary stones (or *kudurru*), virtually all royal, defining the area of the estate and cursing those who interfere with the rights of the owner.

Secondly, the areas themselves, often of valuable irrigated land, required setting down in writing; a tablet from Lagash (*c.* 1980 BC) lists five fields with their irregular dimensions; the area is calculated by reckoning it as a rectangle or regular figure, and then adding or subtracting such parts of the field as lie outside or inside these lines (British Museum catalogue 1963, no. 5). While these calculations did not require writing as such, they did involve a development of precise graphic representation that seems to follow the application of graphics to language. Such representation appears in turn to have led to the working out of the Pythagorean theorem in Mesopotamia though it was never laid out in the explicit form in which it later appeared among the Greeks (Neugebauer and Sachs 1945: 42–3).

Thirdly, the introduction of written contracts led scribes to formalize the formulae and elaborate procedures for their transmission (Veenhof 1972: 345). A tablet from Nineveh (eighth century BC) provides a late copy of an Old Babylonian list of legal words and phrases both in Sumerian (the dead classical language) and in Akkadian. It belongs to a series of such tablets called after the opening phrase, *Ana ittišu* ('at its fixed term') which was used in schools to teach scribes the terminology of contracts and other legal documents. Practice led to training and in the long run to the formal development of the academic, 'decontextualized' (or segregated) study of legal matters. Writing led eventually to the rise of specialist lawyers in the Ancient World as well as to the teaching of laws, which was especially necessary where many of the formulae were enshrined in a dead language whose preservation, indeed existence as such, was a direct result of writing. You cannot decode, decipher, an oral language that is no longer spoken.

Fourthly, the fact that some land was taxed and some was tax-free, that some temple land was worked directly by servile labour and some rented out, implied a set of records or accounts to keep track not only of contributions but of the differential status of the land and the holders of rights in it (Landsberger 1937). The burdens on land were of two main kinds: rents or tithes to the temple (or landowner) and taxes to the state. Both involved accounting. Hammurabi had the temple managers and cattle-masters of the Shamash temple brought to Babylon to have their accounts checked; one Kassite king granted immunity from all taxes to the estates of the god Marduk, while others granted the temples supplies out of the civil revenues. Immunities reached such a level that the Mesopotamian state had to rely upon sources of revenue other than the tax on land and people, especially on direct labour. Building works, canal cleaning and road making were carried out by calling up local people and sometimes by summoning specified numbers of labourers from a distance, a practice going back to the beginning of the irrigation system. If such labour was needed, the cultivator might be shown "a properly signed and dated summons" – "Task: brick-carrying for one day" (Woolley 1963: 628).

The introduction of written title into a society where rights and duties were held orally had a far-reaching effect which was particularly devastating for those without access to the new media. Indeed this shift can be seen as crucial, in the present as in the past, in the appropriation of rights by landlords, ecclesiastical as well as secular. Men of power, especially conquerors, have always taken over land by force, but the value given to deeds by the courts has provided a widely used mechanism for legitimizing the transfer of untitled, therefore ownerless, land to those who commanded, directly or indirectly, the means of communication. It is a problem to which I will return in considering 'The Letter of the Law'.

Reciprocity and balancing the books

As a result of the larger number of transactions that could be handled, from the standpoint of the actor, reciprocity (and credit) in commercial transactions could be more easily extended beyond the more immediate context. I am not referring here to the long-term reciprocities to which anthropologists refer in discussing systems of generalized marital exchange and similar transactions, since these are often either implicit for the actor or exist only at the level of the observer. In the former case we can again see writing as tending to make explicit what was hitherto implicit and as changing what it touches in the process, for example, by the introduction of a greater measure of 'calculation'. No single act (or pair, or limited set of acts) had to equal another, providing the 'books' balanced over the longer term; that is to say, the potential cycle of accepted reciprocities was extended, or, alternatively, asymmetry was fully recognized. On the other hand the reciprocities and obligations themselves became more precise when they were set down in writing rather than being held in the storage system of the brain with its homeostatic tendencies. It is a process that I have elsewhere illustrated by an analysis of the influence of writing on LoDagaa funeral contributions (1972b: 46), where the written record reminded past receivers how they should act as future givers, rather like the lists of Christmas cards that are kept as a guide to next year's postings. The calculus of precise reciprocities has replaced, in part at least, that of the closeness of relationship. A fascinating parallel is provided by Janssen from Egyptian *ostraca* which record gifts given when a man became a grandfather, or gifts to the father (in-law?), which he describes as an *aide-mémoire*; they were intended to jog the author's memory at some later date because the gifts were not free but had to be returned (1982: 256).

Writing and the economy in Africa

A consideration of the potential changes that writing may make in systems of reciprocity suggests that we should look at the recent evidence from Africa in order to bring out the potentialities of writing and the limitations of the oral economy.

Many African communities have been involved in long-distance trade for a very long time; indeed it has been seen as one of the major characteristics of the so-called 'African mode of production' (Coquéry-Vidrovitch 1969). Nevertheless the extent and complexity of that trade was certainly on a different scale than in the Ancient Near East. Where it was probably at its most complex, down the East African coast, across the Sahara and in the Western Sudan, it is significant that Muslims, foreign and indigenous (and before them Egyptians, Greeks and Indians), were involved and that meant at least a minimal use of literacy for commercial purposes. Throughout Africa there were relatively segregated media of exchange – cowry shells, manillas, bars of salt, cloth; on the East African coast in the medieval period we find stamped metal currency. Throughout Africa we find trade and sometimes credit; in the more elaborate commerce across the Sahara we also find written bills of exchange, as well as maps, itineraries and passports being used by merchants. In oral societies one can certainly find analogies, precursors, to all of the practices of the merchants of the Middle East, but writing permits a development in complexity that would otherwise be impossible.

Take the simple matter of credit. Owing to the limits of human memory, the Ghanaian ladies observed by Hart who provided food on credit to employees in a transport yard, and collected payment at the gates at the end of the month, could handle only a restricted number of customers and a restricted number of different types of transaction. Unless they keep a book, shopkeepers too have difficulties with the profit and the loss. But the advantages of writing lie also in the realm of evidence and agreement. Of course writing can deceive as profoundly as spoken words, especially when in the hands of the favoured few. But when both transactors are literate, a written bill provides an opportunity to scan and check the contents, which in itself gives it more authority with both buyer and seller, apart from any subsequent use in the case of dispute.

In the context of both intellectual and practical developments, it is important to stress that a significant attribute of writing is the ability to communicate not only with others but with oneself. A permanent record enables one to reread as well as record one's own thoughts and jottings. In this way one can review and reorganize one's own work, reclassify what one has already classified, rearrange words, sentences and paragraphs in a variety of ways, some of which can now be more effectively carried out by using an electronic typewriter or personal computer. The way that information is reorganized as it is recopied gives us an invaluable insight into the workings of the mind of *homo legens*. At a simple level this is what the Vai merchant, Ansumana Sonie, was doing when he sat down and reorganized his daily accounts, as well as the accounts and membership lists of the 'friendly society' or brotherhood of which he was secretary. Writing enabled him to reclassify not only for accounting but also for recall and conceptual clarification (Goody, Cole and Scribner 1977).

An examination of the account books of Sonie led us to consider some of the cognitive implications of different means and modes of written communication, especially in respect of formal operations. This is not the place to summarize, much less pursue, that discussion, nor yet to consider the question to which I referred at the outset of this chapter about the level of literacy required for 'development', much less for the 'take-off'. My argument has been that writing makes not only a 'direct' (though rarely immediate) contribution at many levels but also cumulatively through the written corpus itself; so it can be important for accumulating and storing knowledge quantitatively as well as for its qualitative development, a subject that could lead us to consider the whole influence of the written tradition, including scientific knowledge, on the economy.

The general point is illustrated by the way that knowledge about agriculture is collected, organized, developed and distributed by writing. Partly this is a matter of recording existing botanical categories and information which can be read, thought about and reorganized. Partly it has to do with writing down the results of new departures, 'experiments' and trials. Partly it is the dissemination of information to specialists and to the public. Let us take an example of the drawing of conclusions from written records. In medieval England one handbook recommended the recording of milk yields of cows with a view to improving the quality of the herd. As for dissemination, at roughly the same period (the twelfth century) one Chinese subprefect at Hangzhou, being concerned with the welfare of those under his jurisdiction as well as with establishing a charitable estate for his lineage, commissioned "a series of diagrams on cultivation and weaving to encourage improved techniques in agriculture and sericulture by illustrating methods and attaching poems to them" (Walton 1984: 45); the diagrams on weaving consisted of twenty-four sketches, from washing the silkworms to cutting the cloth, and were aimed at improving the lot of the farmer and his wife, whose "clothes do not cover her body", whose bellies are not filled. It is also the case that the adoption of new crops and techniques may be speeded up by the more extensive networks promoted indirectly by writing, whether through trade or diplomatic exchange. Neither long-distance trade nor irrigation follows from writing, possibly the reverse, but in early times writing assisted in the collection and ordering of botanical and zoological specimens and information. One result or concomitant was the exotic garden of the Ancient Near East, where new plants and trees were collected from foreign parts and raised in those walled and watered havens that gave us the idea and name of 'paradise' from the Old Persian original. Thus in the seventh century BC Sennacherib planted Indian cotton in his royal garden. Much earlier in Egypt we find the solar temple of Neuserre of the Fifth Dynasty with its meticulous zoological observation in pictorial/textual form, and the botanical garden of Thutmost III which contained all the plants the king brought back from his campaigns.

The advanced agriculture these gardens represent, using the control of water (irrigation) and of non-human energy (the plough), produced enough to support a segment of the population not directly involved in farming. Apart from artisans these were characteristically the warriors and literates, whether administrators or priests, palace or temple, who so often constituted the ruling estates, although the relationship between the groups differed drastically over time. Nor were those in possession of the means of destruction always in control, except in the 'last instance', of the means of communication, let alone literate themselves. While the palace lived partly off booty production (which had its own literature, the listing of captives and captures, partly for prestige, partly for accounting), the temple was more dependent, directly or indirectly, upon the collection of a surplus by a variety of means, by rent, by tax, by tribute or by gift, made usually to the gods. Such transactions in gift and tribute are found in indigenous states of Africa but there the surpluses from agricultural production were usually small, the recording devices simple, and the ability to support full-time specialists limited. Booty and taxes on trade contributed to the running of the chiefdom but there is a sharp contrast with the Ancient Near East where the growth of the 'household' economy of priests (the temple) and of kings (the palace) was greatly facilitated by the use of accounting procedures and a more complex economy. Literacy clearly had to live off the land but at the same time it assisted the process of acquiring and collecting that living and promoted forms of complex exchange and production which in turn provided additional opportunities for taxation. Indigenous states in Africa, on the other hand, with the partial exception of those who accepted the writing system associated with the religion of Islam, lacked the availability of such a catalytic agent for internal purposes, although a number of peoples were in fact influenced by literate cultures to whose pressures they have remained very open. Indeed part of the phenomenon called neo-colonialism has to be seen in terms of this very openness which is associated with the absence of a strong, written tradition that can stand up against the written cultures of the world system. There are important distinctions to be made between different socio-cultural regions of the Third World, of the world system, not simply in terms of their relationship with the metropolis but in terms of their own indigenous, socio-cultural organization, in terms of communications as well as the economy. While the major societies of the Asian continent were strongly affected by the expansion of Europeans, they were more rarely 'colonies' in the African, American and Oceanic sense; nor are they today neo-colonial from the cultural standpoint. Their written traditions have provided them with a more solid basis for cultural resistance than is the case with most oral cultures.

3

The state, the bureau and the file

How has writing influenced the polity? Or to put it another way, how do regimes with writing differ from those without? The answer has to be many layered. Modern nations are obviously highly dependent upon writing for their electoral systems, their legislatures, their internal administration and their external relations. For the distribution of information on which decisions are based, the ideologies that govern the formation of parties, not simply writing but the mechanical reproduction of the word through printing, is critical. Obviously the whole constellation of modern political institutions and behaviour is part of a developing tradition in which changes in the mode of communication play an important role.

But how about the earlier polities? Once again I want to look at selected features of the first literate states of the Ancient Near East, rather than the more recent examples of Greece and Rome, on the grounds that they are closer to the largely oral states of Africa and more likely to pinpoint particular differences to which writing has contributed.

In examining the influence of writing on the polity, I am looking mainly at aspects of political organization rather than political process. I mean by this that while politics as the struggle and use of power pervades all levels of the social system, political organization generally refers to the most inclusive one. When social anthropologists in the course of the 1930s studied the large-scale African kingdoms with differentiated political institutions, they looked for a framework within which to compare the 'tribal' systems that had hitherto occupied much of their attention. Radcliffe-Brown offered the following minimal definition of a political system that would embrace the various societies found in Africa. "In studying political organization, we have to deal with the maintenance or establishment of social order, within a territorial framework, by the organized exercise of coercive authority through the use, or possibility of the use, of physical force" (1940: xiv; Colson 1968: 191).

The definition still raised problems about its applicability to 'tribal' societies, as did the parallel definition of 'law', the settlement of disputes in courts backed by that same coercive force. Subsequently M. G. Smith, whose work had mainly been in centralized states, followed Weber in distinguishing between the distribution of power in political competition and that of authority within an administrative system, claiming that this distinction could also be found in tribal societies. "Political organization consists in the combination and interplay of relations of authority and power in the regulation of public affairs" (1968: 194).

So at the very broadest level of anthropological concern, the comparative study of politics, defined 'substantively' rather than 'behaviourally', has been dominated by the division between states on the one hand and acephalous (that is headless, sometimes segmentary – what I have called 'tribal' above) societies on the other. Research among the latter has been aimed mainly at analyzing how the problem of order (and hence of disorder) is resolved in communities that have no overarching structure of leadership and authority, no sovereign, no chief, no king, no permanent council to direct or co-ordinate their affairs. This issue was one to which Aristotle and Ibn Khaldun were attracted, to which Hobbes and Locke addressed themselves, which exercised Rousseau and Austin, and which is critical, as Parsons insisted, to the work of Durkheim in *The Division of Labour in Society* (1897), just as it is central to the interests of Parsons himself in *The Structure of Social Action* (1937) and *The Social System* (1951). So it is not surprising that the contrast became a major focus for the work of Fortes and Evans-Pritchard as summarized in the introduction to their *African Political Systems* (1940), where many of the guiding concepts such as 'segmentary' and 'moral density' came straight from Durkheim.

Efforts were subsequently made by anthropologists to specify the types of group that determine the major fields of social action in acephalous societies, whether these were lineages, age-sets or village formations, and the way in which these groups operated in a type of regime that has been described as one of 'ordered anarchy'. At this level literacy played no part in the polity, although some desert or mountain tribes, especially in the Islamic world, may have been influenced by the written cultures of adjacent states.

The explicit contrast was with a state polity where the major locus of social control was the hierarchy of authoritative roles embodied in the system of government, behind which stands that final arbiter, the organized control of 'legitimate' force. Consequently the anthropologist's 'state' tends to appear as an undifferentiated category – apart from some minor exceptions (since they have not been elaborated in a comparative direction) that include Barnes' 'snowball state' of the Ngoni (1954), Southall's 'segmentary' state of the Alur (1953), the 'over-kingdom' of Gonja (Goody 1967), the 'primitive state' of Kaberry (1957) and perhaps the 'theatre state' of Geertz's Bali (1980). Whether in discussions of the origin of the state or in comparative enquiries, that single category stands in contrast to the heterogeneity of acephalous societies on the one hand, and on the other to the more complex typologies of political scientists (who in turn tend to treat all 'tribal' societies as a residual category).

Bureaucracies

Even in examining the simpler states there are clearly a great number of distinctions to be made in the nature of the regimes, depending, for example, upon whether the administrative system is controlled by a dynasty, a dictator, the military, the church, or by representatives of some more representative assembly. Then there is the distribution of functions and power in the various sub-systems of the polity: the administrative, the legal, the military, the government and the electoral and legislative bodies.

The segregation of administrative activities in a specific organization, the bureaucracy, is an extension of the distinction between the relation of authority and power discussed by Smith. But it is a segregation that is critically dependent, in this extended form, on the capacity for writing to communicate at a distance, to store information in files, and to tend to depersonalize interaction. But this represents only one axis of differentiation within the political system. Radcliffe-Brown's definition (like many others) points to the connections with law on the one hand and war on the other (the latter forming part of the more inclusive set of international relations). The segregation of legal action leads to the separation of the judge's court from the king's court which forms the subject of the following chapter. The specialization in war leads to the emergence of the military in the shape of the standing army. In addition there is the separation of the formal political competition for power (and of popular participation) in the electoral and legislative institutions.

At one level the distinction between the administrative/ executive, the legislative/governmental, the electoral/participatory, the legal and the military/police, represent aspects that can be hunted out in the political systems of all human societies. Their organizational separation represents an aspect of the process of differentiation that complex human societies have undergone. As with religion, writing has tended to promote the autonomy of organizations that have developed their own modes of procedure, their own corpus of written tradition, their own specialists and possibly their own system of support.

In recent comparative sociology little systematic work has been carried out on these differences among pre-modern states and, in the absence of an accepted conceptual framework capable of including the whole range of political systems, people have tended to cling to the general notions of nineteenth-century writers that were developed on what would now be considered a thin empirical base. For comparative sociology the result has been some rather too facile applications to Africa and elsewhere of Euro-centred categories and sequences, which have made use either of the comparison with Western feudalism (Goody 1963) or, yet more disastrously, with the idea of Oriental Despotism (Wittfogel 1957; Murdock 1959; Suret-Canale 1961; Godelier 1977). Apart from overlooking the implications of important differences in the productive systems, another factor that these attempts at assimilation neglect is the actual or potential effects of changes in the modes of communication on patterns of government. Even though the role of writing, the desk and the bureau is critical to Weber's concept of a bureaucracy, even though filing systems were basic to the development of the 'civilized' states of the Near East in the early Bronze Age (and later, for example in Crete, Chadwick 1959), scholars have described African kingship as examples of Baganda or Akan bureaucracy (Southwold 1961; Wilks 1966). Like some accounts of the myths and philosophy of the Dogon of Mali, such descriptions were ideologically part of the admirable effort to gain proper recognition in Western circles for the indigenous beliefs and practices of other cultures, an effort of intellectual decolonization that is often so fruitful for comparative studies. But such attempts constantly have to be examined to see if they have neglected historical derivations as well as differences in scale and operation. The broad usage of the term 'bureaucracy' would seem to give too little weight to the importance of the consequences, causes or concomitants of communicative systems and associated factors in the sphere of government. In the words of one historian of early society: "The emergence of a large-scale, centralized, bureaucratic institution . . . might itself have been a consequence of the creation of tools which empowered its functioning. Certainly writing enabled the administration to grow and, through written liability, to maintain direct authority over even the lowest levels of personnel and clientele" (Green 1981: 367).

One major sociological or anthropological question about the relation between writing and the polity has precisely to do with state formation, bureaucracy, and the subsequent role of early writing in helping to unify large empires such as China. It has been claimed that "the earliest stages of literacy in most of the 'primary' civilizations were exactly contemporaneous with pristine state development" (Adams 1975: 464; Wheatley 1975: 229). Historically the association may be accidental, since, in effect, the first we know of states comes from the written record. For it is certainly true that in Africa, Polynesia and in the Americas, states arose that had no access to writing in the fullest sense, although some developed forms of 'record' keeping. The limitations that oral communication places on the organization of the polity is what I want to examine in the course of this chapter, arguing that writing is critical in the development of bureaucratic states, even though relatively complex forms of government are possible without it. And the adoption of writing for various purposes associated with the polity has implications, at least at the level of potentialities, for the conduct of its affairs at all levels.

Writing was not essential to the development of the state but of a certain type of state, the bureaucratic one. The difference is clearly brought out in the study by Fallers of the Busoga of East Africa entitled *Bantu Bureaucracy* (1956), where he examines the differences between the conflicting roles of Soga lineages, the state and the introduced bureaucracy of the colonial regime. These differences he relates to the modes of authority, to the existence of the patron–client relationship in the traditional case as against the impersonal, situational authority of the salaried office-holder; the first is an example of the 'particularistic', the second of the 'universalistic' type of social relationship. While Fallers has correctly pointed to some of the intrinsic differences between traditional and modern African states, he has, like Weber, left implicit the implications of different modes of communication, and specifically of writing.

In the chapter that follows I want to try and spell out some of these implications for political systems in three ways. First I want to return to a discussion of the role of writing in the government of the early literate states of the Ancient Near East, partly because we can there see the genesis of certain social institutions ('the elementary forms of the literate life', to adopt a phrase of Durkheim's) and partly because pre-colonial Africa provides very limited examples of the uses of writing for political and other purposes, and those mainly derivative from the Near East, both in form and in application. The second section will be devoted to discussing the administration of African states in order to bring out some of the specific features of those polities without writing (or with only minimal writing). Thirdly I want briefly to consider the effects of Islam and Europe on the extension of the uses of writing into African societies by colonial and national regimes.

The administration of early states with writing

It is above all the role of writing in the administrative sector that stands out, including its use in the state economy which I have already mentioned. Writing of course played an important part in the legal system, as we will see. But there was little parallel to the uses of literacy in assemblies, in the wider circulation of information at the ideological level, nor yet for consultative procedures – these developments were related in the main to the wider availability of skills and reading matter, rather than to a social system using a difficult logographic code.

Internal administration

Taxation, accounting and the census

Since the polity of the states of the Ancient Near East was so closely involved in economic and religious operations, some major aspects of the uses of writing in government have already been discussed in the previous chapter. In Egypt a central storage economy of considerable scale and complexity was supported by accounting procedures that tried to balance the books, to assess the incomings and the outgoings. So too was the 'household' of the king in the palace economy of Mesopotamia. Both were also supported, in a looser sense, by the backing of the sacred authority of priest and temple, identified as this was with the written word, which legitimized the role of ruler and at certain periods trained the specialists needed for the bureaucracy. Those aspects of the polity I have already touched upon. I have also called attention to the close connection between taxation and the census, the numbering of the people and the collection of their 'surplus'. At this point the interests of these states force their way down into the domestic structures of the community in a way I find to be very different from an African kingdom, where census and taxation were generally of minimal importance.[1]

In discussing the ancient economy I have dealt at some length with the part played by writing in national (or rather 'palace') accounting, both of taxes and of booty. Interestingly, booty production also exacts its own inventories, often in pictorial form, which at once enhance the prestige of the conqueror and at the same time offer some kind of accounting procedure for gains that have to be shared by military, royalty and often by the church or temple that has served to support the victorious forces, just as it throws the mantle of legitimacy over the great organizations in general.

Of course war was not pursued for gain only by the kingdoms of

Asia and Europe. The production of booty was an important aspect of the political economy of pre-colonial African states whose supplies came mainly from raiding neighbouring acephalous communities for that end. In the absence of much movable wealth suitable for appropriation, the booty took the form of slaves which were then distributed to the participants in the raid and their backers, to be used personally or to be sold in the market either for local use or for export to the Americas, to the Mediterranean and Middle East or to other African countries. In the Ancient Near East, as in the Spanish conquest of the Americas,[2] the booty was in land and movable wealth as well as humans, while the system of distribution was more complex; the *rex* was rarely the *dux* (the leader in war), even nominally, and had to be rewarded at a distance. In this context the glorification and accountability of booty took on a new significance.

Numbers and the control of time

The fact that accounting played such a prominent part among the uses of writing in the political economy of the Ancient Near East had a number of consequences for the cultural system. It meant that there was a great emphasis, not on the more complicated narrative, descriptive or literary uses of language, but on those of a non-syntactic kind that characterize book-keeping and accounts. In contrast to the way writing influences the structure of religious norms in the creation and reproduction of texts and in the organization of teaching (the reproduction of the readers), the language employed for book-keeping and accounts is much further removed from speech, being largely composed of lexemes that are lifted from context and of numbers that form so distinct a 'set' of their own that this can be developed without a full writing system. This fact is of special importance for the analysis of the centralized polities of Pre-Columbian America. For a system of tokens, or even a knotted code (or *quipu*) of the sort described by Murra (1980: 109–10, 161–2), may serve many of the same purposes as writing – not only for the economy, but for the type of complex calendrical calculations developed in Central America (Morley and Brainerd 1983: 512ff.; Zuidema 1982).

The development of these complex calendrical systems is critically dependent upon graphic representation, including numeracy (Goody 1968). For example, the concept of an era requires some notion of a starting point, the drawing of a line, a precise beginning to which numbered reference can be made. The arbitrary but essential reconciliation of the lunar and solar calculi is needed because writing down the system of time-reckoning encourages the interlocking of units of different cycles. The formalization of graphic representation presents one with a forced choice – that is, whether you have variable 'months' or variable 'years'; though a reconciliation is doubtless possible in oral communication, it is visual representation that explicitly calls for a formula. In addition, numbers were applied to the units of time and their divisions, years, months, days and hours, some units being arbitrary, others not, so that, with this formal interlocking, society is able to gain more control of time through the calendrical system. And that is also a question of politics. One is used to thinking of a political system controlling space, a territory. But the control of time enters into the same frame. Whoever controls the calendar, the mode of reckoning time – whether the priesthood in Egypt or the court in central America – acquires a power that extends throughout the social system, reaching into each of the domains of politics, religion, law and the economy. Changes in technology are of course important. It was above all the mass-manufactured watch, to a lesser extent the clock, that democratized the 'objective', mechanical, calculation of time. But it remains true that it is the polity that can put the clock back or forward, introducing new holidays and cancelling old, even setting the calculation of years by the beginning of a reign or regime.

When I worked among the writingless, watchless, LoDagaa of West Africa, they seemed ready for a more systematic form of reckoning, as I was always being asked the time of day and more importantly how many months away were the first rains. Strictly speaking a full writing system is not required for this development, nor yet, as I have suggested, for numeracy, perhaps not even for the book-keeping that played so prominent a part in the Ancient Near East. Nevertheless the relation between these forms of simple representation and writing itself is very close both in historical and in logical terms.

Full writing systems developed early in the Ancient Near East but for many purposes, especially for long texts of a religious or literary kind, their use followed an extensive period dominated by less speech-like forms in economic and administrative contexts as well as in the control of time and space. Indeed some of the major potentialities of writing for literary, philosophical and other ends were realized in the Near East only with the development of the simpler, more user-friendly, syllabic and alphabetic scripts and of the new materials like pen and paper that encouraged, among other things, greater access and possibly the more rapid transcription of speech. But it cannot be too strongly emphasized that little such use was made of writing in the early phases though these other uses gradually proliferated over the centuries. The transformation of political life was a slow process, depending upon the creation of a literate tradition. However it is equally true that the Chinese accomplished many if not all of these tasks using a logographic system of writing. While the extensive code that this involves limited the rates of attainment of fluent literacy, the achievements of those who learned to write were as great in China as they were elsewhere.

Administrative correspondence

In the great archives of the Syrian kingdom of Ebla (*c.* 2400–2250 BC) we find not only 'economic texts' dealing with taxation and trade, but also 'letters, edicts and treaties' (Matthiae 1980: 164). The letters are mostly despatches sent by officials to the king about administrative problems. Subordinates were able to communicate with their superior at a distance, as well as in a formal manner, so that both question and answer could be permanently set down and become an object of future reference, as a clarification, a guarantee and a precedent.

The exchange of correspondence requires some postal arrangements operating between major centres, such as were set up by Sargon I of Akkad (2334–2279 BC) (Johns 1904: 308). In the vast majority of regimes, ancient or modern, whether capitalist or socialist, the postal service is organized by, and in an important sense on behalf of, the state, carrying its paperwork by priority and without payment. Right at the beginning such a system involved the upkeep of roads and canals so that deliveries could be effected in reasonable time (Oppenheim 1964: 103).

The Ebla archives include messages sent by the king either to officials at missions abroad or else addressed directly to other kings, probably archival copies of the original despatches; the notion of 'making a copy' was an early feature of literate government, which clearly encouraged strictness in the 'literal' interpretation (that is, to the letter) of edicts and treaties. And if communications were to be rendered permanent and interpreted by the letter, they had to be more carefully phrased by specialists in the written word.

The edicts found in the archives were royal ordinances, though ones that often regulated private matters: for example, the distribution of cities of the kingdom among members of the royal family and the award of a cluster of villages to a princess as dowry upon her marriage, a gift that would have been of little value unless it had been capable of producing an income in tax or in kind.

External administration

International treaties

International treaties, which are a type of contract, were widely used in the Ancient Near East, including those terminating a state of war (Oppenheim 1964: 284). They are a type of contract set down in writing.[3] There are, of course, forms of contract in oral societies, but here, as elsewhere, writing makes explicit what was otherwise implicit. It provides a written constitution instead of an oral understanding, with all the implications that this carries. For a constitution is a type of 'social contract' which if it can be said to exist in oral societies does so only in an analytic sense, by which I mean that its tacit existence is 'read back' from written cultures.

In the Ebla archives there are but few examples of such treaties, and these appear to be abbreviated extracts of the original documents that were probably engraved upon stone and deposited in sanctuaries. However, throughout the ancient world of the Near East writing was used to set out alliances between states in a manner that sounds, and is, very contemporary, apart from the resort to religious sanctions.

"In international as in private law", wrote Woolley (1963: 504),

a contract had to be set down in writing, and it had to be sworn to by the parties concerned in the presence of divine witnesses. In the case of a treaty of alliance preliminary negotiations were carried on by ambassadors exchanged between the two contracting powers; each party would have drawn up his own draft version of the text, and the duty of the ambassadors was to reconcile those in the final version; any important disagreement they would refer to their principals; thus Shamshi-Adad of Assyria received from his envoy a copy of a proposed treaty with Eshnunna as drafted by the other side and at once objected: "The matter which I removed from the tablet is still there. The men of Eshnunna are making difficulties."

In other cases the ambassadors were plenipotentiaries and arranged a satisfactory text between themselves, after which the date of ratification had to be fixed, a date not only convenient to both rulers but also approved by the oracles as auspicious.

The ratification was a solemn function introduced by a sacrifice. While the treaty was made out in the names of the kings who were to be bound by it, and was introduced by their full names and titles, no small part of its text consisted of a list of the gods and goddesses invoked as witnesses, the deities of each country separately described, followed by the curses which devolve upon the violator of the contract: "He who shall not observe all these words written upon this silver tablet of the land of the Hatti and of the land of Egypt, may the thousand gods of the land of the Hatti and the thousand gods of the land of Egypt destroy his house, his country and his servants", and the corresponding blessings: "but he who shall keep these words which are on the tablet of silver, whether he be Hittite or Egyptian, and shall not neglect them, may the thousand gods of the land of the Hatti and the thousand gods of the land of Egypt make him to be in good health and long life, as also his houses, his country and his servants". It was an oath of the most solemn sort, so much so that the ceremony of signature was, by Babylonians and Syrians, called "the touching of the throat", for when the sacrificial victim was killed, the king, in the presence of the gods and of the ambassador of the other contracting power, drew his hand across his throat, symbolizing his willingness to die in the same manner if he broke his word. The treaty tablets, once signed, were laid before the state gods of the two countries" (p. 504).

Such treaties sometimes specified a set of continuing exchanges between the parties, including the negative one, the right to the extradition of subjects who had fled to the other kingdom, especially runaway slaves, a feature of quite recent treaties (as well as magical formulae) in North and West Africa. The resulting alliances might be further strengthened by marriage and maintained by the exchange of gifts and letters.

This chancery correspondence was carried by special messenger and sometimes dealt with by a resident ambassador who would undertake the negotiations with the ruler to whom he was accredited. In this way a network of formal international relations developed that depended largely upon written communication. Throughout the Fertile Crescent, Akkadian, written in the cuneiform script, became the diplomatic language employed even by the chancery of the Egyptian Pharaohs. And the use of the same script was accompanied by the employment of similar forms of safe-conduct as well as of treaty formulae.[4] Not only the forms but the norms too were similar; for the regulations that governed Sumerian international trade were adopted by many other states.

In other words, writing not only entered substantially into foreign affairs, but governed the form and language of the discourse because one system dominated the external relations of a large area of the Near East. Once again the uses of writing affected not only the forms of interaction but also helped to change the nature of its rules, substituting the fixed text for the variable utterance.

The administration of states without writing

In this section I want to examine some of the characteristics of African states from the standpoint of their mainly oral mode of communication and the costs and benefits that this entailed. I say mainly oral because in fact the presence of Islam, with its insistence on the ability to read the Book and its long history of central administration and law, did influence the conduct of affairs in many states. So that it is interesting to look at the instances where writing was adopted as indicating the points in the oral system where there was pressure towards a change in the mode of communication. For writing was in principle available to the states of the West African savannahs since the beginning of the second millennium AD, just as it had been used by Europeans on the coast since 1500. What did they adopt writing for and how did it affect the working of the polity? The answer is somewhat different from the case of the Ancient Near East since the initial development was mainly in the realm of 'foreign affairs'.

External administration

Treaties, etc.

The evolution of human society has never been a neatly layered process. Even though one can discern general trends, one form of society does not everywhere replace another at the same time. Not all change, or are posed to change, at identical moments, so that most have to interact with systems of quite a different type. The cultivators of Ethiopia have to interact with the pastoralists of Somalia, the religions of the Book with pagan cults, and centralized governments with acephalous tribes. In the same way societies with writing have relationships with those without; this has been a recurring condition of the spread of writing, affecting both societies in various ways, as I tried to show in looking at the uses of writing in northern Ghana (1968a). For instance, the magic of the word spread its power to non-literate peoples and the consequent demand affected the supply and the suppliers. The situation of encounter is parallel in a formal sense to that which forms the starting point for many theories about the Third World and 'unequal development' (Frank 1981), about the articulation of social formations (Semenov 1980) or about the importance of external as well as internal contradictions in accounting for specific social formations (Godelier 1977).

When writing became available to the peoples of West Africa, some centralized states took it up as a means of communicating with their neighbours, engaging in correspondence and fixing treaties; Muslims, who acted as scribes, provided each other with passports and itineraries to undertake long journeys, whether for trade or pilgrimage. There is more evidence, at least initially, for the external than for the internal use of writing. This is partly a matter of the preservation of the original documents. We know of the correspondence of the late nineteenth-century empire-builder, Samory, with the British because his letters are preserved in the archives of the Public Record Office. We possess the correspondence between the kingdoms of Asante and Gonja from the beginning of the nineteenth century that found their way into Danish archives (Levtzion 1966), as well as fragmentary chancery correspondence of other kinds.

Such correspondence took place not only between those states strongly influenced by Islam but even between states with and without writing, the latter engaging individual literates to pen their letters. One result of this type of international correspondence was an initial tendency on the part of states without writing to interpret the written treaty as if it were subject to exchange or capture like other material objects. When they came into contact with the British and other Europeans on the coast of Guinea, the Asante displayed great concern over the notes, 'books' and treaties which they found being used there. Agreements between these foreign powers and the local rulers were recorded in writing, giving a precision to their arrangements and providing an 'objective' record of agreement in the case of dispute. The Asante soon became firmly attached to this new mode of communication and tended to give its products a greater permanency, concreteness and generality than the originators had intended, for the 'notes' were regarded as subject to exchange or acquisition (Collins 1962). If the Asante conquered a neighbouring power, they took over its 'books' and expected the literate makers of the treaty to continue to observe the same stipulations that had held for the group they had conquered. Much misunderstanding arose from this tendency to equate the paper with its contents, the medium with the message.

The substantial reasons for the predominantly external orientation of writing in these circumstances are of some interest. In the first place, these kingdoms were reacting and adjusting to the use of writing by European powers or by those Muslim states in which Islam played a dominant as distinct from an auxiliary role; *they* used writing, so must we. But perhaps more importantly, in the case both of the passport and of chancery correspondence, it was a question of sending one's word where one could not oneself go, of personal communication at a distance, not yet a telephone but more authoritative than a messenger. While it would demean royalty to visit a neighbouring king, except as a conqueror, the monarch can send his own message without having to rely upon an intermediary whose tongue is capable of misrepresenting his meaning. Instead the very words of the master were encapsulated on an inanimate tablet, a leather hide, a sheet of paper.

The treaty represents a specific arrangement between two sovereign powers, where there is by definition no sanction of legitimate force to support their agreement; such a sanction operated within polities, not between them. Outside their boundaries it is necessary to spell out the contract, and sometimes even the non-contractual elements of contract, and this has to be backed up by non-legal, non-political means, unless war is to be regarded as the continuation of politics by other means. Those means may lie partly embedded in the authority of the written word itself, especially the Word of God when He stands as the guarantor of the covenant. But religious sanctions operate in a yet more general way in this domain of early international relations, as we see in the oaths and the blessings, in the lists of gods and goddesses invoked as witnesses or in the deposition of the original treaties in sanctuaries (as was also done with the tables of monastic accounts in medieval Sri Lanka).

One other aspect of the tendency of writing, in this type of situation, to be used for relations between rather than within is the high degree of variability of external contracts. When the content and provisions of a new social relationship, such as marriage, are relatively constant (as with bridewealth), there is less need for a record than there is in the case of dowry on an interpersonal level or of an alliance between states on an international one, the stipulations of which vary according to the particular circumstances of the partners.

War and peace

Treaties are concerned not only with the positive side of the relations between states but with the negative aspects too, since their breach leads to conflicts and war. The conduct of war in early times required rations and communications, of the same kind as the palace itself, and in these respects, as well as in accounting for booty and in the celebration of victory, writing played a notable part. In Mari, for example, enemy captives were even listed by name (Dalley 1984: 145).

With the advent of the world religions (and written ideologies), inter-group conflicts were affected in quite another way, both inside and outside political units. Internally one consequence of the increased autonomy of church and state, of the boundary-maintaining quality of written religion, is not simply the tension, the struggle, between the two 'great organizations', but the conflicts between the adherents of different 'world' religions, culminating in wars of religion.

In the simpler societies ancestors and gods are often called upon to support one group, usually a territorial or kinship group, in its struggles with another. In African states, supernatural beings are brought in to uphold one regime against another. Even Islam and Christianity are called upon to play this role, as for example in the legendary account, given in the eighteenth-century Gonja chronicle (Goody 1954), of the assistance in the conquest of that country provided by the Muslims; the account was of course written by the Muslims and is brought out annually on the festival of the Prophet's birth, partly to encourage and justify gifts from the chiefs. When a named religion takes this role, it is the beginning (in a morphological sense) of the *Jihād*, of ideological struggles in which differences in practice or belief, between Protestant and Catholic, Sunni and Shiite, play a determining part. As we see all around us, in India, Ireland and in the Middle East, the conflicts between the adherents of these religions is an aspect of the autonomy those systems have acquired, of their power to convert and to create minorities and majorities who regard themselves as the sole possessors of the truth.

Internal administration

Taxes, etc.
I have been talking here of the priority given by pre-colonial African states to the adoption of writing for external communication. Its employment internally was more limited, partly because its incorporation there was more complicated and partly because of the nature of the political economy. African states such as Dahomey and Asante developed simple systems of taxation and tribute, though the productive surplus from agriculture was usually small (Goody 1971: 21–38) and its uses were limited. In some situations of central accumulation, writing is of little consequence, when the

items collected consist of the type of produce that deteriorate rapidly, the problem of recording is of less importance since the goods cannot be 'saved' but must be redistributed within a short space of time. It is the transaction not the storage that is significant – that is, the immediate rather than the delayed transfer; hence accounting is less central. With durables such as Asante gold, accountability was necessarily a matter of trust rather than of auditing, though the Sanaahene (the chief of the gold, the treasurer), like the ruler himself, had to keep the personal and public purses apart at the risk of being dismissed from office. In oral societies an individual can usually memorize his personal transactions, political and economic, perhaps with the aid of witnesses, where the transfer establishes a specific relationship of credit or debt rather than a generalized one of dependence. Transactions between a maternal uncle and a sister's son, for example, are embedded in a multiplex relationship, in Gluckman's phrase (1955: 19), which means that a debt is only one strand among many, a situation that promotes trust among the transactors. But for larger units, or even for the one-off, single-stranded transactions that occur in many tax or 'market' operations in contrast to the more regular transfers of tribute, recording has many advantages. On the one hand a written receipt shows that levies and taxes have been paid, a procedure that places a potential check on the collector as an intermediary in the transaction and renders the tax-farmer accountable, at least in principle. It is a use of writing that becomes more manifest the larger the organization involved and so is of greater significance to an empire than to a city state.

On the other hand, more important politically than the receipt for the giver, the taxed, is the account for the recipient, the taxer. By means of a written record of income, an organization can increase its control over the internal allocation of funds – for example, in calculating the amount to be spent on investment or set aside for saving as distinct from the sum needed for meeting the running costs and consumption needs. All societies require some forward planning from their members, some allocation of resources over time, some husbandry. But for an elaborate organization, budgeting increases its 'efficiency', its 'rationality', and extends its depth of control. This was the case with the temple estates of Mesopotamia which recorded the input and output of goods and services; similar records accompanied the expansion of merchant enterprises throughout the Ancient Near East. As far as government is concerned, today as yesterday, the documents accounting for tax and its expenditure constitute the core set of files required for the establishment of local authorities and the nation itself. In the course of this process the office becomes the location of the desk (the *bureau*), the clerk and the file, which is the way the true bureaucracy begins.

The individual and the office

While some features of the Weberian concept of bureaucracy (1947b: 196ff.; 1947a: 329–41) are certainly present in oral societies (M. G. Smith 1960; Southwold 1961; Wilks 1966), the absence of writing inevitably places limits on the efficacy of government (especially as regards the storage of information) as well as of business firms, churches and other large-scale organizations. As Weber pointed out, one major feature of such administrative organs is the ability to separate 'person' from 'office', people from corporation, and so to establish 'universalistic' as against 'particularistic' relationships. Without such a separation, a family firm may well cease to exist with the death of the head, if his interests are carved up among close kin. The firm continues only if the split is averted by treating the continuity of the organization as a different question from the division of the property between the heirs.[5] The failure to distinguish private and public interest often affected kingdoms as well, especially in the early phases of a particular dynasty, where conquest has blurred the lines between private and public; the state of the conqueror, as in early Norman England, tends to be split up into the estates of the sons; this son gets Normandy, that England, and that Ireland; what was one becomes many. The principle of equal division, taken from the personal realm of inheritance, was applied to the public domain of succession, confusing the singularity of kingship with the plurality of parenthood (Goody 1966).

A separation of public and private is a frequent feature of many states without writing, where the king is nearly everywhere distinguished from the kingship, the chief from the chiefship, the office-holder from the office (Fortes 1962). Some states carried the separation a step further by distinguishing a man's private wealth (including his wives) from what he acquired as an office-holder. In West Africa Asante chiefs were at times dethroned for confusing the two.[6] It is a separation that remains a cause of tension and dispute as it can never be altogether complete, if only for the reason that children are brought up in a particularistic setting in which the two aspects of the parent's status cannot be kept entirely apart.[7] But the further degree of separation characterizing organizations of the kind Weber was discussing seems to depend upon another factor, namely, the increased formalization of administrative procedures that writing promotes and that was so noticeable in the early empires of the Near East. Here affairs of state were embodied in written records which tended to distance them from the personal affairs of the office-holder and to offer some kind of accountability. Again writing tends to make explicit what was implicit in oral communication.

Communication: the message and the audience

The use of writing by the state has a number of other implications for social action, providing a way of controlling spatial as well as temporal relations. In societies of the smallest scale, internal communication can be maintained by direct face-to-face contact between, say, a lineage and its elders. But for a state, even a simple one, the increase in scale, the intervention of spatial distance, the inclusion of larger numbers of individuals in the organization, mean that communication between its members requires the use of intermediaries, representatives, messengers and the like. Communication is still oral and so requires the movement of persons rather than of media; but the contact between ruler and ruled is now indirect, being carried out through a hierarchy of officers (such as subchiefs) distributed throughout the realm and by means of the intermediaries needed to transmit messages between them.

The alternative is to communicate at a distance by raising the sound level and sending simple messages by means of what we regard as 'musical' instruments. Among the acephalous LoDagaa the xylophone is used like church bells in Europe to convey the news of death or rejoicing. Among the centralized Asante talking drums convey more specific messages, sometimes by imitating the tonal patterns of a sentence and sometimes operating in more arbitrary fashion. Typically the talking drums belong to the chief, who acts as a focus of news and rumour, for it is he to whom strangers are first brought, to whom local inhabitants take their grievances and information, and whose court therefore forms the node of the network of oral communication.

When a message has to be delivered either by an intermediary or by the physical appearance of the subordinate before the superior, the immunity of the messenger and the attendance on the superior are of central importance to the running of the kingdom and both are surrounded by important sanctions of a religious and secular kind. More acute problems of security arise with the dispatch of ambassadors to lands which, while not completely hostile, are neither entirely friendly. Once again their mission and their persons are surrounded with formality and prohibitions.

Let me expand upon the topic of attendance at an audience, a hearing. When a divisional chief of Asante takes office, he swears an oath to his overlord, the Asantehene, which is essentially the same as his junior chiefs will swear to him. The elders come before him one by one. Each subchief bends his head which the chief touches three times with the sole of his right foot, a widespread act which expresses submission on the one side and dominance on the other. Then standing upright before his lord, the subject takes the ceremonial sword, points it towards the chief's breast and declares in a loud voice:

I speak the forbidden name of (using the appropriate oath), I speak the great forbidden word. I am the Chief of the rear-guard and I protect your back; as my Elders help me, so will I assist you. If I act towards you like one who says to a man, "Look at your hands, look at your hat" (i.e. I ask you to look both ways at once); if I give you advice and you do not heed it, and I get angry, and go to my house, and do not return and again give you the same advice; if you come and summon me at night, if you summon me by day, and I do not come, then (I have incurred the penalty), for I have spoken the great forbidden word, I have mentioned the forbidden name of —. (Rattray 1929: 86–7)

Movement into the presence of an authority figure is a feature of all hierarchical organizations, modern as well as intermediary and simple; one moves forward and one moves up; one approaches a member of the hierarchy from below, and with gestures of obeisance, which involve lowering oneself since otherwise the approach might be construed as threatening. But in oral societies yet greater emphasis has to be placed on the physical coming together of persons or groups,[8] simply because there is no alternative. Hence the importance of the 'audience' given by a king. The superior may summon the junior by a messenger carrying a special emblem such as the state sword or the messenger's staff,[9] and the obligation to obey the call is binding. In Asante it was an act of rebellion not to 'come in' when called and British administrators later used the same technique with local chiefs; even today prime ministers and presidents expect an equally prompt response to their commands.

Not only did a subordinate chief have to attend when summoned, he also had to be present on set occasions which served communicative as well as formal ends. In the kingdom of Gonja in northern Ghana, junior chiefs living in and around the divisional capital had to attend upon their senior twice a week, on Mondays and Fridays, the days when the great talking drums were played to greet both the dead and the living. On these days a divisional chief was expected to sit in the meeting room (*lembu*) at the entrance to his house, discuss affairs with his subchiefs and be ready to receive any of his subjects. These were the occasions on which much of the work of the division was done.

Communication: national ceremonies

The annual ceremonies, on the other hand, were national as well as divisional. While they were more ritually oriented, secular affairs also played an important part. At the time of the Damba festival, a rite which derived from the Maulud of Islam and celebrates the birth (or circumcision – it depends on the time and place) of the Prophet, all subordinate chiefs had to come to the capital and greet their divisional overlord, and at times these divisional chiefs had to attend upon the paramount himself at the national capital. Among the Asante to the south, the equivalent occasion was the Odwira, the New Yam festival.

Since 1931, when the British rulers tried to reorganize the kingdom more centrally to create a subordinate administrative structure, the paramount has held a Damba ceremony at the capital of

Nyanga (and from 1944 at Damongo). His subchiefs do not all come every year. Often they dance Damba in the divisional centres, attended by their own junior chiefs from outlying villages; it is an index of the greater decentralization of the Gonja,[10] as compared to the Asante kingdom, that at the parallel Odwira ceremony in Kumasi, subordinate chiefs were apparently always required to be present.

In Asante attendance was enforced not only by earthly sanctions but by supernatural authority as well; for the Odwira or New Yam Ceremony was the time when the ancestors returned to earth, to receive among other things their share of the new crop. But the political aspect, that is, the renewal of obeisance and the establishment of communication, is much in evidence. As Bowdich, the leader of the first European mission to Asante, remarked, this festival, "which all dependants and tributaries" were required to attend, appeared "to have been instituted like the Panathenea of Theseus, to unite such various nations by a common festival" (1819: 256).

National ceremonies of this kind, whether in Moscow's Red Square, Accra's Black Star Square or on London's Horse Guards Parade, always play some affirmatory role as far as the existing structure of dominance is concerned – especially as armed might, the final arbiter of political power, is so often a major feature of display. One can also discern an element of 'play' in the investitures and similar ceremonies of Western nations. But in simpler societies, the communicative, or rather 'informational', aspects of ceremony, of mass rituals, are both more specific and more intrinsic; this was the time and place for reaching decisions, for getting news, for conveying information, for reaffirming relationships, as well as for the outbreak of disputes.

Whether these occasions are regular or occasional, one aspect of their political function is similar: they ratify in a face-to-face situation, in direct communication, the relations of super- and subordination that exist across the kingdom. But the requirement that all subchiefs should be present does not merely represent an insistence upon gestures of submission. The chiefs are called because their advice, their counsel, is required by the paramount; to this day in Gonja the occasion is used to make decisions and to settle (or advance) such disputes as the new dispensation of the nation-state allows its component structures to adjudicate.

With the advent of bureaucracy in the shape of the national government, the number and nature of decisions that chiefs in northern Ghana now make is very much more restricted than in the past, but they still have to hear disputes about offices and jurisdiction. These conflicts are often very deep-rooted affairs that arouse much tension and hostility. While not necessarily soluble, the problems are brought for discussion by those concerned in front of the paramount himself. In some of these instances the paramount acts more as a chairman than as an overlord. The disputants state their case not so much to him, as *through* him *to* the assembled multitude, and consequently in many cases his decision reflects the sense of the meeting. His role in such discussions will vary according to his personal abilities; but he would hardly have become chief at all, had he not been able to hold his own in verbal confrontations of this sort, and as in Asante, preference is supposedly given to those who are not hasty in their speech, though this stipulation is more often an ideal than an actuality. So the matter of hearing disputes is more an exercise in political judgement than a way of deciding on rights and wrongs according to some strictly defined code, although with the growing insistence that 'customs' be reduced to writing, this situation is changing, even in remote areas. While it is true that colonial rule and independent government have progressively eroded the position of the chief, his role was rarely tyrannical. There is little evidence to support any general notion of African, let alone Oriental, despotism as being a major mode of political organization in earlier times. Oral consultation ensured a wider participation in decision-making than this phrase suggests.

Communication: centre and periphery

The question of the means of internal communication and the mode of decision-making touches upon the nature of relations between the centre and the periphery discussed by Shils (1962) and others. Where the administration of a state is dependent upon the 'audience', the 'spokesman' and the 'messenger', this link is bound to be fragile compared with the potentialities offered by a literate bureaucracy. The state was therefore more liable to split apart and the possibility of fission in one form or another constantly exercised the central authorities. Acts of rebellion were often aimed not at taking over the whole government but at breaking away from it; by fission a subordinate division established a regime independent of the mother country. Under conditions where both communication with the centre and identification with the state tended to be weak, "the tyranny of distance" (to use the title of Blainey's study of Australian economic history, 1982) is allowed full play.

The point is clearly brought out in Abrahams' discussion of succession among the Nyamwezi of Tanzania (1966), where we find that characteristic African phenomenon of 'proliferating chiefdoms'. According to the Nyamwezi myth, the original Kamba chiefdom grew so large that the chief no longer received his proper tribute of lion skins from the outlying villages. As a consequence he allocated these distant areas to his sister's sons so that they could set up separate chiefdoms.

The chiefdom is seen to expand up to a certain size until it comes up against an organizational block. It can no longer grow without fission. From one point of view these proliferating chiefdoms are examples of a failure to develop an organization that could include more people or larger areas; they are examples, that is, of political devolution. I refer to the rise and fall of African states such as the Interlacustrine kingdoms, as well as of the Kachin of Highland Burma (Fallers 1956: 248; Leach 1954; Friedman 1979). But the multiplication of separate political units was not the only course open to an expanding state. The system of rotational succession found among the Gonja and elsewhere (Goody 1966) is a device that permits the retention of a wider political frame, a more inclusive state system, although necessarily one of a loosely centralized character implied in the notion of an 'overkingdom' (Goody 1967). The centre may be ritually strong but politically weak and in the longer run decentralization may lead to an effective split (as occurred between East and West Gonja) within a nominal unity.

These proliferating chiefdoms are related both to what Southall speaks of as the "segmentary state" of the Alur (1953) and to Barnes' "snowball state" of the Ngoni (1954), being a widespread feature of the non-bureaucratic states of Africa. Other examples are provided by the Azande and Nzakara where chiefdoms split off in a process of expansion, leading eventually to multi-chiefdom tribes rather than to unitary states of wider dimensions (Evans-Pritchard 1971; Dampiere 1967). The presence of a literate bureaucracy, on the other hand, militates against these fissiparous tendencies, providing a consolidating factor in state building – not only because of the fact and content of communication within the political hierarchy and down into the domestic domain, but also because the use of a common written language (as in medieval Western Europe) or a common logographic script (as in China) helps to overcome the diversity of spoken tongues and dialects, and to some extent of cultural practice as well.

Some African states, influenced by Islam, had gone part of the way along this road, especially the Sokoto Caliphate of Northern Nigeria established as a result of the Fulani *Jihād* at the beginning of the nineteenth century. Islam had already been present in the western Sudan for some 800 years and its spread depended upon a knowledge of the Book. But the Book was written in Arabic and that was the language one had to learn to become a reader or a writer, so that advanced literacy skills were limited to a few Islamic scholars. Works were copied and even composed in West Africa but the uses of literacy for the purposes of government were few. While Hausa and Fulani were later written in Arabic script, even with the establishment of the Sokoto Caliphate the language of state remained Arabic (Last 1967: 192). The use of writing was restricted as a result of its origin in the word of God.

A considerable number of chancery letters were composed in the household of the Vizier of Sokoto, mainly to the Emirs of the constituent Hausa states; they are short, often consisting only of greetings, while others contain complaints, mainly about runaway slaves, although further inter-emirate problems are sometimes raised. No copies of outgoing letters were kept; in some cases the letters were actually delivered by the writer, the Vizier being on tour in the emirates for much of the year (Last 1967: 189), so that the degree of bureaucratization was small. Moreover, while these Muslim states tried to impose the taxes prescribed by Islam, no records appear to have been kept of income and expenditure. The finances of the state seem to have been based on tribute and gift-giving rather than on taxation; nevertheless these and other funds did support a certain amount of scholarship.

The effects of writing were more extensive in the literary fields. The learned men who led the *Jihād* aimed at restoring purity to the Islam practised in the Hausa kingdoms. In conformity with the ideals expressed in his works on Islamic law and practice, the Shaikh created "an elementary administration" (Last 1967: 229). Books were composed for the guidance of administrators; more were copied. Histories were written to justify and explain past actions, and we also find a good deal of miracle literature, genealogical works, polemical verse, a guide to letter writing and even personal poems. The use of literacy was perhaps stronger on the ideological and religious front than on the administrative. Only with the twentieth century did a true bureaucracy develop.

Writing in the colonial and national administrations

Whatever use some West African states in the savannah zone made of writing, the advent of colonial regimes brought an extraordinary quantum jump apparent to anyone who has studied the documentary records of the African scene over the last century. Here as elsewhere in colonial regimes, the administrative system in northern Ghana underwent a sudden transformation in the formalization of the bureau and in the quantity of paperwork.

This shift took place despite the fact that the new administrators were professional soldiers who preferred deeds to words, action to paper and were often temperamentally interested in setting up only a minimal level of bureaucratic organization and activity. Nevertheless, immediately they appeared on the scene, systematic records had to be kept of disputes heard, of taxes collected and of money expended; monthly, quarterly and annual reports had to be submitted to the Chief Commissioner at Tamale, who had to report to the Governor of the Gold Coast and he in turn to the Colonial Secretary in London. The information was sifted as it passed up the system. During the course of the military conquest itself in the last decade of the nineteenth century, virtually every written communication, every report, every dispatch, every telegram was passed back to London eventually to be published in Parliamentary Printed Papers. With pacification the paper proliferated even more, but some of it was retained in local files. Each district kept record books village by village; letters maintained a constant two-way flow of information between headquarters and outstations, even after the telephone or radio had been installed; subsequently the 'informal diary' provided a means of communicating less immediate types of information in a more casual way.

In the early 1930s the Government decided upon a policy of Indirect Rule, which meant setting up a subordinate level of administration based on indigenous customs and known as Native Authorities. This proposal entailed a flurry of literate activity on the part of administrators who were called upon to report (in writing) upon local practice. Then it meant not only recognizing some form of chiefship (even where this did not exist in pre-colonial times) but handing over some responsibilities of a judicial, fiscal and administrative kind. Such responsibilities were necessarily seen as involving the maintenance of similar records, since only in this way could one report to higher authority and ultimately to the British Government.

In northern Ghana, there were at first no available clerks who had been through school, so in Gonja the Native Authorities employed those who could read and write Arabic. For reporting upwards to their superiors, this was not the most useful of languages, and the posts were soon filled by young men who had graduated from one of the few schools in the north, in which English was the medium of instruction.

The clerks to the new Native Authorities were asked to submit the same type of record and report as the District Commissioner had to submit to his superiors; indeed the one supplied the information for the other. They were even encouraged to keep informal diaries similar to those of their superiors. The first clerk to the Yagbum Native Authority, that of the paramount chief of Gonja, was J. A. Braimah, who later became an MP (like a number of other Council Clerks from the north), then Minister, Regional Commissioner and finally succeeded to the paramount chiefship himself in 1982. When he took over the office of clerk in 1936, he was encouraged to keep a diary of events, which included comments on the health of the

Native Authority bulls. Each of the subdivisions of Gonja kept its own diaries, which had to be submitted quarterly (there is a reference to the receipt of one from the Tulugu division on August 15, 1942). The habit of writing stuck with J. A. Braimah, and he continued to record events until it became clear during the Nkrumah regime that diaries might be used by the political authorities to check on one's activities. These administrative tasks seem to have developed Braimah's own talents and helped him to become a prolific author of published and unpublished work. It certainly stimulated a vigorous interest in records, in dates and in timing.

What was established in the colonial period, it must be insisted, was only the sketchy beginnings of a modern bureaucratic system; a single expatriate officer undertook virtually the whole spectrum of tasks involved in administering and developing a sizeable area of an unfamiliar country. Over the eighty years that have elapsed since the conquest, the lateral and vertical differentiation of the administrative set-up has grown enormously, leading to a complex network of communicative acts in the hands of a wide variety of specialized officers, international advisors and political representatives, each communicating with their own ministers, bureaux or agencies. At the same time, the advent of universal suffrage, of the mass participation associated with 'democracy', was closely connected with the spread of literacy. Registration of the electorate had to be established by census procedures and, while voting could be organized by means of counters and boxes on which graphic symbols were displayed, the registration and counting were in the hands of literates. More importantly, only literates could function effectively in the new political system given all the paperwork that government and party produced. To be a candidate for office, high or low, you had to know how to read and write.

In Africa the expansion of written records under the colonial governments is especially noticeable because of the paucity of indigenous ones. In India, on the other hand, substantial written records were already being used during the Mughal period, not only at the national level but in the form of village revenue accounts. Nevertheless bureaucracy took a major leap under British imperial rule, which Smith (1985) has described in terms of the complementary aspects of rule-by-records and rule-by-reports. Records in this sense were records of rights and of liability to revenue, building on earlier precedents, compiled by local 'accountants' and based on the notion of the independence of the village community. Reports were kept in English at the district level by expatriate officers, being records of the customs of the people and collected to improve the knowledge of the rulers and increase the governability of the ruled; the zenith of these reports was the Indian Census of 1872 and the accompanying Ethnographic Survey, which dealt in the statistics and distribution of larger social groups – that is, castes. The gathering of both sets of information was regulated by a series of manuals which rationalized and standardized the form in which the information was to be collected; for example, the compilation of genealogies, "crucial to the manner in which local society came to be represented" (Smith 1985: 167) and essentially a graphic form of representation, came by 1880 to be an essential part of Settlement Records.

The emergence of regulation and of rules from these formalized accounts is critical to the development of the relationship between ruler and ruled in complex literate states. The etymological link between ruler and rules emphasizes the nature of the backing one gives to the other; writing makes those rules explicit, leads to their formalization in a variety of ways and thus changes the relation between ruler and ruled.

The argument is parallel to that of Foucault (1979), who proposed that in Europe during the seventeenth and eighteenth centuries it was the development of statistics (aggregate written knowledge of a population in numerical form) that led to a transformation in the notion of governments, as indicated in the change of meaning of 'economy' from household management to the regulation (rule) of society. The increase in knowledge by the state represented an increase in its power to govern; as in both India and Africa knowability meant governability, and both entailed the extensive use of the written word.

Written education, mobility and control

In this way new channels of mobility and control were created in Africa. Not only were literate specialists now eligible for high office alongside hereditary chiefs and foreign administrators, they were yet more important as 'leaders of opinion', helping to form or express the views of those who had begun to exercise some political control through the ballot.

The introduction of voting as the dominant mode of succession to new political office (at least in the initial period of independence, for at the time of writing physical force is more in evidence) boosted the role of the mass media; the control of these channels of communication, first in the written form of the press, then in the spoken and visual shape of radio and television, became a main focus in the struggle for political and economic power. Whereas in the mid nineteenth century a revolt often involved the seizure of the seat of government, the routine of mid-twentieth-century Africa centred upon the capture of the media buildings – the radio station, the television studio and the newspaper office. In the latter quarter of this century another shift has occurred; the struggle is likely to involve the armoury and the barracks, with the media playing a secondary role. The consequences for political and administrative action are severe, since legitimacy lies hidden in the barrel of a gun and implementation of a political programme depends on the increasing participation of police and army. The legal system, which Fallers (1969) regarded as among Africa's greatest achievements, has suffered deeply, especially in the Uganda which he studied, while in Ghana today (1985) the role of lawyers in the courts has greatly diminished. Military and peoples' tribunals have tended to replace the judicial forms of earlier regimes.

Stratification

Both in respect of channels of mobility and control of media, writing had an important effect upon the system of stratification.

Writing has long endowed its practitioners with high status. Early on in Ancient Egypt elite positions were completely identified with writing (Baines 1983: 580), for the titles of 'scribe' and 'administrator of scribes' applied to people of the highest rank. In peacetime at least, the commanding heights of the social system were occupied by officials listed under the king. In the new nations of Africa not only is literacy required of leaders at all levels but mass literacy is seen as linked to mass democracy and that in turn to a modern occupational system, thus linking education, politics and economics, and making the connection between status and literate achievement even tighter. Under this new dispensation the positions of politicians, priests, professionals and business men all depend upon the ability to read and write, and the universalization of these skills is part of the unquestioned credo. However, the optimistic notion that literacy would lead to some form of democratic government on behalf of an informed electorate receives a blow with each new military coup, although some soldiers, some officers at least, have to be literate in order to govern the country and run the army.

The impact of mass literacy and education on the systems of stratification is significantly different in Eurasian and African societies, a point alluded to at the end of the last chapter. Although the social and political situation in Europe changed in important ways with the advent of universal suffrage, the ruling estate of earlier times, the landed aristocracy and gentry, long maintained an important position because of its control of scarce resources. In pre-colonial Africa, however, land was rarely such a scarce resource; the power of a chief depended more on his control of people than of land. Consequently when the political system changed, with the advent first of the colonial regime and then of a national government, local rulers had little to fall back upon except tradition. The literate skills acquired in school were a more powerful determinant of 'class' than was the case in Europe or is now in South America; the ladder of educational mobility has been more accessible at least until the groups with literate skills succeed in making their position a quasi-hereditary one, until the elite becomes a class, since access to power is less constrained by existing class or ethnic interests. It is true that the colonial rulers encouraged the sons of African chiefs to go to school, but in many cases other children were sent in their place; moreover, there was little those from chiefly houses could take with them into the new situation, where they found themselves on the same footing as the children from other groups. From the beginning education had a solvent and in some ways homogenizing effect on the social structure.

The presence of roles demanding literate skills introduces a further dimension of complexity into a system of stratification. This was so in embryonic form even in those states of pre-colonial West Africa that made more than a minimal use of the writing offered them by Islam. Among the Nupe of Northern Nigeria (Nadel 1942), ability to read out or interpret the Holy Book was important not only for the adjudication of legal cases but also as a source of secret knowledge and of religious wisdom. The literate professions provided a ladder of achievement as well as a system of 'values' which were in some measure autonomous, lying partially outside the major hierarchies of the political and economic domains. But they had considerable influence upon those hierarchies, not only because they were the interpreters of the written word, as law-givers or as ritual experts, but also because as viziers and scribes they undertook administrative tasks on behalf of the ruler (Last 1967). However, in addition there were a few people, women as well as men, who created the written word, producing not so much the matter of daily political intercourse but new works of scholarship or literature as well as commentaries on the old. Some of these offered criticism, others suggested reforms of the polity, and this was precisely the base from which the Fulani *Jihād* started. These literati were the representatives, in embryo, of a new class, the intellectuals.

As intellectuals they were associated with alternative views, 'ideologies', and built up a written tradition of critical comments that formed the basis of future action. In this way writers have influenced political systems throughout the history of the written word, not only by administering and supporting these regimes but by extending the range of criticism and opposition. Contemporary examples of the power of such criticisms and ideologies are only too easy to observe, but the importance of the written tradition in modifying political action and social life more generally extends back to Plato and Aristotle in Greece, to Mencius and Confucius in China, to the reformers inside and outside Hinduism, though the extent to which there were yet earlier precursors in the Ancient Near East is a matter of doubt. It is a question of building up a tradition of such commentaries within the written mode.

Writing and the political process

Debating assemblies

There are, of course, other ways of looking at 'politics'. But whatever focus one chooses, organization and behaviour are significantly influenced by the use of writing. For example, Finley (1983) sees debating assemblies as being the essence of 'politics' and as the invention of Greece and Rome. This is very much how contemporary English-speaking West Africans use the term 'politics', to refer to those periods of the recent history of their nations, not all that frequent, when one is able to exercise one's right to vote for candidates of one's choice so that they may act as representatives sitting in a relatively free assembly.

Even if we limit the notion of politics to that of popular participation, this was not altogether absent from earlier societies. Jacobsen (1943) writes of a primitive democracy in Ancient Mesopotamia where an assembly of free citizens also acted as a court of law (Larsen 1976: 10). This assembly of householders functioned, according to Oppenheim (1964: 112), as "a tribal gathering reaching consensus under the guidance of the more influential, richer and older members"; they write letters, fight for tax privileges and accept a corporate responsibility for crimes.[11] That such assemblies were not merely forums for consensus but arenas for debate is clear from a poem quoted by Jacobsen (1943: 163):

> Do not go to stand in the assembly;
> Do not stray to the very place of strife.

Just as the Israelites too had their tents of assembly, so too the Mesopotamian gods met in council in which issues were debated, the political struggle pursued. At least for simpler, if not for historically earlier polities, the point is made by the reference to 'tribal' gatherings. While for most groups the notion of the tribe as governed by a democratic assembly is no more accurate than that of one dominated by an autocratic chief, and while the notion of consensus should perhaps be rejected in favour of 'the sense of the meeting', consultations and debates are found in all such societies, being the precursors of the more structured assemblies of later times and of more complex societies. Many well-attested examples of these oral procedures are to be found in accounts of African societies in recent times, the most detailed study being Bohannan's analysis of the moots of the Tiv of West Africa (1957). Writing is clearly not essential to the development of democratic assemblies on a small scale, but the idea of a representative assembly or of secret voting exert some pressure towards the use of the new form of communication. Like the power of the gun, writing can be a democratic force, especially for a community of greater scale than can be managed in face-to-face relationships. However, it had no immediate consequences for democratic government. It needed some 5,000 years to expand the ability to read and write throughout the social system, to make it an instrument of democracy, of popular power, of the masses. Even then its egalitarian implications were strictly limited, since literacy creates another axis of differentiation involving the access to, and the creation of, texts. Today this is largely a matter of the extent of the literate education one has received; until recently writing created a radical divide between literate and illiterate elements in a population. The proportions of those who could read and write fluctuated greatly with the advent of phonetic systems of writing, especially with the alphabet. While in medieval Europe the figures were low, in Athens the level of alphabetic literacy was probably high, and even for Roman Egypt (where it was largely a question of literacy in a foreign language), Hopkins (forthcoming) has suggested a rate of 20%. Athens was a small-scale society and Roman Egypt hardly a democracy.[12] For processes of informed consultation to operate in larger units, at least before the radio, the widespread use of the written word as a method of indirect communication is a virtual necessity, and that means not only alphabetic writing but printing as well.

The development of the ballot in nineteenth-century Europe spread together with the schooling of the populace. Both were linked to the circulation of information by means of mass-produced newspapers, reviews and books. However, writing gets used not only to promote government and participation in government but to attack the existing regime, by mass communication where the democratic system permits, by *samizdat* publications where it does not.[13] Scepticism, criticism and disbelief are not, of course, absent from oral societies but their expression tends to get rubbed out at each generation, even where it does become explicit. There is no accumulation of non-conforming ideas. Attacks against the present political dispensation tend to take the form of rebellion aimed at re-establishing the old order, rather than at reform, let alone revolution. In literate cultures the individual commentaries of philosophers and preachers are given permanent form which, with the widespread circulation of the printed word, may more easily crystallize into conflicting ideologies. Dreams of nowhere materialize into accounts of Utopia and more practical alternatives take a shape that enables their message to travel widely both in space and time. The articulation of dissent in written form leads to the formulations of dissent groups; the Manifesto, the Party Programme, the Writings of the Prophet, each can form a point on which dissenters can focus, giving rise to a social aggregate, a collectivity of protest. As we have seen, objections to killing exist in the simpler societies, but their adoption by dissenting groups seems to require a crystallization in written form. Indeed, since these are minority groups, whose members are widely dispersed, it is not until the printing press provides a regular mode of communication and exhortation that dissent really comes into its own. Again, it is a case of the changes involved in the process of making the implicit explicit.

Lower-level politics

In the widest context, the political is seen as the struggle for and the use of power, which is an aspect of most social behaviour, around the parish pump as much as on the national scene. I would argue that even if we are dealing with political behaviour in this very general sense, writing remains a significant factor since it constitutes an important dimension of power at any level. The composition of the agenda and the written report structures the decisions a committee makes; those who read and study the papers are in a position to exercise power. The taker of minutes is not simply a service role but one that can influence the decisions made.

Even at the societal level, writing is connected with the distribution of power to the other semi-autonomous 'great organizations', especially the church. For it sets down beliefs and practices, ideologies and programmes, as well as demanding the attention of specialists. The autonomy of the church and hence, to some extent, its power within the society, is predicated upon the written word.

The role of the schooled

As a way of summing up this chapter I want to refer to the influence of writing on the political processes in a different geographical area: that of the Kuna Indians who inhabit the Caribbean Islands of Panama.

The political role of literate, 'schooled' members of a community otherwise largely dependent on oral communication is well brought out in Howe's studies (1979; 1985). I say largely because the Kuna did themselves develop a form of graphic representation of a pictorial kind which seems to have served as a mnemonic for the singing of chants and the reciting of myths and legends (Nordenskiöld 1938; Kramer 1970; MacChapin 1983). These representations seem to have been similar to those on the birch-bark scrolls of the Ojibwa (Dewdney 1975), serving ritual and mnemonic rather than wider purposes.

The Kuna Indians have been in contact with Europeans since the sixteenth century but situated in difficult country; adroitly manipulating one external group against the other, they have maintained a considerable measure of autonomy to this very day, evolving their own political system as a result. In discussing these developments, Howe notes that it is hard to see how they could have occurred without the intervention of writing. For while most Kuna are illiterate, "villages have used their literate members extensively, to record cases, laws, judgements, and permits, to organize village finance and labour, and to keep up extensive external communication". On a more general level, he sees an increased "*formality* and *routinization* of political procedures. Lists, schedules, written laws, and standard operating procedures have replaced (though only partially) diffuse expectations and tacit agreements. None of the labels for systems that have undergone such change – secular, modern, bureaucratic, or Weber's loaded and ethnocentric 'rational' – is entirely satisfactory, but the general trend is obvious." At the same time Howe identifies progressive *secularization* and *individuation*. The first two of the features, formality and routinization, are clearly linked by the author to the existence of lists and schedules, which were some of the earliest features of

Mesopotamian writing; the latter are ones we have also identified as related to developments in the written tradition. In so far as secularization is linked to the separation of church and state, it has formed one of our major themes. As for individuation (not necessarily the same as 'individualism', being a process rather than an ideology), we can best understand the way this is connected by considering the notion of responsibility (Fauconnet 1920).

Writing and responsibility

One aspect of the introduction of writing is the greater precision it gives to orders from above and to pleas from below. It is less easy to evade an order that has been committed to writing and carries an authoritative signature. Such personalized commitment 'in writing' also means that responsibility for giving and receiving orders is more highly individualized. In a chain of oral messages (as with myth and folk tales), the identity of the originator of a specific command can easily get lost; such ambiguity may serve to protect the paramount (who 'can do no wrong') from the results of unfortunate decisions.[14]

The same search for a precise record took place in the context of external relations. The value of providing a written record of agreement (the equivalent of the written contract between individuals) was soon recognized. As in the case of contract itself, the written form enables a more complex, more variable, more individual bargain to be struck. The nature of contract is clearly central to the legal system, itself basic to the system of governmental control and a domain in which Maine (1861) saw the development of 'contract' out of 'status' as being the great revolution of man's social history. As we will see in the next chapter on law, that notion requires some modification; nevertheless the written contract generally involves a greater allocation of personal responsibility than is characteristic of oral societies.

I have spoken of the impact of writing on politics primarily in the early phases of this process. I did this largely to point up the potential differences which its advent could make, to delineate the general features of the contrast with polities where communication is limited to speech. But it is clear that the effects of writing are cumulative in a number of ways. First, the content of the written tradition (what is stored in writing) is continually increasing; not only does the office file become transformed into an archival specimen, but ideas, plans and ideologies are given a continuing existence by being set down in writing, by which they achieve a certain immortality as well as forming the basis for later and possibly newer formulations of those ideas. Secondly, changes in the form of writing, as well as in its diffusion, make it more accessible to the majority of society's members. Thirdly, its uses proliferate over time; print, the mechanical reproduction of the written word, makes possible the spread of information about events and policies. Writing affects the means by which control of the polity is carried out through the secret, written ballot which is deliberately opposed to the open gesture of the raised hand or the verbal exclamation as a truly democratic technique, reflecting the real opinion of the individual members of society, expressed without fear or favour, privately rather than publicly.

I will return in the final chapter to the general way in which early states differ depending upon the presence and use of writing. Here I will take up again the issue I raised at the beginning of the present one, concerning the question of their organization. When social anthropologists have discussed political systems they have generally concentrated upon differentiation in the second half of the binary division enshrined in *African Political Systems*; this division was in fact tripartite (embracing band organizations as well) but is perceived, and indeed phrased, as one between polities of type A and type B. States tend to be treated as a unitary category, even a residual one, so that, for example, enquiries are aimed at the origin of *the* state instead of at the origins (or perhaps development) of different forms of states.

From a socio-cultural as well as from a historical standpoint this categorization is inadequate and requires much more elaboration than it has had. The more historically based notions of the development and classification of states that are widely used by other comparative sociologists and historians are hardly more satisfactory, since they are so Eurocentric in taking the rise of the West as their paradigm of development. In doing so they tend to skate over important differences among earlier states and so omit a consideration of crucial mechanisms. The application of the terms 'feudalism' and 'bureaucracy' in a blanket manner has lead to a neglect of the role of differences in productive systems. More importantly, especially in the latter case, too little attention is paid to changes in the modes of communication. An administrative system without writing differs radically from one that employs literates. Moreover this difference is more than a matter of social organization in any limiting sense of that phrase – it affects cultures and their ability to resist the establishment of hegemonies, a potentiality which has in turn a formidable political dimension. To take an apparently trivial example, in an earlier study (1982) I tried to point out the role of cookbooks in the resistance to the outside pressures of politically dominant societies. Cookbooks are literary products which in turn are linked to the development of an *haute cuisine*. While it would seem ridiculous to associate the *haute cuisine* of China with its capacity for resistance to pressures from the West, the written cultures of China, Japan, India and the Middle East have buffered those societies against not always the military but to some extent the cultural conquest by European powers, limiting the hegemonic effects of such contact. By contrast the cultures of the indigenous societies of Africa and America have been affected in much more devastating ways by the advent of European colonialism. For this, the absence of a written tradition, also related to differences in the economy, was at least partially responsible.

4

The letter of the law

In this chapter I want to consider, as I have done with the other topics, how far the concept of law itself is influenced by the presence of writing, then to go on to discuss its relation to the logic (or rationality), the procedures, the institutions and the content of law. While there is much to say about the application of writing to the law in the Ancient Near East, not to speak of Greece and Rome, I want to draw my contrast largely between the recent situation in Africa on the one hand, and that in Europe, including England in the early Middle Ages, on the other, partly because this contrast has been in the minds of those authors like Bohannan, Epstein, Fallers, Gluckman and others who have contributed so much to its analysis. Indeed it would be impossible to examine the situation without reference to European, and more specifically Anglo-American, legal systems.

The first problem, which is at once one of genesis and classification, was raised in a direct way by a writer on the legal system of Babylonia and Assyria. Of the earlier period, he asked, "the question remains, was it 'right' or 'law'? Were there enactments by authority, making it clear what was right, and in some cases creating right, where there was none before? There was much to suggest the existence of enacted law, even of a code of laws" (Johns 1904: 39).

When social scientists deal with enacted, codified law, they sometimes take the view that this segment of social action is of a formal, technical type that is better left to specialists. But I would argue that here we are dealing with problems, as the very terminology reveals, of right and wrong as well as rights and duties, of laws and rules as well as torts and crimes, of customs and norms which have been seen by some as the basis of the study of social life. We are dealing with

ideas of justice and how society should be run. Nor are the particular
usages of such terms and concepts confined to one language. In
French *le droit*, like the parallel English and German usages 'right'
and *Recht*, refers to direction as well as 'conformity to a rule'
(Robert) and derives, like the adjective *droit*, straight, from the low
Latin, *directum*; later in the sixteenth century, *la droite*, the right
('that which is on the side opposite the heart'), displaced the Old
French *destre* (cognate with 'dextrous'). As with the English custom
(via French from the Latin *consuetudo* – the word *mos* gave
another related set of derivatives) and law, there is a kind of
parallelism with *la loi*, which generally refers to the written law, or
anyhow that which is 'established by the sovereign authority of a
society and sanctioned by public force' (Robert). The contrast is
neatly made by Planiol in his *Traité de Droit civil* (vol. I, no. 10): "le
droit qui dérive de la coutume s'appelle *droit coutumier*; le droit qui
dérive de la loi s'appelle *droit écrit*". Thus 'droit' forms an inclusive
category above 'law' and 'custom'.

Whereas 'law' appears to come from a Scandinavian root meaning 'to lie' or 'to fix' (there was also 'ae' and 'doom' in Anglo-
Saxon), *loi* derives from the Latin *lex*, which is possibly linked with
legere, to read (Ernout and Meillet 1951: 630), whereas *ius* is the
more inclusive concept; 'consuetudine ius est id quod sine lege'.
Custom results from tacit agreement whereas 'Le caractère spécial
de la loi explique au contraire qu'elle doive être écrite et promulgée'
(Ernout and Meillet 1951: 630). Hence *legem figere*, 'to engrave the
law on bronze and fix at the forum', and *legem delere*, 'to erase, to
break the law', *ius*, whence justice, is the inclusive term; *lex*, like the
French '*loi*', the German *Gesetz* and to some extent the English
'*law*', refers to the fixed, written component. But the important
point for the immediate context is that we are dealing with a cluster
of concepts, somewhat overlapping, that refer to very central processes in any form of human interaction. The term *droit* comprises
regularities as well as justice. It refers to the rights of man as well as
to the rights of states to impose customs duties (*les droits de douane*)
and taxes (*les impôts*), from which some are free (*francs*). In
German *das Recht* is again concerned with right as well as with
rights.

Secondly, as will become clear, in dealing with the influence of writing on law, we are examining new modalities by which a society can organize its affairs, involving the ultimate creation, in the process of the separation of the court of law from the court of kings, of another 'great organization' with a certain measure (variable in different societies) of structural autonomy. But thirdly, apart from the partial autonomy of the organization, there is also the related problem of the partial autonomy of the text. As suggested in a much earlier article (Goody and Watt 1963), by creating a text 'out there', a material object detached from man (who created and interprets it), the written word can become the subject of a new kind of critical attention. That is not only because it is 'out there', but because we cannot, as Plato observed, pose questions which the text itself can answer back, unlike the human beings to whom we talk. Moreover the text is often more difficult to understand since it lacks the context of speech, may well be abbreviated, cryptic and generalized, and may not relate primarily to the present at all, being, for example, a law left on the statute books since the sixteenth century. In all these ways the text requires interpretation, explanation, even translation. Moreover the creation of the legal text involves a formalization (e.g. a numbering of the laws), a universalization (e.g. an extension of their range by the elimination of particularities) and an ongoing rationalization. This latter must be understood not in the sense of a process opposed to the modes of thought of oral communities, but one that reorders and reclassifies, sometimes in ways that do not necessarily clarify, the words, phrases, sentences, items with which the text is dealing, as well as leading to further commentaries, either written in the first instance or summarizing the oral elaborations of scholars upon the original work.

Let me begin with the problem of the definition of law, since however fuzzy a concept of the actor or observer we may think it is, there is nothing to be said for avoiding the issue altogether.

The definition of law

In Europe the distinction between law and custom is ultimately based on what was written and what was not. To codify custom is to set it down in writing before proclaiming it as law.[1] The term 'law' has a range of meanings, many of them wide in scope, but, as we have seen, an important component of many of these has to do with the code. In the jural systems of societies without writing, there can be no effective distinction of this kind between law and custom. So much is clear from Gluckman's careful analysis of legal action among the Lozi of Zambia (1955) in which he translates the corresponding concept, *mulao*, as rules of right doing, covering both law and custom.[2] The two are one. But when the jurisdiction of a written code is promulgated over a wide territory, there is bound to be some conflict, at least initially, between national law and local custom (and in some cases with religious 'law'). In medieval France this division took on a territorial form, depending upon whether code or custom was stressed as a source of judicial decision; the country was split between the southern part, known as *le Pays du Droit Écrit*, acknowledging Roman Law and contiguous Italian practice, and the northern part, *le Pays du Droit Coutumier*, which emphasized local usage. England was closer to the northern practice. The English Common Law was established in the thirteenth century by means of the determined application of writing to create a law common to the whole country, set above local, customary, differences but on the other hand not dependent upon Roman models.

The difference between these regimes seems to be related to Weber's observation about the development of 'rationalized legal subcultures' as proceeding along two different routes. In England and other common-law countries it was the work of a guild of lawyers in the service of private clients, while on the continent it was the creation of university-based scholars charged with training officials for a state or ecclesiastical bureaucracy (Fallers 1969: 329; Weber 1947c: 42, 89). The result was different concepts of codification; there was the Code based upon the Roman model as distinct from the codification by statute of English law, both employing writing in the creation of a code, but in rather different ways.

More usually the difference between law and custom has a hierarchical dimension. In his study of the Basoga of Uganda, Fallers wrote: "Customary law is not so much a kind of law as a kind of legal situation which develops in imperial or quasi-imperial contexts, in which dominant legal systems recognize and support the local law of politically subordinate communities. Like the peasant community with which it is so often associated, it is characterized by its relation to a wider, more learned, and politically more powerful system. Usually what is called customary law is unwritten, but it is significant that those who write about law that is unwritten but yet has not been in some sense 'received' into the superordinate system, tend not to use the term; Barton writes simply of 'Ifugao law', Pospisil of 'Kapauku law'. Customary law is folk law in the process of reception" (1969: 3). In other words as a within-society distinction it tends to run parallel to that between 'magic' and 'religion'. Custom is what is not included in the code or its equivalents.

The view of customary law as folk law in the process of being 'received' into the main body of national law represents one possible outcome of the imperial situation, one that appeared likely in the later, benign, phase of British decolonization in Africa; it is doubtful if an examination of more recent events would lead to the adoption of such an optimistic vision of the future. Two other possibilities have arisen: in some cases local practices have been reinforced by being written down, and in others national law (as distinct from fiats or the decisions of military tribunals) has tended to wither away. The era of decolonization has provided the data for much anthropological and sociological theorizing, but few would now argue that this fascinating period was anything except a historical interlude which produced highly specific social forms.

Looking at that period, Fallers argued that law is both cultural and social, concerned with the institutionalization of values "to which the people themselves are sufficiently committed to be willing to impose them upon themselves in an authoritative manner" (1969: 2). The notion that law reflects social and cultural structure in quite the way Fallers suggested (p. 315) would no longer be entirely acceptable. The homogeneity it assumes may provide an adequate model for analyzing an acephalous, unstratified community like the LoDagaa of northern Ghana. But even for simple states like the neighbouring Gonja, which is a multi-ethnic society, it cannot adequately characterize a judicial process which is neither always popular nor always accessible (p. 315). In bureaucratic states the legal and other interests of the dominant groups may diverge in even more radical ways from those of subordinate ones. Such differentiation is a matter both of the historical record and of contemporary experience, and a holistic approach cannot be allowed to sweep the fact under the mat – even in the domain of marriage and the family. But quite apart from hierarchical differentiation, law may possess, though usually less than religion, a limited degree of autonomy linked to a written tradition which gives 'Roman Law', like 'Roman Catholic Religion', a certain independence because of its own rules, its own tradition and its own organization. This limited autonomy is encapsulated in the recourse to the written precedent of case law, characteristic of England, where there is neither written Constitution (unlike the United States) nor Code (unlike French). But all these systems are more directly influenced by the wishes of the political authorities, who have to support the courts' decisions, than is the case with religious activity.

In discussing comparative legal systems, anthropologists have rightly attempted to re-assess some of the concepts that have emerged in the study of European law. Malinowski extended the definition of the term 'law' outside the usual sphere of application to societies having codes, courts and constables. He wanted to make the point that the sanctions on human behaviour should be considered as a total set, and hence applied the word 'law' to any norm that was not merely 'neutral' custom, just as Llewellyn and Hoebel (1961), inspired by American legal 'realism', saw law as a rule whose breach invokes an active response, a breach that somebody does something about.

Courts, constables and codes

The point is well taken. But to make it, as Pound (1942), Radcliffe-Brown (1933), Seagle (1937), Fallers (1969) and others have pointed out, one does not have to dispense with the useful distinction between societies with courts and those without, between 'legal' and 'jural' norms. The distinction is not entirely binary for there are intermediate institutions and practices. But important differences exist as can be seen even in the descriptions of post-colonial courts which show the formerly acephalous Tiv (Bohannan 1957) and Arusha (Gulliver 1963) to differ in significant ways from those of the Lozi and Basoga.

The worthy attempts of anthropologists to see the common

elements among forms of dispute and their settlement in different cultures have led to the treatment of law as a fuzzy set that covers all or most forms of social control. The approach is associated, by and large, with an anti-evolutionist bias, usually thinking of that notion as linked to one of progress, but which is often ahistorical as well. In an interesting introduction to a volume entitled 'The Discourse of Law', Humphreys characterizes law as a form of discourse (1985: 254) while at the same time rejecting the need to define the concept. The all-embracing view is fine for some purposes but certainly not for others. Globally it leads to an impoverishment of analysis, partly because it fails to give a satisfactory account of the intervention of courts, governments, lawyers and people in the legal process, partly because, if law is a form of discourse, it must change with the ways that discourse is carried on – for example, when 'rules' are presented in a written form. Referring to the work of E. P. Thompson (1975), Humphreys notes that "the clarification" of property rights in seventeenth–eighteenth-century English law led to the delegitimation of use rights previously enjoyed by the rural population and the redefinition of the exercise of such rights as theft, poaching, etc." (1985: 247). This change is interpreted as the result of defective drafting of laws by lawyers. We may also see it either as a deliberate effort to restrict popular rights or as the largely unintended result of the use of written language (both of which may occur with systems of land registration). But the point is that the encapsulation of oral practices as written rules has far-reaching consequences for the members of a society. The written code does not initiate either oppression or justice; it gives them a different format, which relates to the modes of communication and is not merely a matter of changing one set of cultural clothes for another. It is because of its failure to give sufficient weight to the broad differences as well as the broad similarities in human societies (an uncomfortable task of striking a difficult and in the end unattainable balance) that modern social science in its structural and functional forms has contributed less than it should to advance the study of society. On the one hand we have cultural particularism; the contention that every society differs is a truism of little worth that applies equally well to every individual. But do they have to be considered separately in every context? At the same time particularism runs head into its direct opposite, a universalism employing concepts that tend to be given a too general application.

Let me return to that second element in the crude characterization of law with which I began, as a form of social control embedded in one of the specialized 'great organizations' and operating through the medium of courts, constables and codes.

The first has already been discussed but the presence of constables provides another discriminating feature of legal systems that runs parallel to that of courts. The role of law-enforcing officials implies a degree of monopolization of force (or perhaps better, 'paramount control', Yoffee 1979: 16, following Fried 1967: 237) that characterizes states which operate some means of procuring the authoritative settlement of disputes (Radcliffe-Brown 1940). Although some social scientists tend to write as if coercion was a marginal phenomenon, as if political decisions were always made on the basis of 'models', ideologies, choice, nevertheless force is always there, sometimes in the background, often in the foreground; it is its application and distribution that differ in centralized and tribal (acephalous) systems.

In the most general sense of the term the third feature, the code, is equally important in comparing and distinguishing legal systems, and one that is central to the present discussion. The very fact that laws exist in written form makes a profound difference, first to the nature of its sources, secondly to the ways of changing the rules, thirdly to the judicial process, and fourthly to court organization. Indeed it touches upon the nature of rules themselves.

I am using the word 'code' in the very general sense of the application of writing to a body of rules, although it is clear that in many early systems of law, writing was much more extensively used for the transfers involved in marriages, sale, debts and testaments. But 'code' has a more precise legal meaning, as in the Napoleonic Code which, issued over 150 years ago, "still keeps its universal value, with items simply being adapted, added or subtracted, according to the development of social problems and the reaction of the legislature" (Bottéro 1982b: 413). In considering that most famous of the early codes, the Code of Hammurabi, Bottéro queries the application of both the terms 'code' and 'law'. For it is incomplete, had no 'legislative' value and was recopied unchanged for other reasons; it did not represent an attempt to present the totality of a country's laws. Not, claims Bottéro, if a law is defined as "an imperative rule of conduct, laid down and enforced by legitimate authority", because its statements are neither general or universal but derived from the situation itself (p. 416). Moreover they lack the 'logic' of most collections of laws since one injunction appears to run counter to another (p. 417). What we have is a set of decisions of the king, court decisions from which the specific details of the case have been removed; it was a model of a treatise on the exercise of judicial power.

The relation of the early codes to 'law', in the sense of judicial decisions, is even more problematic in the European case. Anglo-Saxon codes after Aethelberht's day have been described as "literature rather than law" (Diamond 1971: 53). Some codes are 'literary exercises' used to teach reading and writing and as a means of general education; where there are specialist law-scribes, they tend to become law-books, feeding back into the training of practitioners and the public at large. Some appear to represent collections of judgements; others are statements of what law ought to be rather than what it is; few if any are what Maine suggested, mere collections of existing customs, since writing transforms what it touches in various ways, for example in establishing fixed penalties where variable ones prevailed.[3] This is simply one aspect of "the very rigidity which is inherent in the idea of a code", that is, a code in the full, practical sense (Epstein 1953: 95).

Early codes were not of the Napoleonic kind nor did they take the form Maine assumed, a written version of custom, although this constituted one element. On the other hand they made important contributions to the development of jurisprudence. My own use of the term 'code' covers this whole variety of forms as well as alluding to the codification of procedures, which were often of greater significance in social life.

Sources of law and changes of rule

As I have noted, in societies without writing, even where courts exist, there is no effective distinction between 'law' and 'custom' as sources of judicial decision, although certain rules may be seen as justiciable and others not. While there may be some specialization of remembrancers and judges who know more than other people about rules of right-doing, everybody relies on their transmission through the oral channel. As a consequence, the sources of law see to it that a relatively close link is maintained with the other aspects of the social system. For example, the amount of bridewealth may rise over time if there is an increasing flow of the relevant goods within the economy. Or payments may be substituted for bride-service when many men have migrated or work outside the local agricultural sector. Both processes have occurred in northern Ghana in recent times. But such changes do not require the intervention of a deliberate process of organized decision-making in order to bring about a raising of the amount of bridal prestations in tune with inflation, nor yet to legitimize a shift from the transfer of labour to that of goods. What happens is that a gradual adjustment can take place between income, work and marriage as the result of many individual or household decisions, which are subject to common influences. I do not argue that such adjustments are inevitable, nor that deliberate 'legislative' decisions do not occur, but that there is greater flexibility in the oral context.

Contrast the situation in a legal system with a written code. If the marriage prestations or obligations are specified in writing, then some means has to be found of deliberately altering (or ignoring) the code. In modern parliaments a great deal of decision-making by the representatives of the people involves changes of precisely this kind, the deliberate removal of 'anomalies' that in an oral society would have tended to disappear by themselves in a quasi-automatic manner. But once committed to writing, 'customs' cannot just fade away. So while writing greatly increases the amount of information held in store, and in this sense enhances the potentialities of the human mind, it also makes the problem of erasure much more difficult, in other words, deletion represents the other side of the storage coin. To take one notable example, the English law of blasphemy, though no longer providing for capital punishment (*de haeretico comburendo*) since 1677 (29 Charles II c.9), still remains a crime under Common Law. In practice the written rule is rarely, if ever, applied. How do we manage to modify or ignore a law of this kind? In giving a judicial decision, the judge will take into account sources of law other than the written code itself. One of these is precedent, comprising an earlier ruling given by an authoritative court. Another factor is the recognition of changes that have taken place in the climate of opinion. While shifts of this latter kind take place in non-literate societies, there is less room for direct conflict, for open confrontation, between the old and the new. The old fades more quickly into the background; it is, quite simply, forgotten.

One example of this process of merging is described in Fallers' account of the neo-traditional legal system of the Basoga of East Africa. He argues that "formal leases – constraints for the use of land for determinate periods and purposes – violate the received conceptual scheme" (1969: 322). Nevertheless the binding (and restrictive) nature of this kind of contract has developed 'imperceptibly' out of previous practice in accord with the increasing commercialization of Busoga's economy. Had the law been written, it would not have changed 'imperceptibly'.

In written law precedent is one way in which a rule may be modified, once a previous court has made a decision that can be used in future judgements. Gluckman (1955: 23–4, 256–8) has observed that this source of law is little used in non-literate societies. The reason is basically the same; verbal precedents are either forgotten or else merge into future judgements; they do not comprise a distinct category, except perhaps for a short space of time.

The relation of precedent, and indeed of the nature of legal reasoning, to writing is brought out in Epstein's analysis of urban 'customary' courts in southern Africa where he draws the contrast with European courts whose judgements

have been *recorded* for centuries. The cases have been abridged, annotated, presented in digest form and been the subject of prolific commentary. Through the passage of time, and the efforts of a specialized class of lawyers, the law has become highly categorized. In these circumstances the task of the court is to some extent simplified because, as novel situations arise, the facts they disclose may be fitted into existing categories . . . Within these categories the courts are at once able to seek out analogies with previously decided cases, and to apply the appropriate *precedent*. African customary law, on the other hand, is *unrecorded*, and while particular offences have their respective vernacular terms, litigants do not have to bring their case within some specific form of action. Nor, so far as I have been able to discover, do individual decisions constitute any binding authority for the deciding of subsequent cases (1954: 27, my italics).

Precedent apart, Maine distinguishes three ways of bringing law into line with changing practice: by Legal Fictions, by Equity and by Legislation. By Legal Fiction he understands "any assumption which conceals or affects to conceal, the fact that a rule of law has undergone alteration, its letter remaining unchanged, its operation being modified" (1931: 21–2). Both English case-law and Roman Responsa Prudentium are general categories of such fictions, and he cites the practice of adoption as a specific example of their use. Are we not clearly dealing here with the relative fixity of written law over time in contrast to the relative flexibility of practice, of custom?

The second 'instrumentality' by which the law is adapted to 'social wants' is Equity, defined as "any body of rules existing by the side of the original civil law, founded on distinct principles and claiming incidentally to supercede the civil law in virtue of a superior sanctity inherent in those principles" (p. 23). Finally, there is Legislation, the enactments of a legislature, whether in the form of an autocratic prince or of a parliamentary assembly. Both of these instrumentalities are required because the law has been set down in writing and has to be modified as circumstances change, either deliberately by legislation or informally by introducing considerations of general equity.

In the second chapter of *Ancient Law* Maine makes the point that one general difference in the forms of law consists in the mode of changing them. "When primitive law has once been embodied in a Code, there is an end to what may be called its spontaneous development. Henceforward the changes effected in it, if effected at all, are effected deliberately and from without" (1931: 17). He goes on to elaborate this statement, claiming that while changes occurred in earlier times, they were rarely subject to a 'set purpose'; for they were "dictated by feelings and modes of thought which, under our present mental conditions, we are unable to comprehend. A new era begins, however, with the Codes." After the code comes into existence, 'legal modification' can be attributed to the "*conscious* desire for improvement" (p. 18, my italics).

Though Maine points to the problem, he does not fully appreciate that the spontaneous development on which he comments is the imperceptible process of adjustment of norms that constantly takes place in oral societies in response to external pressures or internal forces. The process is imperceptible because norms have only a verbal, an oral existence, so that rules that are no longer applicable tend to slip out of the memory store. But write down the norms in the form of a code or statute and you then have to make deliberate and conscious efforts to effect any alteration. That is to say, government in written cultures has to concern itself with legislating for changes in the law that custom would have adapted more or less automatically. And where the written law has not been formally changed, legal fictions and other sources of law are called upon to adapt it to actual situations. Though Maine and later Gluckman pointed to those differences, they did not specifically relate them to the presence of writing. The differences between 'primitive' and 'advanced', 'simple' and 'complex' systems of law are described without making explicit (conscious) the influence of this major contributory mechanism.

Sources of law are of course specific to particular societies. Nevertheless there are some aspects found more widely distributed in systems of written law. In the theory of Sunni Islamic jurisprudence, the Qur'ān, the prophetic traditions (*hadith*), the application of analogy (*qivas*) and scholarly consensus (*ijma'*) are the four recognized sources of law, in addition to the hermeneutic use of reason (*ra'y*). Custom, notes Udovitch, is not in theory an accepted source of positive law. Yet especially for the Hanafi school, and especially in economic life, custom (*'urf*); or the practice (*'ada*) of merchants, is constantly used as a guide to conduct inside and outside the courts, so that effectively it becomes a source of law (1985: 447, 457). That is to say, 'local knowledge' modifies the "universally valid system of law . . . where inspiration, origins and, one might even say, ultimate authorship go back to God" (p. 446). God 'writes' the Book of Law and He is first and foremost "universal in character", to which he adds the significant qualification, at least in a monotheistic system. In both law and religion, the 'universality' of the written has to be supplemented in practice by the particularity of the local -- that is, of custom.

Legal reasoning

The recourse to precedent and to legislation are associated with differences in the nature of legal reasoning and indeed in reasoning itself. Such differences are not, of course, linked to innate mental ability, but to the tools, concepts and programs available for intellectual activity. The point emerges clearly in Fallers' account of neo-traditional Busoga law which is entitled *Law without Precedent* (1969). He draws a deliberate contrast with Anglo-American law because he sees the case-by-case form that precedent takes as linked to legal reasoning in changing societies. New situations arise, people's ideas change, and these changes are accommodated by the use of ambiguous concepts and what he describes as a "moving system of classification" (1969: 18).

Although Soga law is case-law in the sense that it makes little use of statutes, it "contains no explicit doctrine of precedent of any sort" (p. 19), partly because judges assume continuity. He argues that the process of legal reasoning by means of 'categorizing concepts' is similar but that it differs in its operation. For "there is no explicit doctrine of precedent and no machinery for case reporting to put such a doctrine into systematic practice. The courts have excellent records [this is obviously a recent feature of the neo-traditional courts, J.R.G.]; but there is no provision for selecting precedent-setting cases and bringing them to the attention of the judges. In addition, the concepts themselves are somewhat different – less abstract and generalized" (p. 21).

The jurist Hart has argued that communication of "general standards of content, which multitudes of individuals could understand", is essential to law and that such communication is effected by legislation and precedent (1961: 121). The Soga lack these procedures, regarded by Hart as essential for orderly change. Instead each sitting of a Soga court represents a fresh start – there is no authority outside the court to decide about the rules. Fallers explained this difference in terms of static and changing societies; but it is surely a question of the way change, operating at different speeds, is conceived and handled in communication. Written records of court proceedings are now being made and, as Fallers suggests, these eventually will be used for creating precedents. "The use of writing serves to improve record-keeping with respect to 'facts', but it does not – at least not yet – increase the explicitness of communication with and about legal concepts" (1969: 314). This process is precisely what took place earlier in the creation of Anglo-American law and will be repeated in Busoga. Because it is writing that lays the groundwork for the differences that Fallers notes "between legal systems . . . that have trained judges and advocates, law reports and law schools; and those like the Soga system that lack these facilities but are, nonetheless, engaged in what is, on some level, the same kind of work" (p. 20). Legal reasoning, which Fallers defines as "the application to the settlement of disputes of categorizing concepts that define justiciable normative issues" (p. 32), is different because the European judge can carefully rework previous decisions (precedents), thus preserving "the conceptual framework of the law while making the minimal changes necessary to deal with the matter at hand", while the Musoga judge remembers similar cases but "assimilates each case directly to a set of concepts which he carries in his mind" (pp. 32–3). It is the question of the way we assimilate experience and modify concepts that constitutes the significant difference, following on logically from the application of writing. Assimilation is achieved by playing down difference and change, which are obviously less easy to contemplate if records are either absent or disregarded. The Basoga do discuss cases of dispute but the legal system leaves so much implicit and its proceedings rarely involve the explicit statement of rules (p. 36). Fallers relates the absence of explicitness to the absence of professional thinkers-about-the-law. But it must be remembered that their very presence is in turn related to the elaborate institutional organization of European law, which is essentially based not only on reporting in the sense of 'rendering an account' (an activity common to all human discourse) but on the contemplation of the *written* record. Let us follow his description in more detail. "Reporters collect, analyze, and publish important cases. Scholars organize legal ideas and legislative and judicial acts into coherent 'fields'. Philosophers reconsider the moral and intellectual bases of legal thought. Legislatures and appellate judges, from time to time, tidy up sections of the law. Politicians and publicists debate legal 'principles' in the public forum" (p. 35).

While my argument is implicit in Fallers' discussion of the absence of precedent and legislation in Soga law, I do not see the difference simply as a matter of making explicit categories and rules (by writing, I argue) that were always present. It is here, I think, that I depart from the assumptions of many of my colleagues. I see the notion and nature of concepts and rules as actually changing in this process, changing as regards both form and content. Epstein makes a similar point in his study of urban courts: "Since customary law has remained unwritten its categories have never been formalized" (1954: 29). The system as a whole is never subject to review to bring out inconsistencies. Not that the basic mental processes and institutional analogues are absent from simpler cultures. But the difference between implicit and explicit reasoning, between the contemplation of the text and the pondering of the utterance, between the capacity to review a statement visually as well as internally, by eye as well as by ear, while in some respects small, is of fundamental importance for the development of what we think of as reasoning. The reading permits a greater distancing between individual, language and reference than speech, a greater objectification which increases the analytic potential of the human mind.

Of this difference Fallers provides an excellent example. "To anyone used to thinking of legal argument as containing an element of explicit discussion of rules or concepts of wrong", he says, "the transcripts of Soga trials read like one non-sequitur after the other. Sometimes the non-sequiturs are interlarded with apparent contradictions . . . " (1969: 320–1). He goes on to say that "neither non-sequiturs nor the contradictions really are such". But surely they both are and are not; they become so with the explicitness of writing (not necessarily immediately, as Fallers points out on p. 314), which turns them into non-sequiturs and contradictions as we know them. And that way of knowing (affecting our epistemology) is highly important for the development of social action and for cognition in the wider sense of our understanding of the world.

Court organization

Writing affects not only the sources of law and reasoning in law but also the organization of law. The relationship of law to society becomes formalized with the advent of writing. Since there is no longer a quasi-homeostatic adaptation of norms, the written law achieves a kind of autonomy of its own, as do its organs. The judicial court gradually becomes separate from the royal or chief's court, acquiring its own highly literate specialists, some of whom are experts in the oral presentation of cases, arguing and advocating the client's cause, others in giving advice.

The development of specialized advocates, as distinct from advisors, was a notable feature of classical Rome, though these also seem to have been present in Mesopotamia. In Athens, however, advocacy was not a profession; a litigant had to conduct his own case in person although he could divide his allocated time between himself and supporting speakers. The testimonies of witnesses were not included in this allocation of time but from 378 BC onwards these testimonies took the form of a written statement prepared in advance which the witness had to affirm or deny on oath when he appeared in court.

We have about 100 speeches (or large fragments) addressed to law courts, attributed to ten famous speech writers, though sometimes dubiously. These speeches were sometimes retouched for publication and circulated among the Athenian public (Humphreys 1985, forthcoming). Already, then, we find both law reports and speech writers, the latter being a very strange occupation from the standpoint of oral societies.

The internal organization of the court also becomes elaborated because the use of precedents, and perhaps judge-made law on any scale, requires the keeping of records. But that is not the only role of the law reports for they can also be useful for the subsequent checking, control and reviewing of judgements by appeal courts or by administrative officers, as well as for more philosophical purposes.

Written records imply the presence of clerks whose work gives a permanent form to the verbal duels and decisions. Judges too need to understand the written word as law is increasingly incorporated in digests and *summae*. Under these circumstances the legal profession becomes an occupation for literate specialists, and law is increasingly taken out of the 'amateur' hands of the man in the street. Legal norms no longer reside in the memory of each and every individual (at least of every elder) but may be literally buried in documents to be disinterred only by specialists in the written word. Custom becomes a matter of what people know and do, law what appears in the code, whose content may depend upon the specialist's interpretation of popular will, of political dominance, of bureaucratic convenience or of the internal 'logic' of legal reasoning. The long-term implications of such dissociation of law and custom, which is at the same time a differentiation of the two realms with the written word usually being given priority, are radical for the development both of society and of the individual.

Legal forms

Writing encourages formalism of another kind. Certain aspects of Western legal procedure, more in systems of statute than of case-law, have been inherited from Roman Law, the early phases of which were characterized by 'actional formalism'. This phrase refers to "its tendency to endow every act in the law with a definite form" (Schulz 1936: 24), a process that seems to grow out of writing, even though writing was not always considered essential to the legal act itself. According to Schulz, documents were of purely evidential value, although they preserved additional details to which only passing reference was made in the oral formulae. Nevertheless there was a general shift of direction. The use of writing served not only to formalize legal procedures in general but to change them in substantive ways. For example, the document might serve to simplify the spoken formula which referred to it for details, while a projected *lex* was publicly advertised in writing before the votes were cast.

Contract

One of the most obvious interventions of writing was in the field of contract. According to Maine the great revolution of mankind was from status to contract. Forms of contractual arrangement do of course exist in oral culture. As these bring into being new and often temporary relations between individuals or groups, the transactions embodied in the agreements often need to be referred to at some future time. For this, one has to depend upon the memory and longevity of the 'eye-witness', although this mode of remembering has limitations that are often recognized by the actors themselves because of the many conflicts that ensue, a fact that makes such societies open to adopting improved forms of testimony or record. Contracts involving a complicated series of variable arrangements are patently more difficult to keep track of in oral societies that follow 'customary' practice. They are certainly more susceptible to reinterpretation by each of the parties involved, being more open to the present disposition of power; the initial ambiguity may be no greater but the room for selective reconsideration, conscious or unconscious, is inevitably wider.

The absence of a written record places a limit upon the range and variability of oral contracts. For example, in the event of a marriage, the family of the groom will pass four cattle to the family of the bride. The written contract (as distinct from the written code) increases the potential range of specification, since each contract can be tailored by the parties to the present situation. I do not wish to claim that variable marriage payments are a feature only of societies with writing; if there is any positive association between the two, it is almost certainly due to other factors. Moreover exceptions are many: in Asante, the nature and amount of the marriage prestations depend upon the status of the bride. However, such variations as exist in this type of transaction in oral societies usually have to be formulated in a fairly straightforward manner. Those involved in, say, Melanau marriage in Sarawak are much more complicated (Morris 1953: 129–33), and when a record of these gifts has to be kept in case the marriage is dissolved, writing permits a greater range, a greater certainty, in these transactions within the framework of an agreed formula, the contract.

Contract, then, was not absent in oral societies but in urban situations its incidence increases, since interactions tend to be more single-stranded, especially where writing serves to focus attention on a specific aspect of a transaction, one that no longer takes place between kin but between strangers. On the one hand tribal law often fails to enforce executory contracts (Epstein 1953: 93); on the other hand written law elaborates the "lawyer's conception of contract in the abstract. This is a technical and theoretical conception arrived at by a process of abstraction from an increasing number of

facts and suitable for application to the innumerable forms of transactions" (Diamond 1971: 379). The importance of writing in the
form of the contract, the elaboration of the notion through a process
of 'abstraction', through the making of 'an abstract', and the
emergence of specialist notaries is clear and the case stands
as a paradigm of the uses of literacy in social and intellectual
development.

Maine's insistence on the importance of the change from status to
contract, Durkheim's discussion of the role of contract in the move
from mechanical to organic solidarity – both were influential ways
of describing major shifts in legal systems. The increase in contractual relations was certainly connected, as both Spencer and
Durkheim indicated, with the shift from a domestic to a manufac-
turing and trading economy which employed wage-labour; free-
men, not slaves, make contracts. On the other hand, the proliferation of formal contracts also followed upon the use of writing.
Think only of the development of written marriage contracts or
settlements in Ancient Egypt, in Judaism, in Christian Ethiopia,
under Islam, in Greece, Rome, in eighteenth-century England, in
the 'writings' of County Clare. It is true that today Anglo-American
unions have effectively abandoned formal contracts regulating
marital property, although implicit understandings (the non-
contractual elements of contract) and legal controls are many. Nor
were they ever as important as under a system of local notaries. But
in France and other countries that follow the Napoleonic Code,
such contracts concerning the ownership and distribution of property are a *sine qua non*, and were so in many places long before
Napoleon. And far from being confined to affinal relations, written
contracts between adjacent generations in the same family,
between, say, father and mother, and son and daughter-in-law,
were widespread in continental Europe, when the parents handed
over the farm or other property to their offspring. Instead of trust-
ing the children, the latter had to enter into a written contract (a sort
of mortgage) which could specify the details of what food and
clothing had to be provided for the old people, what rooms and
doors had to be used by them. Reading such documents (and they
continue to exist in rural France as elsewhere) one is astonished to

see the way that filial piety has to stand up and be counted, spelt out in exact quantities and decked out in a lawyer's jargon.

In commerce, the influence of contracts was even more extensive, as we have noted in discussing the Old Assyrian caravan trade. The practice continued throughout the history of the Near East. Centuries later Mahomet declared, "Oh ye who believed, when ye contract a debt to one another for a stated term, write it down" (Qur'ān, Surah II: 282). Why write it down? Above all, it seems, because that avoids quarrels (even between close kin), and it avoids usury (*riba*), a concept that covered a number of commercial 'sins', and finally it facilitates the development of commerce (Udovitch 1985).

The influence of written language on contracts was not limited to form or content but extended to the search for clarification, just as some have argued is the case with learning to program computers. "In the (written) contracts", writes Johns (1904: iv), "we find men struggling for exactness of statement and clearness of diction . . . Every phrase is technical and legal, to an extent that often defies translation." The struggle for clarity, the development of a specialist field, these are constant themes in the analysis of the influence of writing on law.

Testaments
In using writing for marriage or mortgage, transactions may become more complex, in some ways more binding, since they are more explicit in terms of legal action. At the same time transactions tend to be less so as far as supernatural sanctions are concerned, for these latter are usually hinted at, suggested, rather than spelled out, so that the reduction to writing reduces their effectiveness; the separation between law and religion, both at this level and at the level of the great organizations, is also a process of secularization.

There is a similar domain where writing gives an increased flexibility to individual choice, binding the next generation rather than this. By means of the written will or testament, non-standard decisions of the actors cannot so easily get swallowed up by 'custom'. Let me give a concrete example of what I mean. When I was in Birifu, a settlement of the LoDagaa of northern Ghana, I was friendly with an elder called Bonyiri. Unlike the situation in most families, his eldest son San, who lived in the same compound, was farming separately because of various quarrels they had had in the past. When San began to farm on his own, he was given land by his father. But the major part of Bonyiri's land was retained by the old man, who cultivated it with his other sons. As far as Bonyiri was concerned, San had already received his share of the patrimony, even though it was smaller than would have come to him by the principle of equal shares. But after I had raised this matter in discussion, some elders of the same clan section took me aside and told me that, whatever Bonyiri's wishes, the land would be distributed equally after his death; they explained that otherwise the ancestors would trouble those who remained behind if the land was not divided according to the existing norms, those norms by which it had already been handed down to the living by those very ancestors. The result was that at his death the old man's wishes about the disposition of his property were effectively ignored.

The possibility of 'alienation' of family property by a kind of testament does exist in some oral cultures. In Asante there is a procedure known as *samansie* (literally, that which is set aside by the dead man) whereby an individual can bequeath property to certain categories of 'non-inheriting' relatives, providing the transaction is properly witnessed by representatives of those liable to lose out. But as with the LoDagaa such gifts are always subject to subsequent review after the testator's death, a fact that is incorporated in the proverb that runs – "When a ghost has made an improper distribution of his . . . property, the living will make a new one" (Rattray 1929: 339).

Such forms exist, but the use of writing adds another dimension to teatamentary disposition. Even today no will is necessary provided an individual is satisfied with the norms of what lawyers curiously, though predictably, refer to as 'intestate' inheritance, that is, inheritance by the customary norms without a written testament provided by the literate specialist. The question of a will arises only if one intends to modify that understanding and leave more to a mistress than to a wife, more to a servant than to a son; or if there is property that one wishes to distribute in particular ways, or if one wants to be more certain that one's will be done.

A contemporary example of the probable effects of the introduction of a written will is provided by Colson in her account of the Tonga of southern Africa. Here she notes that the written form of testament tends to designate a single heir, or in any case to cancel the more general rights which kin may have in the property of the deceased. The very notion makes the transmission of property depend upon the wishes, the will, of the testator rather than be part of immemorial custom. Not that oral societies completely ignore the desires of the testator, but these tend to get more easily over-ridden than when they are expressed in writing,[4] although even here the law tends to place restrictions on an individual's capacity to disinherit 'natural' heirs.

Because the will may be seen as expressing the wishes of the testator in opposition to custom, it is often an instrument of social change. The written testament, drawn up by a professional literate and witnessed by an outsider's signature, makes it simpler to settle one's property in a flexible manner, as well as to provide for more elaborate and more individualized arrangements. It is the same with the alienation of property during one's lifetime. In Anglo-Saxon law, book-right was a method of breaking the customary mode of inheritance and hence was much encouraged by the church in whose favour such freedom of disposition was frequently exercised; this written act of 'free disposal' permanently alienated the property from those who held the customary rights. Such a procedure was again an individualizing one, enabling people to make special arrangements which would be secure after their death, difficult to set aside because of the written format and the legal sanctions. As we have seen, the individual wishes of the testator in oral cultures, while perhaps no less freely expressed, tend to get swallowed up in the practice of the group, which sees 'justice' and 'freedom' in different terms.

The significance of the written will, with its freedom of testation, is nowhere clearer than in the opening clause of the Lex Baiuvariorum (Diamond 1971: 51), which runs as follows:

Whenever a free person makes a will and gives his property to the Church for the redemption of his soul [see Proverbs 13:8], let him have leave to do so with his own share after he has made division with his sons. Let no one prevent him; let neither king nor duke nor any person have power to prevent him. And whatever he has given – houses, land, slaves or any other property – for the redemption of his soul, let him confirm in writing by his own hand, and let him bring 6 witnesses, or more if they are willing, and let them put their hands on the writing and mark their names at his request. Then let him put the writing on the altar, and so let him hand over the money in the presence of the priest who serves in that place. And thereafter let him have no power over it, neither he nor his posterity, unless the defender of the Church be willing to grant him the favour, but let the things of the Church be defended by the bishop, whatever is given by Christians to the Church of God.

A similar situation is emerging in contemporary Africa, where the will is often used to prefer children to brothers or to sisters' sons. There has always been tension in patrilineal systems between adelphic and filial transmission, and in matrilineal ones between transmission to children and to sisters' sons. The tension increases when greater differentiation occurs, especially in wealth. I have remarked (1962) upon these problems for the LoDagaa, and Colson also noted that among the Tonga it is the rich (and their sons) who want to be allowed to make wills in order to circumvent matrilineal inheritance while the poor wish to maintain the present system (1950: 31). For in this way collective rights (or better, the rights of more distant kin in the descent group) can be set aside in favour of individual rights (or better, the rights of closer kin outside the descent group). She sums up the probable effects of the change in the following words:

1. The influence of the matrilineal groups will be weakened and the linkage of the various matrilineal groups to one another will probably fall away.
2. There will be a concentration of wealth over the generations instead of a general distribution at each death. This may lead to cleavages in Tonga society between the farmers and the majority of the Tonga who still control little property.
3. There will be a shift to the inheritance by sons and daughters.
4. The authority of the father will be strengthened.
5. The focus of witchcraft fears will shift into a man's own family.
6. There is likely to be an increase in witchcraft charges and possibly in actual cases of poisoning.
7. The position of those children who do not live with their fathers – children who have gone with their mother on divorce, illegitimate children, etc. – is likely to be worsened as will that of

divorced and otherwise single women who will no longer have as sure a claim on the matrilineal group (p. 34).

Of course there are advantages as well as problems in the registration of wills, title to land, birth, marriage and divorce. For the national and colonial administrations the general pressures towards such bureaucratization are self-evident. But there are also more specific reasons concerned not only with statistics for planning and taxation, the avoidance of disputes and the system of appeals (where case records are important), but to do with the allocation of benefits. This is especially true in the more anonymous life of the towns. In a village everyone knows who is married and who divorced; in a town a certificate has an added value, both for individuals and for the courts. "The effect of registration", writes Epstein, "is to relieve the courts of the task of establishing the validity of marriage by an arduous process of examination and the calling of necessary witnesses. It provides an easy *mode of proof* of marriage" (1953: 60, my italics).

The mouth and the hand

The use of writing involves a partial shift of the human instrumentality from mouth to hand which has a significant effect on legal forms, especially 'symbolic' ones. When an Asante was condemned to death, his mouth was immediately closed by means of a skewer, thus preventing him from cursing the chief who had judged the case. The power, in the sense of efficacy, of the curse is seen to depend not only upon a particular view of the interaction of forces in the universe but on the idea that a special strength attaches to certain verbal formulae, whether these be curses, oaths, spells or blessings, capable of acting upon the individual involved. Those who are reluctant to accept this causal chain treat them as expletives, disrespectful to man and possibly to God, but whose efficacy lies in the offence taken.

The oath, curse, spell and blessing are all utterances for which the mouth takes on a special significance. In the language of the LoDagaa, the phrase *kuono nuor*, 'cry the mouth', describes the making of an oath or a curse; to end the situation created by this verbal act one has to 'take out the mouth', a procedure which removes the danger of mystical action.

For the written channel, the corresponding organ is the hand which constitutes a parallel focus of meaning in phrases such as 'in my own hand'. Handwriting acquires a special weight as indicative of 'character', and the equivalent of the oral oath is the signed confession. The signature effectively becomes a substitute for the person, at least at the bottom of cheques. But it is not only a card of identity, as individual as the print of the finger or the hand, but also an assertion of truth or of consent.

Evidence

In the case of procedural formalism, contracts, testaments and, as we will see in the next section, the registration of title to land, so critical in the contemporary transformations of the Third World, written evidence in courts is characteristically given greater truth-value than oral testimony. This was so from the beginning. Among the first types of text proper to emerge, by the end of the Old Kingdom of Egypt around 2150 BC, were "copies of legal decrees and proceedings and important private contracts, which could be displayed in order to make their terms public and operative in perpetuity" (Baines 1983: 577). Later on ethical precepts, which were apparently associated with the attempt to avoid litigation, began to enter into the record. Quite apart from the monumental versions of legal documents and the written court proceedings of the Old Kingdom, one finds "the use of documents as overriding evidence . . . , the citation of precedent and of statute . . . and a law code . . . Elaborate record storage served legal institutions . . . Legal matters could be 'published' in monumental form in a protected but accessible place" (p. 589).[5] While Baines sees most of these practices as responding to needs that can be differently catered for in a non-literate society, with the advent of writing "they acquired a notable rigour and generated new modes of intercourse, as in a subject's right to petition the king in writing" (p. 589). He considers that the creation of wills (which were technically deeds of delayed transfer, and included wills of and for women) may have reduced conflict. Certainly wills were of great importance, in increasing flexibility as well as in reducing conflict. However, there are other areas in which the use of writing makes a significant difference to a legal system even when compared with such a legally conscious but oral state as the Lozi (Gluckman 1955, 1965). Let us look, for example, at its influence on notions of relevant evidence, a question discussed by Epstein (1954) and Gluckman. I do not wish to deny the validity of the link they establish between ideas of relevance and the predominance of multiplex as against single-stranded relationships. They argue that in the former situation it is 'logical' for judges to listen to a wide range of talk, of evidence, in order to establish the facts, since the dispute concerns people whose relationships overlap in numerous ways. But in 'modern' courts, the very specific concept of evidence is not simply attributable to the precedence of single-stranded relationships. In addition, the situation is affected by the new channel of discourse. The very admission of written evidence promotes a closer definition of relevance if only because the documents have to be sorted through beforehand and are the subject of precise decisions. Control over the evidence is certainly less easy with oral witnesses whose testimony tends to ramble on unless aided by the policeman's notebook or the lawyer's question.

In this way the influence of writing enters into the court proceedings themselves, not only in the keeping of case records, which may serve as the basis of precedent or appeal, not only for recording transactions and for purposes of proof, but also for narrowing down the area of dispute and the issues at stake, with important consequences for the notion of relevance. Epstein points out that we have to look for the essence of the mode of dealing with cases not so much in a body of rules, the content of law, but in the "procedure within which claims are disputed and cases settled" (1953: 25). For example, since there are no legal practitioners, the court proceedings take the form of statement rather than examination. This is partly because of the absence of 'pleadings' in customary law, this being the technical term for court documents that relate to the case and lay out its parameters. In oral proceedings, on the other hand, the nature of the case and the remedy sought often only emerge in the course of the hearing (p. 26).

As a consequence those proceedings operate in a wider context and with a broader idea of relevance. The court members are "not unaware of the right-duty element of the case with which the English court would be most concerned" (p. 29), but they aim at measuring the conduct of all parties and seeking a reconciliation.

This is largely a function of the multiplex social relations that are involved. But it is also the case that the use of documents serves to narrow the issues and promote more precise notions of proof and of truth.

The shift to writing emerges as a driving force towards a more formal concept of evidence, and in a certain sense of truth itself, just as we have seen that on the level of reasoning it helps to transform ideas of how we can use the past (by precedent) and arrange the future (by legislation). For the legal process is closely related to the notion of truth. The Anglo-Saxon *riht* means law as well as right, custom and justice (Diamond 1971: 60). The Law Code of Kiev was known as Jaroslav's Pravda. And when writing appears, the concern with truth in time becomes closely linked to the use of written evidence, an idea that is clearly stated in the very detailed Visigothic Code of Reccessiwinth ('the Law of the Book') promulgated in *c.* AD 654:

> Let the Judge, so that he may grasp the case well, first question the witnesses and then ask for the documents, so that the truth may be more surely discovered, lest it may easily come to an oath . . . But let oaths be given in those cases where the judge's investigation elicits no writing or proof or sure signs of the truth. (II.1.21; Diamond 1971: 304)

The oath of purgation is conceived of as second best to other forms of proof and 'sure signs of truth', of which writing is the most acceptable, especially for transactions in land.

The registration of title

Of all the legal procedures that writing affects, the changes involved in the tenure of land by the registration of title are some of the most far-reaching for society as a whole. When I first went to work among the LoDagaa of northern Ghana in 1950, a flourishing Agricultural Station had been established in the vicinity for some ten years. The land had been acquired for this purpose by the Government after consultation with the local people. Acquisition is perhaps the wrong term, since the Colonial Government had from the beginning declared all land to be Crown Property. Nevertheless money had been set aside in the funds of the Local (Native) Authority to compensate those who had rights to the land – that is, who were the 'owners' in local terms. However this money had never been claimed, since there was no customary way of alienating land, certainly not by sale, although an individual might be allowed to work a particular plot to which he had no previous claim but which over time might gradually and implicitly be accepted as his in most relevant respects.

One reason for the absence of complete alienation is that, as many observers have pointed out, land does not have a single 'owner'. A large number of people have different claims on the same parcel, giving rise to what Maine called a 'hierarchy of rights' that in subtle ways highlights important social relationships (Gluckman 1947; Fortes 1945). When registration of title takes place, whether under conditions of conquest, of expropriation or of modernization, these complex arrangements often have to be summed up in a single entry in the register that attempts to allocate 'ownership' (that is, the total nexus of rights) to one individual rather than specifying all the claims of kith and kin. Whatever end we are aiming at, what we end up with is a list, a table, that places a designated area of land against the name of a single person, and sometimes of a corporation or similar body. The differentiated hierarchy or segmentary distribution of rights tends to get lumped together in one formula.

I need to clarify the general point. A written contract can introduce elements of variability and perpetuity which are less likely to be found in an oral society. But when it comes to the summary of complex situations in administrative lists, the opposite is true; writing strips the social relationships of its complicating context and 'murders to dissect'. For example, the contract in neo-traditional Soga law is entered into by individuals but the consequences inevitably extend to other kin who are not included (Fallers 1969: 317). How are these rights to be incorporated in a written contract, much less the columns and rows of a land register?

The implications of registration are dramatic. I have already mentioned the use of writing by ecclesiastical bodies to acquire land from family units or corporations. In Anglo-Saxon England 'bookland' stood opposed to 'folkland', the latter held under customary (orally transmitted) tenure, the former acquired by the church. Thus writing was a means of certifying and legitimizing the alienation of land that would otherwise be subject to familial claims. It excluded the interests of the wider family.[6]

In northern Ghana in recent times the appropriators of unused, 'communal' lands were farmers who wanted to cultivate larger areas of new crops with the aid of non-human sources of energy (Goody 1980). They needed to register the land in their own name in order to raise loans from a bank or from a governmental agency to purchase a tractor. Customary tenure gave you neither enough land nor an individual claim which could serve as a guarantee to the loan. In order to obtain a loan to buy a tractor, it was necessary to have a document in which the name of the applicant, the 'big farmer', appeared together with the amount of land he 'owned', setting aside all claims of kin and community. Registration was thus a form of alienation, resented by the have-nots and resulting in protests that took the familiar form of crop-burning. Throughout the world, written evidence of tenure has been demanded by literate commissioners, judges and colonialists. Because of this, whether in Fiji, in Puerto Rico, or in the American Southwest, non-literate, illiterate or partly literate peoples have been deprived of land that was originally theirs.

The particular example I want to take is from the Central American Republic of Panama, since it represents a general pattern of colonial conquest. The present system of landholding is closely related to the country's colonial past. As with the British in northern Ghana, at the time of the conquest all rights in land were taken over by the Spanish government, which then granted large tracts to favoured subjects who had served the government through military service or in the civil administration. These grants formed the basis of the holdings of the present-day elite (Weil *et al.* 1972: 111) who recently controlled 56% of the privately owned land, although the area of such land was much less than that of the state lands. In other words through conquest the new government took over all rights in land, passing down some to those who had rendered it service. Although the previous occupants, the conquered indigenes, continued to exercise rights of use, they had no title that would stand up in court since this generally demanded some form of written authority.

The same was true not only of the 'natives' but of many

'peasants', *campesinos*, usually *mestizos*, offspring of immigrants, Indians and Africans, who farmed land without any recognized, that is, court-recognized, title. A survey in 1966 showed that 66% of the country's agricultural workers were squatters of this kind, the remaining 34% being tenants and owners. In 1970 only 15%, at most, owned their land, most of it in small parcels.

This situation persisted despite the introduction of laws for agrarian reform designed to facilitate the transfer of title to occupied farms and despite the availability of ample cultivable land. When, with independence in 1903, the government took over crown lands, it made an effort to increase peasant ownership. Already some land had been sold to villages as collective estates, which were then worked communally or assigned to (not owned by) individual families. Now plans were made to break up communal holdings and government-owned tracts for peasant use. However the *campesinos*, "illiterate and uninformed, have mostly failed to apply for title or take steps to acquire the property they may have lived on and worked on for generations" (Weil *et al.* 1972: 111).

As a result 'squatter occupancy' is the most prevalent form of tenure, with landless families moving into vacant lands, constructing their houses and establishing their homesteads. Usually they are not ousted, partly because of the ever-present difficulties in dislodging farmers, partly because the land might not otherwise be in use. Meanwhile the squatters do little to alter their status. "Although many could acquire their own land through agrarian reform grant or purchase, they prefer the familiarity of their established arrangement", which gives them mobility as well as freedom from taxation and other impositions (Weil *et al.* 1972: 111–12).

But apart from the advantages to the 'squatter' of escaping these responsibilities, there is the question of the legitimacy of the existing system. It is the republic (earlier the crown) that took control of an area by physical force, that then legitimized that control by means of paper claims, and that later redistributed the land so acquired to create large landowners. It is hardly surprising that non-literate Indians or illiterate peasants pay little attention to such claims unless forced to do so by the might of the politically organized state that depends not only upon force but upon written rules and written judgements.

An analogous situation exists with regard to rights of a repro-
ductive rather than productive kind. Indians, *mestizos* and Blacks
all entered into 'regular' and semi-permanent unions in which children were born and raised. But the new dispensation of the written
law defined marriage in terms of ecclesiastical prohibitions and later
of a church ceremony in which details of the marriage (as in Europe
from the sixteenth century onwards) were first recorded in the
parish records and later in civil registers. All unwritten marriages
are consequently defined as common-law unions or as some form of
concubinage. Under such a system, "Are you married?" means
"Have you got written proof of having spoken certain written
formulae?" When a section of the population, even the majority,
has another, unwritten, way of defining a conjugal union, its legitimacy, and that of the children, may lack 'legal' recognition and
from this point of view remain in doubt. The written law is thus
highly partial in every sense of the word, favouring the literate few
at the expense of the illiterate many. While such 'illegitimacy' may
not matter if these people also have no property rights that the
written law would recognize, their children stand to lose any entitle-
ments in the eyes of the law. Yet in all other respects the conjugal
union may be perfectly normal. As the authors of the 1972 handbook on Panama (Weil *et al.* 1972) remark, "Despite changes, traditional Hispanic concepts and attitudes with respect to the family
still largely apply, even in households of common-law unions"
(p. 113). Nor is it remarkable that "In the urban lower class and
among the peasants, common-law marriage is as prevalent as formal
matrimony." However the nature of these unions differs interestingly in the rural and urban areas. In the first, the majority are
durable and entail full responsibilities, whereas in cities (and in
parts of the countryside) "casual arrangements are frequently less
permanent, and paternal desertion is quite common" (p. 113). In
the villages the sanctions of kith and kin help to maintain conjugal
unions but in the anonymity of the town, where 'legal' sanctions pre-
vail (and where legality is seen as partial), those unions are more
fragile, more extended in space, partly because of the different system of employment and even support.

Note that there is no necessary connection between unregistered
unions and what has been called the matrifocal family (or the

deserting husband) – one type of single-parent family, since most marriages in the lower socio-economic groups will be unregistered, whatever their constitution. But in a stratified society, especially where few rights to property or status are transmitted between fathers and children, in other words among the property-less lower classes, registration makes little difference. So that unregistered marriages, like the unregistered title, may be seen as relatively free of responsibility, at least on the part of the male, and as permitting the kind of 'mobility', especially in a Catholic society, that formal marriage inhibits, even when divorce is permitted. Nor is such 'freedom' a feature only of lower-status marriages, for individuals in higher socio-economic groups may deliberately aim to avoid the rights and duties involved in 'legal' marriage. Traditionally this was the function of one kind of concubinage, including 'clerical concubinage'. In Brazil *fazenda* clergy frequently formed unions of this kind which were also common among the general population of Whites as well as Blacks, although for different reasons.

The expansion of writing and law in medieval England

On the matter of rights in land, changes of a similar kind took place in medieval England. Unwritten law had been prevalent in the eleventh century. "Nevertheless two centuries later, by Edward I's reign, the king's attorneys were arguing in many of the *quo warranto* prosecutions against the magnates that the only sufficient warrant for a privilege was a written one and that in the form of a specific statement in a charter" (Clanchy 1979: 3). Since written title had only recently come into use, these prosecutions threatened to disenfranchise most of the magnates. Indeed the English 'common law' represented the crown's reaction to the independence of this nobility in dispute settlement. Not surprisingly there was a strong reaction from the haves against these procedures, which have elsewhere been used against the have-nots, whether tribesmen or peasants. In this respect at least (to quote a sixteenth-century cliché) the pen certainly proved as mighty as the sword.

Writing has been used in England from the Roman period when we find not only inscriptions of religious and political significance but also the remarkable collection of tablets from Hadrian's Wall which include private letters as well as the kind of administrative account found in Mesopotamian temples and palaces but here used for another 'great organisation', the army (Birley 1977: 132ff.). Under the Anglo-Saxons, writing was employed for charters and for some other legal and administrative purposes, as well as in important literary and religious ways. But with the Norman Conquest there was a quantum jump in its application, for reasons similar to those we have encountered in northern Ghana, to a wider range of activities. The great Domesday Book – popularly so-called because it was likened to the book held by Christ at the Day of Judgement – in which was listed, according to the *Anglo-Saxon Chronicle*, every hide and every pig, was a massive attempt to reduce every man's rights to a definitive form. Those were the words of Richard FitzNeal who, in the following century, declared that King William had "decided to bring the conquered people under the written law" (Clanchy 1979: 11).[7] In fact, the Domesday Book appears to have been little used as a source of law (though it was used in administration) until 200 years later, when there was a further rapid extension of the bureaucratic techniques of government.

The Norman Conquest changed the language of record-keeping not to French but to Latin, probably as a consequence of appointing Normans and foreigners to bishoprics and abbacies. The introduction of these men and the use of this language led to the founding of new libraries and brought the country into "the mainstream of medieval literate communication" (Clanchy 1979: 13), more open to the administrative reforms of the Gregorian papacy of the eleventh century. In Clanchy's view, English bureaucracy really began with the pipe rolls of the twelfth-century Exchequer (p. 21). At least from the 1270s seignorial stewards and bailiffs were required to write down the names of all males over twelve; under the Statute of Exeter of 1285 the king's commissioners had to be supplied with the names of every hamlet. By 1300 beadles and others were accustomed to making lists; books on estate management recommended the autumn listing of everything on the manor. And by this period, the reign of Edward I, even some serfs were using documents (p. 33).

The structure of rural life was deeply influenced by the fact that England never took up the system, revived in Italy and southern

France at roughly this period, by which a notary had to produce and certify documents; instead individuals did so themselves using their own seals. Consequently there was not the same development of village notaries, so well illustrated in Collomp's *La Maison du Père* for eighteenth-century Provence, the land of the *Droit écrit*, where notary and cleric together controlled the major uses of writing in the country areas. The priest noted the events of an individual's life, the major *'rites de passage'* – that is, baptism, birth, marriage and death – while the notary recorded the contracts of marriage and the testaments that accompanied them, as well as sales, loans and other transactions that needed paperwork. In the eighteenth century nearly every marriage in Haute Provence, whatever the social level, required a contract to be written and endorsed in the bride's house. For while the husband became 'le maître de la dot', the wife retained the rights in her property which was always listed separately. The notarial contract preceded the religious ceremony by several hours and the terms of the arrangement were understood to be *paroles de future, verba de futura* (Collomp 1983: 18); in other words they were binding on both parties. The agreement was witnessed by as many signatures as the parties could muster, the number itself being a mark of status. While not everyone could read and write "the value of the entry in the notarial register and the almost magical power of the written word" were one of the bases of Provençal society (p. 19). Once again literacy fingered its way into every corner of domestic life, providing a formidable instrument of control over family affairs.

The contrast between the systems was noted at an early stage. One Italian visitor to England, a Giovanni di Bologna, himself a notary, observed in 1279 that the Italians wanted to have a public instrument for every contract they entered into, whereas in England this was not called for. Nevertheless documentary evidence was increasingly required and by the Statute of Merchants of 1285 "every important town in England was obliged to have a clerk to enrol recognizances of debt in duplicate and write out bills of obligation authenticated by a royal seal" (Clanchy 1979: 37). As early as 1235 a plea was judged to be void because no written document had been produced.

It was in the twelfth century that such documents became

commonplace; it was the thirteenth that saw them archived (sometimes in triplicate, by the 'feet of fines') for reference and subsequent use. Taxation, as Clanchy shows, was the king's main aim in making records (which therefore became a major activity of the Exchequer), but individuals also used records of land transactions and of debts for other purposes.

This proliferation of documents, which prepared the gentry in England for a more general use of writing, was followed by the advent of registers and archives. At the same time the accumulation of books led to the development of libraries, of classification and of catalogues. It also encouraged 'guides' to the literature. The productions of the schoolmen "aimed to cope with the increasing mass of written material by providing guides to it (in Latin) in logically organized treatises; the *Summa Theologiae* of Thomas Aquinas (composed in *c*. 1260) is the best known of such texts" (Clanchy 1979: 84). A *summa*, like a *glossa*, was a standard scholastic form, defined by a twelfth-century bishop as "a concise encyclopaedia" or "a compendious collection of instances"; the prototype was Abelard's *Sic et Non* (composed in the 1130s) which aimed to cut through the 'mass of words' presented to divinity students by bringing together selected contradictory quotations under headings and subheadings. Legal texts took a similar form.

Note what is happening here. The accumulation of documents leads, as at Ebla over three millennia earlier, to efforts to organize them into archives. But the written tradition is cumulative in another way, not only quantitatively, since the knowledge contained in those documents is subject to the same processes. Knowledge accumulates and needs to be summarized. Putting different texts, different points of view, side by side, has the further effect of drawing out, of pointing up, those contradictions which would be difficult to spot in oral discourse, and of encouraging commentaries, arguments and attempts at their resolution, which in the first place were often oral. Not that contradiction and argument, which Lloyd rightly regards as so important in the earlier developments in classical Greece (1979), were absent from oral societies. Anybody who has sat through a lengthy court case in Africa, or even the less formal type of dispute settlement, will be only too aware that arguments and debates are of its essence. But to speak against (*contra dicere*) is one thing, to write against is another. For it is not simply a matter of circulation and endurance; contradiction takes on a different dimension when the text is available as an instrument of comparison. This is because contradictions become more 'obvious' and more 'exact' when placed side by side; that often means their being taken out of context, which is, as any author knows, a kind of falsification. And its effect is especially marked in those fields in which authoritative discourse has hitherto obtained or in which the recognition of difference requires the literal juxtaposition of general statements made over time, a process which becomes possible only with the advent of a quasi-permanent record.

In medieval England it was this relative permanency of the record that was constantly perceived as one of the big advantages of the written word, though the notion had some curious side-effects. The Domesday Book was used as a source of law for over two hundred years (mainly in the later period), yet it had been a survey of the state of the nation at a particular point in time. Consequently its actual truth-value diminished just as its perceived truth-value increased. For the written word was seen as associated with immortality. Bracton's great treatise on medieval English law was an attempt to produce order (a *summa*) from "the ancient judgements of just men" which were "by the aid of writing to be preserved to posterity *forever*" (my italics) – an aim too of Glanvill's work (Bracton 1968: II, 19; Glanvill 1965). It was also recognized, not for the first or last time, that writing immortalized not only words, but the scribe himself. The self-portrait of Eadwine, monk of Christ Church, Canterbury, declared him to be 'the prince of writers', whose praise and fame will never die (Clanchy 1979: 89). Again "with the loss of books", says Ordericus Vitalis, "the deeds of the ancients pass into oblivion . . . with the changing world, as hail or snow melt in the waters of a swift river swept away by the current never to return" (Clanchy 1979: 117; Ordericus Vitalis 1854: II, 284–5). Or in Bracton's words on the permanency of written testimony: "Gifts are sometimes made in writing, that is in charters, for perpetual remembrance, because the life of man is but brief and in order that the gift may be easily proved." In his insightful study of European law in the Middle Ages Kern too has argued that there was "a need . . . to discover some means of imparting permanency and authenticity" (1939: 178), although here he is discussing the gathering together of fragmentary writings in the form of a code. In yet another way his study supports the general thesis, for he points to the role of learned law, written law, in the transition from "custom to statute" (1939: 176ff.). It was learned law that put together the *Corpus Juris* based on Roman law; "being dead law, not living tradition, it compelled systematic study and discovery of principles", giving jurisprudence "its character as a science for the interpretation of comprehensive statutes" (p. 177). The new law became generalized over a large area whereas customary law "is only suited to small local communities". It gave rise to the idea that "the law exists as a complete body in a code" promulgated by the state, that "the written law is comprehensive" (p. 178).

These notions, he suggests, gave rise to the partial separation of law from society on which we have remarked. "For a simple person . . . it is a strange thing that all law should exist in books, and not where God has planted it – in conscience and public opinion, in custom, and sound human understanding. The positive written law brings with it learned lawyers and scholars, cut off from the people" (pp. 178–9). As a result lawyers and advocates are seen as "perverters of justice", dealing with "unintelligible laws . . . made arbitrarily by men . . . resurrected at Bologna". In contrast to positive codified law, customary law

quietly passes over obsolete laws, which sink into oblivion, and die peacefully, but the law remains young, always in the belief that it is old. Yet it is not old . . . Statute law, on the other hand, cannot be freed from the letter of legal texts, until a new text has replaced an old one, even though life has long since condemned the old text to death; in the meantime the dead text retains power over life. (1939: 179)

On this same theme Clanchy comments:

Remembered truth was also flexible and up to date, because no ancient custom could be proved to be older than the memory of the oldest living wise man. There was no conflict between past and present, between ancient precedents and present practice . . . Written records, on the other hand, do not die peacefully, as they retain a half life in archives and can be resurrected to inform, impress and mystify future generations. (Clanchy 1979: 233)

There are other important ways in which the legal system of

England altered under the increasing use of writing. The legal profession, as a body of literate specialists, emerged in the late thirteenth century. Already there were changes in the mode of pleading, bringing in formal ways of procedure, the instructions for which were provided in books. Public speaking was deliberately learned from the written word. The verbal duel, the legal conflict, took on the characteristic of set parts on which Clanchy makes an interesting comment that applies to literature as well. "The idea of each protagonist having a set part written down verbatim, which he must adhere to, was unfamiliar to the non-literate and presented actors, whether in law courts or on stage sets outside churches, with common problems. In a religious drama, *Le Mystère d'Adam* (dating from *c.* 1140), how the words are to be spoken is described in detail. M. D. Legge suggests that writing set parts may have been new; that is why actors are instructed not to add or omit anything, to speak clearly and to say their lines in the right order" (Clanchy 1979: 225), We are back again to the problem of formalization and to the separation of the roles of those who reproduce (and accept) the written word from those who change the old or create the new.

The letter and the spirit of the law

This split between creator and performer, between the *aidos* with his lyre and the *rhapsodes* with his staff, the first creating poetry, the second repeating the authorized version, is drastically widened by the substitution of text for utterance, leading to a division of labour between the process of creation and that of reproduction which we have already noted in the contrast between the prophet and the priest. A parallel contrast exists between the letter and the spirit of the laws. It is because we have a lettered law that we have to have ways of changing and modifying it in accordance with some conception of the 'spirit' of the law. While we may consider this notion of essence or spirit to be a will-o'-the-wisp, an *ignis fatuus*, it nevertheless represents a recognition of the emergence of two paths to truth, the literal truth (the letter of the law) and the underlying truth (the spirit of the law).

We have returned to a central theme of the first chapter, the way in which literate religions, indeed the written tradition itself, encourages generalized statements of norms. We can regard this process, as Fallers does with legal reasoning, as a question of making explicit what is otherwise implicit. I would go further and regard it as transforming normative behaviour, as giving rise to the notion of the rule that Bourdieu (1977) rightly criticizes. Two lines of argument intertwine. There is an important difference between implicit and explicit reasoning (or norms) since the second involves the concept of 'publication', of making public and, more importantly, keeping the product in the public domain by giving it a permanent form. That means writing. Secondly, the process of making explicit does more than change what was formerly implicit, for when anything is put into writing, it becomes the potential subject of further elaboration. Thirdly, the process of putting laws, rules or norms in writing is also a process of universalization, of generalization, in the manner I have already discussed.

The problem is not of course that in oral societies norms are absent. Epstein rightly insists on their 'logical priority' in the dispute process (1967: 206). It is rather a question of the changes that occur when norms are made explicit by being written down. Not only do they tend to iron out local differences and increase 'certainty', but they can also be subjected to a variety of new operations, forms of analysis. "For many jurists . . . the central test of jurisprudence appears as the analysis and systematic exposition of legal rules and precepts, and the deduction of the general principles and concepts that underlie truth, and the way in which these may be built up into a logical and coherent scheme or system" (Epstein 1967: 208–9).

'Principles' emerge by deduction and are built up into 'logical' systems. But such systematization is essentially dependent upon the recorded case and the written word, which can be read, reread, reorganized and abstracted at a more general level. The absence of that possibility and of its potential development meant that while Epstein's discussants would analyze particular cases in great detail, they were reluctant to deal with hypothetical issues. Not because they lacked legal insight "but because their mode of thinking was particular rather than abstract; the rules of law they expounded were not conceived as logical entities; they were rather embodied in a matrix of social relationships which alone gave them meaning" (p. 210).

Their mode of thinking, I argue, is dominated by the absence of writing, that important technology of the intellect, and of the tradition that it makes possible. Without this distancing mechanism cases tend to remain embedded in a matrix of particularities. It is not simply that we are dealing with 'multiplex societies', in Gluckman's phrase, but that an important means of abstraction and generalization at the intellectual level is not available to the actors.

The example of the process of generalization I gave in the first chapter was that of the reaction to homicide where I argued that in real life the assessment of a killing depends upon the context and the category. This is true even in literate societies, the reaction depending upon whether the victim is inside or outside the group, whether the act is defined as war, feud, manslaughter or straight murder. But the written code tends to present the complex set of practices in the form of more simplified rules. 'Thou shalt not do so and so.' Such heavily decontextualized statements are particularly characteristic of written religions, especially the universalistic religions of conversion, since they offer a framework of norms, possibly in the shape of a series of commandments, which is of wider applicability than tribal or national prohibitions. The latter would tend to be more specific: "Thou shalt not do it to others [Jews, Muslims] except under the following conditions . . . " But the complexities are eliminated, so that the norms of written religions often remain guides to ideal rather than to practical action, for saints rather than for sinners. To translate these general norms into everyday terms often requires a set of oral adjustments, or even written commentaries, which may serve both to interpret and even to change the law.

Secular law does not work in precisely the same way as religious injunctions do, but we have argued, like Kern, that while customary law is local, written law generalizes, partly because it is written and partly because it is not church-wide but state-wide. One striking example comes from the post-colonial history of East Africa. While Kenya and Tanzania unified the court system but attempted to preserve customary law by codifying it, Uganda established a national judicial system hoping that customary law would wither away. For example, the code defined adultery as intercourse other than with the monogamous wife but, as Fallers points out, this definition made nonsense of the social life of much of the country (1969: 334). As a result of such legislation we find a widespread conflict with morality (p. 328), but more because of the over-generalization of norms than, as Fallers maintains, because of the necessity of separating off a restricted justiciable sphere.

I have concentrated in this chapter on comparing African law with the legal system as it developed in Europe. This particular procedure has one disadvantage in that it is comparing a relatively late legal system with an oral one. If we were to take an earlier example of law influenced by writing, the comparison would assume another shape, since one could not refer to the developed body of Roman law. The early codes of Mesopotamia, like those of the Germanic tribes, were of a very different kind from the treatises of Theodosius and Justinian. Nevertheless some of the same processes of generalization and abstraction as we have seen at work in medieval Britain and its recent colonies were at work in earlier times.

While Hammurabi's text is a treatise on decisions, according to Bottéro "it omits all features that are individual, contingent or insignificant from the judicial standpoint" (1982b: 428). It is this selectivity that differentiates the 'savant', text in hand, from the spectator, "a way of abstraction that such a process requires, eliminating from a particular item everything that does not relate to a specific intellectual concern" (p. 429). However we may define Hammurabi's compilation, it is clear that it contributed to the development of jurisprudence, and Bottéro compares it to a work of science, and specifically to a medical text which it resembled in structure as well as in procedure, that is, in generalizing from cases by eliminating the particular.

Finally, it is worth returning to the example of Sumer in order to take up the point made at the beginning of this chapter: that, while the writing of codes and the records of cases was important for the development of jurisprudence and the systematization of law for legal reasoning, and perhaps for reasoning more generally, the new technique was at first more influential in terms of legal documents. From Sumer a vast number have come down to us. Thousands of clay tablets are inscribed with all kinds of legal forms – contracts, deeds, wills, promissory notes, receipts, and court decisions. The advanced student of law devoted much of his time to practising the writing of the highly specialized legal terminology, as well as law codes and those court decisions which "had taken on the force of legal precedents" (Kramer 1956: 51). Records of one case, "the case of the silent wife", silent in respect of her husband's murder, are found in more than one copy, indicating that it was "celebrated throughout the legal circles of Sumer as a memorable precedent" (p. 53).

In Ancient Sumer the administration of justice was in the hands of the priests, though it later became the province of a specialized branch of that profession. Cases continued to be heard in, or in front of, the temple, and it was there that the judgements were filed. Gradually, the law passed into the hands of civilian judges (Johns 1904: 83), but the overwhelming concern with written procedures continued. At the trial both sides had to produce their 'tablets', the written deeds relating to the case. Landsberger and Balkan even speak of an attorney, "a special official who offers assistance in legal procedures" (Larsen 1976: 152, 186).

Contrast the situation in Ancient Egypt, where the administration of law was closely bound up with general administration, and scribes and recorders were often involved in both. Again, writing dominated much of the proceedings. For example, "all petitioners for civil redress had to submit their case in writing and, if possible, produce written documents in support of it; since all wills, contracts, tax payments, etc., were also recorded in writing and copies of them filed in the White House, the archive of the government treasury, it should have been easy, in most instances, to establish the truth" (Woolley 1963: 495–6). The truth was at stake, but so was falsehood. For written records could be altered like oral ones, though such alterations are easier to discover. On the walls of one tomb we find the details of a court case brought by one Mes reclaiming an estate which had belonged to his family for a long period, but had been seized and awarded to a certain Khay; Mes won his case on the grounds that not only were Khay's title-deeds forged but there had been falsification of the land register at the time of the former trial.[8] Even at this level, change becomes a more deliberate, conscious and, in this case, illegal process, involving forgery itself. For records were crucial to judgment, and in one case decisions over an estate referred to ones taken over the previous eighty years as well as at the time of its original foundation 300 years before (O'Connor 1983: 218).

The relevant facts in a legal action were extended dramatically in time, just as in space law spread its tentacles from the national to the local. The consequent process of generalization took place at the level both of form and of content. So that there was a fixing of the written format, at least of particular statements, and at the same time both a loss of context and the rendering of implicit norms and procedures more explicit. The employment of writing led to developments in legal documentation on the one hand and legal reasoning on the other, to the elaboration of records, of the code and of its application.

5

Ruptures and continuities

It is dangerous but necessary to return to the aims one set oneself at the beginning of an essay. These were, first, to outline the effects of early literacy on the organization of human societies – early because to consider the effects of a long written tradition would be to take on an even more difficult task. And secondly I sought to indicate how such considerations should not only qualify simplistic Eurocentric notions of the nature of modern and traditional societies but should modify analyses of the classification and development of human communities, by placing more emphasis than is often done on the means and mode, that is, the relations of communication. In this concluding chapter I want to summarize the first, exemplify the second and add some further comments about analytic procedures.

In outlining some of the major differences that writing can make to the organization of social action, I took as a framework the broad level of the institutional categories of religion, economy, polity and law. Even when they take the form of separate organizations, none of these institutions is completely distinct, so that the topics of the chapters inevitably overlap. And when it comes to the simpler societies there is so much overlap that one can treat these categories only in functional terms.

For social organization, the long learning process which early forms of writing involve leads to the emergence of literate specialists who do not participate in the primary productive processes and have therefore to be supported by those who do, by some form of redistribution or endowment. Alphabetic writing does not necessitate the creation of a class of scribes in the same way; nevertheless, a rather similar process occurs when literate schooling is extended to previously non-literate peoples (or even illiterate strata), since the

171

effort required to learn the skill is clearly greater for the first generation than for the second, and their singular position accords them
a special status in the society. But throughout history the specialization of scribes combines with the relative autonomy of the written
tradition to promote the structural autonomy of 'the great organizations' which tend to develop their own literary corpus, their own
bodies of specialist knowledge. The case to which most attention
was given was that of religion; with the emergence of the endowed
temple or monastery, the church becomes a distinct organization
with partially separate interests from those of the state. Any
divergence between the domain of priest and king that one finds
implicit in oral societies now becomes explicit and can take on an
'ideological' dimension. For the written tradition articulates beliefs
and interests in a semi-permanent form that can extend their influence independently of any particular political system. That is where
the phenomenon of conversion comes into the picture, with all that
it implies for religious and ideological plurality, and the liberating
freedoms and savage conflicts to which this differentiation gives
rise.

   In spelling out the influences of writing upon religion, I am speaking of tendencies. Exceptions there will always be. Some religions of
the Book are not religions of conversion; some cults in societies
without writing may seek out adepts. Let us take first the case of
religions of the Book. From some points of view Hinduism looks
like a religion specific to a particular culture. Yet its practice spread
widely through South East Asia in the medieval period, not only to
the mainland of Indochina but also to that similarly named
achipelago, Indonesia, the Indian Islands. Throughout that extensive area the influence of Hinduism was immense, as witness the
totally dominating effect it had on iconography, that is, on sculpture
and painting as well as the temple and literature. It is not only a
question of tracing general influences, but of finding specific scriptures and visual forms of the gods that would be recognized throughout the Indian sub-continent. Buddhism is clearly a religion of
expansion, having expanded even further than Hinduism into East
Asia, incorporating some of the latter's written mantras and spreading writing itself. However, China had its more particularistic
'religions', like Taoism, which used logographic writing for ritual

texts, for divination and for other purposes over an enormous area, but did not expand beyond the confines of the Empire. While some contemporary forms of Hinduism and Buddhism in India, China and Japan appear to be less concerned with boundaries and more with incorporation, there have been periods in the history of these religions when conversion and the fear of apostasy have played more dominating roles. And even today the conflicts between Hindu and Muslim, the emergence of Sikhism, the conversions to Islam, Christianity and neo-Buddhism among some lower castes bring out the boundary-maintaining aspects of these written creeds, each with their own sacred texts, their concern with literacy and with an exclusive mode of worship, notion of salvation and access to truth.

Of the main written religions of the Near East, Judaism nowadays appears as an example of a non-proselytizing creed, since the body of beliefs and practices was attached to a specific tribal group. Nevertheless, the religion does seem to have expanded throughout the Mediterranean in the latter half of the first millennium BC, converting the earlier Phoenician population to its beliefs and practices. The diaspora was not only a matter of the flight from Palestine but also of the conversion or incorporation of peoples in Ethiopia, Arabia, India, south Russia, even China. But in any case, despite the tribally based nature of its message, the Old Testament became a Holy Book for the whole of Christianity and, in some measure, for Islam too, which gave specific recognition to the peoples of the Book.

In the case of the religious systems of societies without writing, I have argued that we lack there a concept of a religion, partly because magico-religious activities form a part of most social action, not being the attribute of a separate organization, partly because of the identification with a people, as in 'Asante religion'. But although religions do not move, cults do. In this context, I mean by cults the practices associated with what are often called medicine shrines in West Africa, though such mobility would also be found with related movements (the word itself is significant) of an anti-witchcraft kind, that spread from place to place, from society to society.

Religion, and later on education, are the areas where structural autonomy is most developed in the early stages of written cultures. But law and the economy both achieve a measure of independence in their different ways. One general theme that the discussion of law brought out was the importance of writing as a way of storing information, thus enabling people to surmount in some measure the homeostatic adjustment that holding it in memory often involves. There is a consequent loss of flexibility which creates problems in a changing situation. On the other hand fixity is advantageous for contractual relations of many kinds, although the very process of setting up a contract (or registering land) tends to lead to the neglect of wider networks of rights and responsibilities, pinning these down to the individual rather than recognizing the participation of the wider kin group; to deal with the latter various complex legal forms of 'corporation sole' have to be reinvented, making explicit what was formerly implicit and transforming the actual situation in so doing.

The potentialities for change are especially apparent with longer texts because writing is obviously easier to review than speech, so that implicit contradictions are made explicit and hence readily resolved, leading to cumulative advances in knowledge and procedures, though such advances give rise in turn to puzzles of different kinds. All this is part of the reflexive potentialities of writing which affect notions of consciousness on both levels, making the implicit explicit and rendering the result more available to reflective inspection, to external argument and to further elaboration.

I have suggested that this process is related to a sharpened concept of rules and norms, a notion which draws us back again to law and politics, if only because of the connection between rules and rulers. All societies are guided by norms and rules of some sort. But where these remain implicit, at the level of 'deep structure', they do not take the same shape, for the actor or for society, as when they are consciously formulated by the ruled or put up in the forum, engraved on plates, by the rulers. First, they are not so 'fixed'; they generally emerge in context (like proverbs), not in the 'abstracted' way of a code. Secondly, they tend to be less generalized than literate formulae; or, rather, their generalizations tend to be embedded in situations. Thirdly, they are not formulated nor yet formalized into neat digests or *summae*. It is writing that enables one to pick out norms or decisions and set them out in the form of a guide, a handbook. When this has been done, law, *gesetz*, *loi*, distinguish themselves from 'custom' within the total body of 'rights', while the written is often given a higher truth value (in a court of law, in literature, in philosophy, in quoting an 'authority') than the oral.

Although it would be wrong to overemphasize the extent to which the institutional differentiation between, say, the polity and law can be attributed to the advent of literacy, two points stand out. Directly or indirectly writing enters into the way we define 'a religion' and 'the law' (as distinct from religion and 'custom'). At a different level, it enters into the way we define bureaucratic polities and a complex economy, one of which would be meaningless without the office and the file, and the other without elaborate methods of accounting for the profit and the loss, of raising credit and organizing investment, and of carrying out productive and mercantile activities by some development of the partnership or firm, organizational forms that are significantly dependent on the use of writing. Hence we find an association between money-lending, banking and literacy throughout human history.

This is not to claim that oral societies do not possess analogous institutions. The arrangements of a group of brothers, or a husband and wife, working together on the farm or in some craft activity bears a close resemblance to a partnership or to a family firm. What the introduction of writing helps to do, however, is to make the implicit explicit, and in so doing to extend the possibilities of social action, sometimes by bringing out tacit contradictions and thus leading to new resolutions (and probably new contradictions), but also by creating more precise types of transaction and relationship, even between trusted kin, that give these partnerships the strength to endure in more complex, more 'anonymous' circumstances.

My second aim in this analysis has been to shift some of the weight that has often been placed on the means and relations of production to the means and relations of communication. By this I understand not only the techniques but also the technology, including the technology of the intellect it directly permits, the libraries of accumulated knowledge as well as the internal cognitive developments, together with the constraints and freedoms that human beings attach to such systems. There has been no intention of confining analysis either to 'materialist' or to 'ideological' factors, a categorization which smacks of by-gone debates, long since by-passed. Who nowadays would think of the intellectual products of the human hand and mind, such as writing, as being purely internal or external, as relating only to matter or to ideas?

Writing of course is a multiple variable, both in terms of technique and in terms of use (restricted or otherwise) and of its accumulated store. The written word takes many different forms, which in turn influence the trends it is likely to encourage. In any case the form it takes is but one factor influencing a particular situation. The ramifications of the impact of writing, the need to take that more fully into account when explaining major social changes, and the partly independent case for reconsidering the nature of those changes themselves, can be brought out by recapitulating and expanding some comments on a situation I touched upon earlier.

In discussing first religion and then law, attention was drawn to the generalizing push that writing tends to give to normative structures, partly because of the relative decontextualization of communication in the written channel, partly because of the wider social groupings within which that communication takes place. The point arose again in reference to the economy of the Ancient Near East. Here writing can be seen as linked to the circulation of goods and to the use of media of exchange (that is, money, specifically silver, *l'argent* itself) in an economy, one important facet of which was oriented to the market. For writing assisted in the development not only of accounting but of the notion of units of account, the reduction of a variety of expenditures to the same base in order to calculate the profit and the loss, or more simply to provide a concise statement of the flow of goods.

A similar trend took place in medieval Europe during the eleventh and twelfth centuries, at the time of the radical extension of the uses of writing that led to the recapitulation of, and building upon, some of those earlier developments that had been experienced by the literate societies of the Near East and the Mediterranean. In his study of the growing use of texts in medieval Europe, Stock draws attention to the parallel growth in writing and in the use of coinage (1983: 85): "The rebirth of medieval literacy coincided with the remonetization of markets and exchange" (p. 32). Of the later eleventh and twelfth centuries he writes, "For the first time since antiquity Europe witnessed the existence of a disinterested market of ideas, for which the essential prerequisite was a system of communication based upon texts. The logical product of the literate organization and classification of knowledge was the scholastic system, just as the market was the natural instrument for the distribution of commodities regulated by prices" (1983: 86). For Stock, the changes result from the operation of 'analogous principles', the relative autonomy of the economy and of scholarship, their organization by means of a set of abstract rules, the externality of market and text, the creation of a level of 'abstract entities' and 'model relations' that correspond to lexical and syntactical structures, social and intellectual processes which entailed a certain degree of secularization (p. 87).

While societies cannot be reduced to systems of communication or of exchange, they must clearly be expected to change in line with changes in these systems, changes which include monetization as well as literacy. The link between the two has resonances in the sociology of Talcott Parsons, for whom "Money is probably the most striking case of an institutionalized medium which . . . has all the properties of a medium and language of communication . . . The essential phenomenon is the *generalization* of commitments and the expectations associated with them" (1960: 273, my italics). At a more concrete level money provides a (more or less) generalized medium of exchange as well as a system of reckoning by means of which a wide range of goods and services can be summarized in the highly generalized terms of a single scale of values. While the process of generalization involved in the written expression of norms and the use of more 'universal' media of exchange are not necessary concomitants one of another, they do in a sense run a parallel course.

The suggested link between money and writing raises the much wider problem of the nature of economy that prevailed in the Ancient World, with its elaborate systems of book-keeping, accumulation and trade. In the Old Assyrian trade, according to Veenhof, "silver served a purely commercial purpose and functioned as money in all the meanings of the word" (1972: 399).

He is not referring to the part it plays in the entire economy over the whole period, but to certain trading operations carried out at a particular time, around 1900 BC, which involved traders, merchants and "the great bankers and money-investors". Here he does not hesitate to speak of markets and market places (as well as of transactions in the houses of merchants), of shareholders and commission sales, of variable prices and of the profit and the loss. As for the relations of production, slaves were employed but so too were free men, that is, wage-labourers. Some cloth was produced in workshops, some in the house, some by putting-out. Just as a range of institutions engaged in economic activity – the temple and the state as well as the family firm and the commercial partnership, so too there existed a variety of forms of labour and of ways of holding land. Métayage could be found alongside service in the royal weaving establishments, hired labour and the *corvée* alongside slavery (Johns 1904: 173, 196). I have argued that the presence of writing was instrumental not only in keeping track of this variety of forms of labour relationship but to some degree in its genesis.

One thing that is happening in these complex trading operations, as Oppenheim points out (1964: 88), is that capital has become a commodity for the use of which interest is charged. As the means and standard of exchange, silver became subject to 'capitalistic' treatment. Not that this development was approved for all transactions, for example those within the family itself. In the words of the Old Testament: "Unto a stranger thou mayest lend upon usury; but unto a brother thou shalt not lend upon usury" (Deut. 23:20). In southern Mesopotamia there seems to have been no such ambivalence, whence the origin of the later theological view of Babylon as the centre of 'capitalistic' ideas about money, although it was basically overland trade to which the Bible objected. According to Oppenheim this Babylonian development may have been linked to the high degree of urbanization and a storage economy associated with mercantile enterprise, an integration that "seems to have favored the use of money, that is, surplus staples" (p. 89). Later on, in the last half of the first millennium, the role of 'private' capital as distinct from investments by temple and palace increased, and there is evidence of a 'banking house' taking over some of the earlier responsibilities of the 'great organizations' (p. 85).

Oppenheim and Veenhof are not the only Assyrian scholars to refer to capitalists as well as to money-lenders. Woolley does so in the UNESCO history (Woolley 1963) to the evident discomfort of his Russian colleagues (1963: 613). But already at the beginning of the century, Johns had written of 'capitalists' in his compendium of Babylonian and Assyrian laws, comparing their agency arrangements with the *commenda* of the later Mediterranean, an institution that has been seen as dependent upon writing. "The agent takes stock or money of his principal, signs for it, agrees to pay so much profit, and goes off to seek a market, making what profit he can" (1904: 78). The comparison with the trading practices of Venice and the Arab Middle East is maintained and extended in the works of Landsberger, Garelli and Larsen (1976: 102). Oppenheim draws attention to similar activities in the Phoenician cities of the Iron Age and among the Nabatean caravans of the first centuries of our era (1964: 92). In each of these cases, partially independent merchants under some degree of protection from the local king or nobility carried out trading and banking operations of a capitalistic kind, a kind that in modern times expanded into manufacture as well as commerce.

That is not to say that the 'great organizations' did not dominate, for the major part of the early period, the processes of production and distribution. But as scholars of Assyrian trade make clear, Polanyi's notion of state-directed, marketless, moneyless, trade (1957) simply cannot be sustained for the whole period. According to Larsen, "the Old Assyrian commercial colonies in Northern Syria and Anatolia were based on a socio-economic system of 'capitalistic' type where long distance trade rested on private venture-taking" (1976: 16). Not only in trade but also in land, labour and in production, we find risk-taking and other forms of economic activity which later in human history came to dominate the social system.

What we do not find of course is an industrial capitalist economy of the modern type. But it is a totally different matter to deny the presence of economic activities of a capitalistic kind. Such a contention represents a hang-over of earlier types of evolutionary theory of human society where the stages tend to overdetermine the nature of social action. An overdetermined stage theory means that, for example, 'money' or 'markets' are held by definition to exist only at certain periods identified in global terms, e.g. under those stages designated as capitalism or feudalism. Much of the data of economic or social history do not justify such radical breaking points, with one system of exchange, such as the redistributive, disappearing to make way for another. Or slave labour vanishing from the face of the earth to be replaced by serfdom. Such assumptions, where they are valid, tend to privilege the particular sequences of events that have been recorded for Western Europe. But in any case when we look at Ancient Mesopotamia, at fourteenth-century China, at sixteenth-century India, or at nineteenth-century Brazil, we find the coexistence of a variety of forms of labour, land holding and exchange, although obviously in different 'mixes'. It follows that social change consists not so much in the splitting apart of social systems under the pressure of internal contradictions in order to adopt new forms of labour, new relations of production, but in the expansion of one existing form at the expense of another. The expansion may be sudden or gradual, but the point is that these alternative forms of social and economic activity were already located within the social system and had been so since the development of 'civilization' in the Bronze Age. And one reason for their early presence was the close connection of monetization, the raising of credit, business partnership and accounts of all kinds with the existence of the written mode.

In his masterly analysis of social and economic organization, Weber argues that "capital accounting has arisen as a basic form of economic calculation only in the Western world" (1947a: 193), that it is a form of monetary accounting which is peculiar to "rational economic profit-making" and "aimed at the valuation and verification of opportunities for profit and of the success of profit-making activity" (p. 191). At the same time he recognized that an elementary form of such activity was to be found in the *commenda*, a variety of which we have been discussing.

In the earliest beginnings of rational profit-making activity capital appears, though not under this name, as a sum of money used in accounting. Thus in the 'commenda' relationship various types of goods were entrusted to a travelling merchant to sell in a foreign market, and possibly he was also commissioned to purchase other goods wanted for sale at home.

The profit or loss was then divided in a particular proportion between the travelling merchant and the entrepreneur who advanced the capital. But for this to take place it was necessary to value the goods in money; that is, to strike balances at the beginning and the conclusion of an enterprise. The 'capital' of the commenda relationship or the *societas maris* was simply this money valuation, which served only the purpose of settling accounts between the parties and no other. (1947a: 196)

As Weber realized when he talked about "the limitations on the development of capitalism" in the Ancient World, activities of a capitalistic kind were carried out long before the existence of the medieval commenda, activities that were dependent upon accounting procedures of a complex kind. Why then is capital accounting as a basic form found only in the Western world? Is it because the critical feature is taken to be double-entry book-keeping, which appears to have been a relatively late Italian invention, first published in 1494 but used for two generations before? Is it because further qualifications are required, that "profit-making enterprises with capital accounting" have to be "doubly oriented to the market in that they both purchase means of production on the market and sell their product there" (p. 201). However, the rationality of monetary accounting upon which Weber insists is clearly present in the Ancient World and did not have to await the Renaissance in Europe, for its existence was directly connected with the application of writing to the income and outgoings of mercantile 'firms' as well as of the temples and palaces of the Near East. Whatever important developments took place at a later period, they did not include the introduction of rationality or accounting.

A consideration of the implications of writing in these contexts leads us to qualify anthropological and historical assumptions in a number of ways. First, we need to challenge the way in which the formal categorization of human activities into, say, redistributive or reciprocal exchange, becomes transformed into types or stages of society in such a way that one type of activity is seen not only as dominating the whole range of economic action but also as excluding other possibilities as well. The possibilities were often already present, even if subdominant. Secondly, it is even more necessary to query those dichotomies and distinctions, based more on feeling than fact, on sentiment than study, which tend to separate us by a profound chasm from our predecessors. The case does not really require making for the classical worlds of Greece and Rome, except by those who see a fundamental divide in mentality as well as in production between modern and traditional, industrial and pre-industrial, capitalist and pre-capitalist. But there is an equally strong tradition of the Great Divide that designates as primitive all that went before fifth-century Athens. Much was undoubtedly contributed to the development of human cultures at each of these periods, but it would seem dangerous to draw too strong a dividing line betwen 'us' and the great civilizations of the Ancient Near East (nor yet of India or China for that matter), for they possessed and utilized one critical invention of mankind in the sphere of communications, namely writing, whose use was not simply cosmetic but penetrated deeply into many areas of social life, permitting the development of new forms of social organization and new ways of handling information.

Once again, one must be careful about drawing the line too sharply. While writing helped to develop new types of formal logical operation, it did so initially by making explicit what was implicit in oral cultures, which were neither pre-logical nor yet alogical except in a very narrow sense of those words.

These warnings are necessary because to overprivilege the European experience by stage theories that cut us off too sharply from other societies leads us to jump to the self-congratulatory assumption that only in one area of the world could modernization have taken place. Before we attribute its emergence to the particular economic ethic of Protestantism, for example, it is worth considering that literate Buddhist merchants in medieval Sri Lanka were not seriously inhibited by their religious precepts, much less those entrepreneurs involved in the manufacture of silk and pottery in medieval China, or of cotton in India, at roughly the same period. Indeed the Buddhist monasteries themselves were run on 'business' lines, with an abundance of records, setting aside the ascetic tradition of the founders, and becoming as Weber himself noted of temples and monasteries elsewhere, "the very loci of all rational economies". Indeed in China and Tibet, as with some orders in Western Europe, they were heavily involved in trade themselves.

And the nature of this 'rationality' was related to the application of writing to ends that were economic as well as religious.

The seeds of many factors that we associate with the rise of the West were sown elsewhere than in Western Europe, elsewhere even than in the cultures descending from Greece and Rome. In the limited sense of rational which the argument of Weber implies (and which is all the notion, like that of logic, is worth analytically), 'rational' economies and 'rational' activities more generally were instituted not by the advent of capitalism in Europe, but by the advent of writing in Mesopotamia 4,500 years before, or rather with the developments that slowly emerged as the 'implications' of literacy. The advent of writing was in turn linked to changes in the system of production, distribution and consumption, but not simply as a passive effect of those changes. Clearly all this did not create capitalism – many further developments took place in the system of production and distribution as well as in that of communication in the narrower sense. But some of the features often associated with those later developments appear at the earlier period in a form that links them to the advent of writing and to the creation of a written tradition. The generalization of media of exchange is one of these; so too is 'rational' book-keeping. For these and other reasons a consideration of the effects of communication may lead to a modification of the sharp dichotomy that so many assume between modern and traditional, industrial and pre-industrial, capitalist and pre-capitalist, a modification that can prevent us from prematurely 'primitivizing' the social life of other 'civilizations'. It is not a question of overlooking but of rescheduling differences, giving more weight to the technology and contents (including the ideological ones) of new systems of communication.

It is not only for the economy that a study of the implications of writing leads to such a revaluation, but for religion as well. As with law, the very concept of a religion is affected. So too is the question of the status of the Church as a partially independent body in society, one of the great organizations. The role of such a Church differs from the 'Church' that Durkheim discerned among the native Australians, having a measure of autonomy built upon its control of resources as well as of an important sector of written communication. Such partial independence means that the Church is never simply an arm of the political system, indeed it is at times its rival, with its temples and monasteries providing distinct foci of local power, especially when central government is weak. Equally when that government is stronger, the resources of the Church offer a tempting prey, to be used to supplement the personal incomes of the rulers, to erect public monuments, to distribute among the laity or to invest in new productive processes, all outcomes that occurred at different junctures in human history.

In the course of this essay I have discussed a number of other issues, but in a fashion so summary that it would be absurd to further summarize what has already been an extremely brief treatment of a vast subject: the influence of a major mode of communication, writing, on social organization. I have doubtless omitted much and included other features where some would have put the emphasis elsewhere. The aim has been to explain some aspects of the difference between socio-cultural systems that others may already have noted but have not linked in this particular way.

In taking one thread, the means and relations of communication, I am not intending to deny the relevance of others. Any impression to the contrary derives from the method of exposition associated with selecting a topic and following it through rather than adopting the different tack of trying to trace all the large variety of relevant factors in a field study or in a historical situation. As I suggested in the introduction, path-analysis would be a way of weighting these various factors but neither the material nor the enquiry lends itself to this technique. On the other hand simply to list every possible influence without weighting any is an exercise of little intellectual value, though it may provide a convenient way out for the over-cautious academic searching around for some kind of explanatory framework. Nor have I intended to claim that the introduction of writing immediately or necessarily leads to the changes I have singled out. The written tradition is cumulative, it builds up over time. I have tried to outline the effects of such a tradition on the evolution of the organization of societies, especially in its transitional phases. But I see these effects as trends rather than as necessities.

I would end with two further comments, one new, one old. In dealing with law I deliberately introduced the data on medieval England to indicate that in matters of media, we were not dealing with continuous, straight-line, unilineal evolution. There are many ebbs and flows, hiccups in the on-going process. Medieval Europe relived, by invention or by adoption, many of the developments in bureaucratic government that had occurred in the Near East some 3,000 years earlier. In the process each region, each country, gave them an individual twist; the effects of writing and the written tradition were not identical in England and in Italy. Nevertheless I believe there is enough in common to enable us to talk of general tendencies.

Lastly, the caveat with which I started. I have been dealing, in part at least, with societal differences that others have already observed and characterized in specific ways, for example, in terms of the contrast between universalistic and particularistic, between abstract and concrete, between flexible and formal. Some of these designations, 'decontextualized' for example, are less than satisfactory, for we are usually dealing in trends rather than dichotomies; nothing is completely 'decontextualized' nor completely 'universalistic'. Moreover these trends may be specific to particular domains so that the greater 'flexibility' given to contracts takes its place alongside the greater formality of the registration of land. It is partly because of these considerations that a summary would only lead to misunderstanding by further endangering the delicate balance that any such enquiry has to discover between the general and the particular, especially in the quality and use of words. It is not difficult to make the text too obscure or overly simplistic. A balance would be easier to maintain if one could make more careful discrimination with the aid of unlovely neologisms. As it is, "I gotta use words when I speak to you", as Eliot's Sweeney Agonistes remarks. That sentence can serve to sum up the nature of my enquiry, which has involved an exploration of the differences in social life when I use words to write as well as to speak, to you or to anyone else.

Notes

1. The word of God

1. M. Bernal, personal communication.
2. For the study of culture contact and for an analysis of the interactions of Black and White in a South African situation, see M. Gluckman 1958. The whole controversy on culture contact had both a practical and an 'ideological' level, since Malinowski's capacity to attract funds for research in Africa depended upon his ability to sell 'applied anthropology' to the Rockefeller Foundation, whereas Evans-Pritchard and his colleague Fortes were highly scornful of such deviations from 'pure' research (Goody, forthcoming: a).
3. See, for example, Woolley's comments: "The Egyptian was not given to reflective thought and was not in the least worried by the fact that his ideas concerning the phenomena of reality were hopelessly incompatible" (1963: 719); "the coffin texts as a whole fail to recognize any close connection between religion and morals" (p. 722). See also his insistence on the use of magic to force the gods into compliance.
4. The question of whether writing encouraged more (literary) production in the narrow sense is doubtful. Assmann and others have argued that 'wisdom' texts had a specifically legal and generally moralizing origin (1983: 80ff.), suggesting that apart from narratives, 'literature' related to monumental display rather than to writing on papyrus. None the less the idea of whole text transmission is very important to literature and relates to the mingling of mathematics, medicine, 'magic' and so on, with the specifically 'literary' texts (J. Baines, personal communication.).
5. One of the most striking examples of the later independence of the temples is the way that they absorbed the change to the Ptolemies and the Roman emperors (J. Baines, personal communication).
6. Humans held the title of high priest but are not shown as performing the cult. This seems to be partly a matter of 'decorum' but its effect on uniformity is great. One text, for example, shows that even in a weak period a provincial temple got its new cult image from the capital city (J. Baines, personal communication).

7. The defacing of Hatshepsut's monuments provides another example of an attempt to eliminate too solid a record of the past (O'Connor 1983: 218–19).
8. The 'monotheistic' trend has also been described as 'henotheistic' by Hornung (1982) and Assmann (1983) (see Baines, forthcoming). Henotheism refers to the belief in a single god without asserting that he is the only God, sometimes seen as a stage of belief between polytheism and monotheism (Oxford English Dictionary).
9. For a brilliant discussion of this process in Europe of the eleventh and twelfth centuries, see Stock 1983. Not the first such development, but as history has at times recapitulated and developed earlier processes, so the long term implications of literacy have been picked up again and fostered at different places and in different periods. There has been no simple line of unfolding.
10. I do not include the term 'magic' in any disparaging way, but only to indicate a range of activities. Judaism, Christianity and Islam contain plenty of the elements often called magical in other societies, though we tend to exclude our own actions from this category, regarding the movement from magic to religion as being a progressive one, progressing from them to us.
11. On the role of priests for the Late Period see A. B. Lloyd 1983: 301–9. Herodotus was struck by their ritual purity, which involved circumcision, frequent baths and the avoidance of fish and beans.
12. In medieval Sri Lanka the monastic hospitals were apparently for the use of monks only (Gunawardana 1979: 147). On the relative autonomy of priests in Mesopotamia, see Yoffee 1979: 16.
13. For relevant comments on sacrifice, see Goody 1981b, and, on the notion of the High God, see Goody 1972: 32.

2. The word of mammon

1. The earliest envelopes known at present are from a Middle Uruk level at Farukhabad.
2. Le Brun and Vallat reject the idea of the tokens as representing anything except numbers (1978: 33–4). For another criticism of Schmandt-Besserat see also Lieberman 1980 and the reply by Powell (1981: 423ff.). For a very interesting analysis of the way the spatial lay-out of early cuneiform writing developed, from token use in response to administrative needs for, largely economic, record-keeping, see Green 1981.
3. Amiet reports some such signs at level 17 but they appear in an 'organized' form only at the following level (Le Brun and Vallat 1978: 40).
4. On the more general problem of the conflict between an accumulating Church and an appropriating State, see Goody 1983.

5. For the early period there is little evidence of substantial temples devoted to the divine cult, except in one or two places; whether or not this material represents a wider distribution of such temples is a matter for debate.
6. On the secularization of land by the rulers of Akkad, see Garelli 1969: 91.
7. See Dyer's study of the Bishopric of Worcester between the seventh and sixteenth centuries (1980).
8. Recent scholarship tends to see the control of irrigation as being locally based, especially in Egypt (e.g. A. B. Lloyd 1983: 326). In Mesopotamia, the later and less favourable timing of the inundation meant that it was essential to prepare dykes and levées to protect the green fields from the water, to build earth works to store and distribute the water and to relocate cultivation from time to time because of progressive salinization. The digging of new canals and the resettlement of the population formed, according to Oppenheim, "an essential part of the economic and political program of a responsible sovereign, rivaling in importance the maintenance of the dikes" (1964: 42). The sovereign was of course generally the ruler of a city state.
9. Woolley constantly attempts to stress the 'capitalist' elements in the ancient economy, to the dismay of his Soviet colleagues. The followers of Polanyi would also emphasize the gap between the economic systems but it is important to try and accommodate both continuity and discontinuity in discussions of modes of production.
   According to Garelli the labour force in the textile workshops was servile and female (1969: 103).
10. This process is especially clear in Egypt. When the Asiatic loom was introduced in the New Kingdom it was operated by men, whereas its precursor had been worked by women.
11. Linen was also used in Mesopotamia and cotton was planted in the royal garden of Sennacherib (704–681 BC, Oppenheim 1964: 94) and in China in the twelfth century AD.
12. "The central government used some of the food surpluses and manufactured goods that it had at its disposal to engage in foreign trade. While there is no evidence that the king claimed a monopoly over this trade, the needs and wealth of the court encouraged the palace to trade on a scale that greatly exceeded that of any other individual or institution in the country. It therefore seems likely that it was through the court that most foreign goods made their way to Egypt, prior to being distributed as royal bounty" (Trigger 1983: 59).
13. Although Larsen regards linen as the dominant textile and wool as subsidiary, Veenhof puts them in the opposite order. In any case looms appear very early on the fourth millennium cylinder seals from the south, where the bulk of these textiles originate (Le Brun and Vallat 1978: 26; Amiet 1972). Textiles were of great importance in trade and

formed the only kind of 'industrial production' in the Near East until Muslim times (Oppenheim 1964: 84).
14. Seven witnesses and a signature were also demanded by written Roman testaments (Guigue 1863: 2).

3. The state, the bureau and the file

1. For an account of the interlocking of taxation, consumption and the census, see Postgate 1974. On the relation of the census to conscription in Mari, see Dalley 1984: 142, including a fascinating account of the resistance put up and the rewards offered for attendance at the numbering (food provided, land redistributed).
2. A striking example from a much later period, that of the expansion of Europe, will reinforce the case. There is little in the history of booty collection to rival the savagery of the conquest of Central and South America by the Spanish conquistadores. The end was gold and valuables; the means included not only conquest but slaughter, capture, enslavement and persistent treachery. Yet these rough and hardened campaigners were restrained by the use of writing in two ways. The Spanish crown took one fifth of all booty and its collection was monitored by royal officials who accompanied the expeditions. One particularly bloody expedition into the interior of what is now Venezuela was led by Federmann, as the direct result of loans made by German bankers to the Emperor Charles V. It is recorded that the royal treasurer, Antonio de Naveros, was shocked at the way Federmann accepted presents of gold without keeping a proper financial record (Hemming 1978: 27). The slaughter was of less concern than the book-keeping.

   Not long after this expedition, the conquistadores captured large numbers of gold objects in their attack on the Muisca of present-day Colombia. In June 1598 the treasure was brought together to be melted down. As on other expeditions, all of which had to be approved by the King, a royal official kept account of what was captured, as did the leader himself. So the first step was to compare the records of the two. Every participant was then searched for hidden gold or jewels. After common debts had been paid, the army was divided into three parts, captains, horsemen and soldiers, each of which named an assessor. When everything had been valued, a paltry 200 pesos was provided for two churches to be used to pay alms for the 500 dead of the expedition. The next day the three royal officials presented the booty to the leader of the expedition extracting one-fifth for the king. The rest was divided among the participants. Despite this careful accounting, the leader, Jimenez de Quesada, was later accused by some men who had been left behind on the way and yet who demanded a share, while the fiscal charged that he had disclosed only a fraction of the amount due to the

Crown. As a lawyer he defended himself brilliantly and got off with a small fine (Hemming 1978: 95–6). The problems of booty production and the importance of an exact record run through the history of the whole process of looting South America of its gold and valuables.

The second way in which the written tradition acted as a restraining factor upon these savage conquerors has to do with religion. Part of the justification for the conquest and enslavement of other peoples by the Spanish and Portuguese had been the belief that captivity conferred upon them the benefits of the Christian religion. The bulk of the slaves came from Africa. Before leaving Angola for the New World the human cargo was usually gathered in a church and told about the Christian religion, baptized and given a piece of paper on which their new (Christian) names had been written (Bowser 1974: 47). Their names, religion, status, all were changed by means of that piece of paper. This was their card of identity. But in addition, their chests were marked with the royal arms of Spain, a proof of baptism but also a brand, a property mark.

While the first conquistadores enslaved many Indians in America, objections of a moral and ecclesiastical kind were later raised by both church and king. As a result of this debate, it was decided that while it was permissible to fight and enslave the infidel Moors of Africa who had already heard about Christianity and rejected it, those who had had no such opportunity were in a different position. So a written proclamation, known as the Requirement, had to be read aloud, through interpreters if possible, before a Spanish attack took place. After being given a brief history of the world, describing the Papacy and the Spanish monarchy, the natives were required to accept the King as their ruler on behalf of the Pope and to allow the preaching of Christianity in their lands. Failure to comply immediately made the listeners liable to attack and subsequent enslavement, the proclamation ending with the words "we protest that any deaths or losses that result from this are your fault" (Hemming 1978: 37–8). The reading not only legitimized the attack but transferred the blame and deleted the guilt. The extraordinary transforming power believed to be vested in the written word verges on the 'magical', although it is illustrative of its authority in the political and legal systems that were about to be established.

3. Of treaties concluded by Mari, Dalley writes that the "agreement was recorded on a tablet which contained the various clauses that had to be agreed in advance. Both parties would seal the tablet since it was a legal contract. Each would possess a copy with identical clauses but a rather different prologue, and we know from slightly later evidence that a copy was deposited in a temple in each country" (1984: 140).

4. "We find in treaties of the second millennium BC expressions taken *verbatim* from those in a treaty of Naram-Sin of Akkad in the twenty-fourth century BC" (Woolley 1963: 507).

5. The difficulty of continuing a commercial enterprise after the death of the founder is always problematic but in Africa there are particular difficulties. There the development of an individual's enterprise into a family firm (which one might call the shift from enterpreneurship to business) is made difficult not only by inadequate bureaucratic experience but also by the prevalence of fraternal inheritance. This type of transmission is related to corporate rights in land, but it is problematic under conditions where an enterprise may devolve upon a 'brother' whose skills are of a different order rather than a 'son' who has been trained for the job (see Goody 1970).

6. The distinction rests upon a more widely recognized one between inherited and self-acquired property, see Fortes (1949). For a discussion of the concept of office in Asante, see Fortes (1962).

7. On this question see the discussion of Fallers (1956: 244) on Parsons and Freud concerning the 'psychogenetic' roots of nepotism and solidary cliques.

8. This is just one meaning of that ambiguous word 'corporate'; see Radcliffe-Brown 1935, and my earlier comment on this point (Goody 1969: 95).

9. The sword was used in the Eastern Gonja division of Kpembe; elsewhere, as in Asante, it was generally the spokesman's staff.

10. I use the term 'decentralization' in preference to non-centralization since the evidence suggests that political de-evolution had taken place before the advent of the British.

11. Oppenheim also calls attention to the work of J. N. Wilson on 'The assembly of a Phoenician city' *Journal of Near Eastern Studies* 4 (1945), as well as the study of a Soviet historian, G. Kh. Sarkisian on 'The self-governing city of Selucid Babylonia' (1952). See also R. M. Adams 1965. It has been suggested that at Assur the system of naming years after officials already represents the abolition of life kingship that may have formed a model for the Greeks (Larsen 1976: 192).

12. In Roman Egypt the 'popular' uses of writing lay in the legal and economic domains. Small-scale as it was, Athens employed writing in a form of voting, while debate was stimulated by the rendering of laws, of information, modes of argument, even the speeches of the orators themselves, in visible language. The power of writing made itself felt in a number of political contexts.

13. One surprising example of the use of writing for such a purpose occurred in the revolt of blacks, both slaves and freedmen, in Bahia, Brazil, in 1835. Captives of mainly Yoruba and Hausa origin were apparently inspired by the *Jihād* of Uthman dan Fodio of 1807 in Nigeria in which texts played an important part in the reform of the country and in the loyalties of the faithful. In Bahia, too, they started Islamic schools, issued written proclamations as well as using writing to organize the revolt. It was widely thought by the authorities that literacy was a major factor in its successful organization, as a result of

which they forced the freedmen who could read and write to return to West Africa (Goody, forthcoming: b).

14. Of course a similar protection of the superior takes place in literate administrations but is less easy to conceal. For an interesting example see Prebble's account of the Glencoe massacre (1966) which turns upon the interpretation (including the neglect) of written orders. In part it is the question of the blind eye, which is often easier to cultivate than the deaf ear.

4. The letter of the law

1. See for instance the action of the two rectors of the Breton island of Hoedic in the first quarter of the nineteenth century who "élaborèrent une 'constitution' commune". They looked at old family practices, usages, rights, and old customs and then 'codified' them (Jorion 1983: 42, quoting Escard 1897).
2. Fallers remarks that he first thought of the concept *mu-lao* as a Bantu form of the English 'law', but Gluckman convinced him that this was not so (1969: 331–2).
3. See Diamond 1971: 45, where he notes a report by Ephorus, preserved by Strabo, to the effect that the Greek legislators fixed the sanctions and no longer left them to be assessed at the arbitrary will of the judges. Equally, colonial legislators in Africa wanted a written code to increase certainty in law, ironing out local variations and seeking 'an authorized version' (Epstein 1967: 209).
4. Among the Tswana an aggrieved person appealed to the chief if a will departed to any considerable extent from the ordinary rules of inheritance (Schapera 1938: 230). For modern Yoruba, see Lloyd 1962: 290ff. (Diamond 1971: 376).
5. Baines points out to me that this document is now regarded as a 'law handbook' rather than 'a code', a shift of opinion that has also taken place with regard to the 'code' of Hammurabi (e.g. Bottéro 1982b, Yoffee 1979: 16). My own use of 'code' has been in a less precise sense than is involved in this distinction.
6. Already in Ancient Egypt title to land and other major property (e.g. offices that could be sold) was 'registered' in the sense that documents were deposited in government departments (Baines, personal communication).
7. The words assigned to William are similar to those credited to the Chinese emperor, Hsiao-wen, in the fifth century. "The [*wei*] codes are the great principles of the state and are the means for ordering the people. If the ruler is able to make good his codes, then the state is in order, if he cannot it is in disorder. Our state arose once in [the area of] Hung and Tai and created institutions as the need arose; these are not an enduring code for all ages. Therefore this summer we have per-

sonally taken part in discussing the articles of law" (cited in Dien 1976: 80). Note that the code is seen as the instrument of ordering social relationships but it does so in ways that do not endure for all ages and that overlook the particular. "We should not upset our institutions merely [to accommodate] one [worthy] man", a theme running contrary to the Confucian tradition of elevating men on the basis of talent rather than birth.

8. Precautions of course were taken against this crime. In Mesopotamia the use of envelopes, of copies and of witnesses and oaths (Johns 1904: 80; Larsen 1976: 187) all helped to protect the document or establish its validity.

Bibliography

Abrahams, R. G. 1966. Succession to the chiefship in northern Unyamwezi. In J. Goody (ed.), *Succession to High Office*. Cambridge

Adams, R. M. 1966. *The Evolution of Urban Society: Early Mesopotamia and Prehispanic Mexico*. Chicago

1974. Anthropological perspectives on ancient trade. *Current Anthropology* 15: 239–58

1975. The emerging place of trade in civilizational studies. In J. A. Sabloff and C. C. Lamberg-Karlovsky (eds.), *Ancient Civilizations and Trade*. Albuquerque

Ames, M. 1964. Magical-animism and Buddhism: a structural analysis of the Sinhalese religious system. In E. B. Harper (ed.), *Religion in South Asia*. Seattle

Amiet, P. 1966. Il y a 5000 ans les Elamites inventaient l'écriture. *Archéologia* 12: 20–2

1972. *Glyptique Susienne* (Mém. de la délégation archéologique en Iran, vol. 43). Paris

1982. Introduction historique. In B. André-Leiknam and C. Ziegler (eds.), *Naissance de l'écriture: cunéiformes et hiéroglyphes*. Ministère de la Culture, Paris

Assmann, J. 1983. Schrift, Tod and Identität. Des Grab als Vorschuleder Literatur im alten Ägypten. In A. and J. Assmann and C. Hardmeier (eds.), *Schrift und Gedächtnis: Beiträge zur Archäologie der literarischen Kommunikation*. Munich

1983. *Re und Amun: Die Krise des polytheistischen Weltbilds in Ägypten der 18–10 Dynastie*. Fribourg

Baines, J. 1983. Literacy and ancient Egyptian society. *Man* N.S. 18: 572–99

1985. Theories and universals of representation – Heinrich Schäfer and Egyptian art. *Art History* 8: 1–25

(forthcoming). Review of Assmann (1983). *Journal of Biblical Literature*

Barnes, J. A. 1954. *Politics in a Changing Society: A Political History of the Fort Jameson Ngoni*. Oxford

Barton, R. F. 1949. *Ifugao Law*. Berkeley

Bernand, C. and Gruzinski, S. 1985. La Famille en Mésoamerique et dans les Andes. *Encyclopédie de la Famille*. Paris

Birley, R. 1977. *Vindolanda. A Roman Frontier Post on Hadrian's Wall*. London

Birot, M. 1960. *Textes administratifs de la salle 5 du palais* (Archives royales de Mari, IX). Paris

Black-Michaud, J. 1975. *Cohesive Force: Feud in the Mediterranean and the Middle East*. Oxford

Blainey, G. 1982. *The Tyranny of Distance: How Distance Shaped Australia's History*. Melbourne

Boas, F. 1927. *Primitive Art*. Oslo

Bohannan, P. 1957. *Justice and Judgement among the Tiv*. London

Bottéro, J. 1982a. Écriture et civilization en Mésopotamie. In B. André-Leiknam and C. Ziegler (eds.), *Naissance de l'écriture: cunéiformes et hiéroglyphes*. Ministère de la Culture, Paris
  1982b. Le 'Code' de Hammu-rabi. *Annali della Scuola Normale Superiore du Pisa* 12: 409–44

Bourdieu, P. 1977. *Outline of a Theory of Practice*. Cambridge

Bowdich, T. 1819. *Mission from Cape Coast Castle to Ashantee*. London

Bowser, F. P. 1974. *The African Slave in Colonial Peru 1524–1650*. Stanford

Bracton, H. de 1968. *On the Laws and Customs of England*, ed. G. E. Woodbine, transl. S. E. Thorne, Cambridge, Mass.

British Museum 1963. *Writing in Ancient Western Asia: Its Origin and Development from Pictures to Letters* [Catalogue with slide illustrations]. Repr. London, 1968

Carrithers, M. B. 1983. *The Forest Monks of Sri Lanka: An Anthropological and Historical Study*. Delhi

Chadwick, J. 1959. A prehistoric bureaucracy. *Diogenes* 26: 7–18
  1976. *The Mycenean World*. Cambridge

Clanchy, M. T. 1979. *From Memory to Written Record: England 1066–1307*. London

Cole, M. and Keyssar, H. 1982. The concept of literacy in print and film [manuscript]. Communications program, University California, San Diego

Collins, E. 1962. The panic element in nineteenth-century British relations with Ashanti. *Transactions of the Historical Society of Ghana* 5: 79–144

Collomp, A. 1983. *La Maison du père: famille et village en Haute Provence au XVII et XVIII siècles*. Paris

Colsoon, E. 1950. Possible repercussions of the right to make wills. *Journal of African Administration* 2: 24–34
  1968. Political anthropology: the field. *International Encyclopedia of the Social Sciences* (New York) 12: 189–93

Coquéry-Vidrovitch, C. 1969. Recherches sur un mode de production africain. *La Pensée* 144: 61–78

Dalley, S. 1984. *Mari and Karana: Two Old Babylonian Cities*. London

Dampiere, É. de 1967. *Un ancien Royaume Bandia du Haut-Oubangui*. Paris

Das, S. K. 1930. *The Educational System of the Ancient Hindus*. Calcutta

Daube, O. 1947. *Studies in Biblical Law*. Cambridge

Dewdney, S. 1975. *Scrolls of the Southern Ojibwa*. Toronto

Diamond, A. L. 1971. *Primitive Law, Past and Present*. London [third revised edn of *Primitive Law*]

Dien, A. E. 1976. Elite lineages and the T'o-pa accommodation: a study of the edict of 495. *Journal of the Economic and Social History of the Orient* 19: 61–88

Dumont, L. and Pocock, D. 1957. For a sociology of India. *Contributions to Indian Sociology* 1: 7–22

1959. On the different aspects or levels in Hinduism. *Contributions to Indian Sociology* 3: 40–54

Durkheim, É. 1933. *On the Division of Labour in Society*, transl. G. Simpson. New York (first French edn 1897)

1947. *The Elementary Forms of the Religious Life*, transl. J. W. Swain. Glencoe, Ill. (first French edn 1912)

Dyer, C. 1980. *Lords and Peasants in a Changing Society: the Estates of the Bishopric of Worcester, 680–1540*. Cambridge

Edwards, I. E. S. 1947. *The Pyramids of Egypt*. Harmondsworth, Middlesex (2nd edn 1962)

1971. The early dynastic period in Egypt. In I. E. S. Edwards, C. J. Gadd and N. G. L. Hammond (eds.), *The Cambridge Ancient History*, vol. I, part 2. Cambridge

Eisenstein, E. L. 1979. *The Printing Press as an Agent of Change: Communications and Cultural Transformations in Early Modern Europe*. 2 vols., Cambridge

Epstein, A. L. 1953. *The Administration of Justice and the Urban African: A Study of Urban Native Courts in Northern Rhodesia* (Colonial Research Studies, no. 7). HMSO, London

1954. *Judicial Techniques and the Judicial Process: A Study in African Customary Law* (The Rhodes Livingstone Papers, no. 23). Manchester

1967. The case method in the field of law. In A. L. Epstein (ed.), *The Craft of Social Anthropology*. London

Ernout, A. and Meillet, A. 1951. *Dictionnaire etymologique de la langue latine: histoire des mots*. Paris

Escard, F. 1897. Paroisses et communes autonomes Hoedic et Houat. Solutions anciennes de la question sociale. *Revue internationale scientifique, littéraire et artistique* 4: 55–78

Evans-Pritchard, E. E. 1940. *The Nuer: A Description of the Modes of Livelihood and Political Institutions of a Nilotic People*. Oxford

1956. *Nuer Religion*. Oxford

1971. *The Azande: History and Political Institutions*. Oxford
Falkenstein, A. 1936. *Archaische Texte aus Uruk*. Leipzig
Fallers, L. A. 1956. *Bantu Bureaucracy: A Study of Integration and Conflict in the Political Institutions of an East African People*. Cambridge
1969. *Law Without Precedent*. Chicago
Fauconnet, P. 1920. *La Responsabilité*. Paris
Finley, M. 1983. *Politics in the Ancient World*. Cambridge
Flanagan, J. W. 1979. The relocation of the Davidic capital. *American Academy of Religion* 47: 223–44
1981. Chiefs in Israel. *Study of the Old Testament* 20: 47–73
Fortes, M. 1936. Culture contact as a dynamic process: an investigation in the Northern Territories of the Gold Coast. *Africa* 9: 24–55
1945. *The Dynamics of Clanship among the Tallensi*. London
1949. *The Web of Kinship among the Tallensi*. London
1962. Ritual and office in tribal society. In M. Gluckman (ed.), *Essays on the Ritual of Social Relations*. Manchester
Fortes, M. and Evans-Pritchard, E. E. (eds.) 1940. *African Political Systems*. London
Foucault, M. 1979. On governmentality. *Ideology and Consciousness* 6: 5–21
Frank, A. G. 1981. *Reflections on the World Economic Crisis*. London
Friberg, J. 1978–9. *The Third Millennium Roots of Babylonian Mathematics*, Part 1. Göteborg
Fried, M. 1967. *The Evolution of Political Society*. New York
Friedman, J. 1975. Tribes, states and transformations. In M. Bloch (ed.), *Marxist Analysis and Anthropology* (ASA Studies 3). London
1979. *System, Structure and Contradiction: The Evolution of 'Asiatic' Social Formations* (Social Studies in Oceania and South East Asia, no. 2). Copenhagen
Fuller, C. J. 1984. *Servants of the Goddess: The Priests of a South Indian Temple*. Cambridge
Gadd, C. J. 1971. The dynasty of Agade and the Gutian invasion. In I. E. S. Edwards, C. J. Gadd, and N. G. L. Hammond (eds.), *The Cambridge Ancient History*, vol. II, part 2. Cambridge
Gardiner, A. H. 1947. *Ancient Egyptian Onamastica*. 2 vols. London
Garelli, P. 1969. *Le Proche-Orient asiatique: des origines aux invasions des peuples de la mer*. 2 vols. Paris
Geertz, C. 1980. *Negara: The Theatre State in Nineteenth-century Bali*. Princeton, New Jersey
Gelb, I. J. 1952. *A Study of Writing*. Chicago (second edn 1963)
Gellner, E. 1978. Notes towards a theory of ideology. *L'Homme* 18: 69–82
Glanvill, Ranulf de 1965. [reputed author of] *The Treatise on the Laws and Customs of England, commonly called Glanvil*, ed. G. D. G. Hall. London
Gluckman, M. 1947. African land tenure. *Scientific American* 22: 157–68

1955. *The Judicial Process among the Barotse of Northern Rhodesia*. Manchester

1958. *Analysis of a Social Situation in Modern Zululand*. *Rhodes-Livingstone Paper*, 28

1965. *The Ideas in Barotse Jurisprudence*. New Haven

Godelier, M. 1977. *Perspectives in Marxist Anthropology*. Cambridge

Goedicke, H. 1979. Cult-temple and State during the Old Kingdom in Egypt. In E. Lipiński (ed.), *State and Temple Economy in the Ancient Near East* (Orientalia Loraniensia analecta 5–6). Leuven

Goody, J. 1954. *The Ethnography of the Northern Territories of the Gold Coast, West of the White Volta*. Colonial Office, London

1957. Anomie in Ashanti? *Africa* 27: 356–65

1962. *Death, Property and the Ancestors*. Stanford

1963. Feudalism in Africa? *Journal of African History* 5: 304–45

1966. Circulating succession among the Gonja. In J. Goody (ed.), *Succession to High Office*. Cambridge

1967. The over-kingdom of Gonja. In D. Forde and P. Kaberry (eds.), *West African Kingdoms*. London

1968a. Restricted literacy in northern Ghana. In J. Goody (ed.), *Literacy in Traditional Societies*. Cambridge

1968b. The social organisation of time. *International Encyclopedia of the Social Sciences* 16: 30–42

1969. The classification of double descent systems. *Current Anthropology* 1961 (repr. in *Comparative Studies in Kinship*, Stanford)

1970. Sideways and downwards: lateral and vertical succession, inheritance and descent in Africa and Eurasia. *Man* 5: 627–38

1971. *Technology, Tradition and the State*. London

1972a. *The Myth of the Bagre*. Oxford

1972b. Literacy and the non-literate. *Times Literary Supplement* May 1972, 539–40 (repr. in R. Disch (ed.), *The Future of Literacy*, Princeton)

1975. Religion, social change and the sociology of conversion. In J. Goody (ed.), *Changing Social Structure in Ghana*. London

1977. *The Domestication of the Savage Mind*. Cambridge

1978. Population and policy in the Voltaic region. In J. Friedman and M. Rowlands (eds.), *The Evolution of Social Systems*. London

1980. Rice burning and the Green Revolution in northern Ghana. *Journal of Development Studies* 16: 136–55

1981a. Alphabet and writing. In R. Williams (ed.), *Meanings and Messages: The World of Human Communication*. London

1981b. Sacrifice among the LoDagaa and elsewhere; a comparative comment on implicit questions and explicit rejections. *Systèmes de pensée en Afrique noire: la sacrifice IV*. Cahier 5, CNRS, Ivry, 9–22

1982. *Cooking, Cuisine and Class*. Cambridge

1983. *The Development of Family and Marriage in Europe*. Cambridge

1986. The construction of a ritual text. *Proceedings of Berlin Conference on Ritual*

(forthcoming: a). The economic base of British Social Anthropology between the wars (m.s.)

(forthcoming: b). Writing, religion and revolt in Bahia. *Visible Language*

Goody, J. (ed.) 1978. *Literacy in Traditional Societies*. Cambridge

Goody, J., Cole, M. and Scribner, S. 1977. Writing and formal operations: a case study among the Vai. *Africa* 47: 289–304

Goody, J. and Watt, I. P. 1963. The consequences of literacy. *Comparative Studies in Society and History* 5: 304–45

Green, M. 1981. The construction and implementation of the cuneiform writing system. *Visible Language* 15: 345–72

Guigue, M. C. 1863. *De l'Origine de la signature et de son emploi au moyen âge principalement dans le pays de droit écrit*. Paris

Gulliver, P. J. 1963. *Social Control in an African Society. A Study of the Arusha, Agricultural Masai of Northern Tanganyika*. Boston

Gunawardana, R. A. L. H. 1979. *Robe and Plough: Monasticism and Economic Interest in Early Medieval Sri Lanka* (Association for Asian Studies No. 35). Tucson, Arizona

Harris, R. 1961. On the process of secularization under Hammurabi. *Journal of Cuneiform Studies* 15: 117–20

Hart, K. 1961. *The Concept of Law*. London

Hawkins, J. D. 1979. The origin and dissemination of writing in Western Asia. In P. R. S. Moorey (ed.), *Origins of Civilization* (Wolfson College Lectures, 1978). Oxford

Hébert, J. C. 1961. Analyse structurale des géomancies comoriennes, malagaches et africaines. *Journal de la Société des Africanistes* 31: 115–208

1965. La cosmographie malgache suivie de l'énumération des points cardinaux et l'importance du nord-est. *Taloha I. Annales de la faculté des lettres*, Université de Madagascar

Hemming, J. 1978. *The Search for El Dorado*. London

Herskovits, M. J. 1938. *Dahomey, an Ancient West African Kingdom*, 2 vols. London

Hocart, A. M. 1950. *Caste*. London

Homans, G. C. 1942. *English Villagers of the Thirteenth Century*. Cambridge, Mass.

Hopkins, K. (forthcoming). Literacy, monetization and obsessional record-keeping in two Egyptian villages

Hornung, B. 1982. *Conceptions of God in Ancient Egypt, The One and the Many*, transl. J. Baines. Ithaca, New York (German edn 1971)

Howe, J. 1979. The effects of writing on the Cuna political system. *Ethnology* 18: 1–16

1985. *The Kuna Gathering*. Stanford

Humphreys, S. 1985. Law as discourse. In S. Humphreys (ed.), The Discourse of Law, *History and Anthropology* 1: 241–64

1985. Social relations on stage: witnesses in Classical Athens. In S. Humphreys (ed.), The Discourse of Law, *History and Anthropology* 1: 313–69

(forthcoming). 'La solidarité de la famille': kin as witnesses in ancient Athenian law courts

Ingalls, D. 1959. The Brahman tradition. In M. Singer (ed.), *Traditional India: Structure and Change*. American Folklore Society, Philadelphia

Jacobsen, Th. 1943. Primitive democracy in Ancient Mesopotamia. *Journal of Near Eastern Studies* 2: 159–72

James, T. G. H. 1979. *An Introduction to Ancient Egypt* (rev. edn). London

Janssen, J. J. 1982. Gift-giving in ancient Egypt as an economic feature. *Journal of Egyptian Archaeology* 68: 253–8

Johns, C. H. W. 1904. *Babylonian and Assyrian Laws, Contracts and Letters*. Edinburgh

Jorion, P. 1983. *Les Pêcheurs d'Houat*. Paris

Kaberry, P. 1957. Primitive states. *British Journal of Sociology* 8: 224–34

Kern, F. 1939. *Kingship and Law in the Middle Ages*, transl. S. B. Chrimes. Oxford

Kramer, F. W. 1970. *Literature among the Cuna Indians*. Göteborg

Kramer, S. N. 1956. *From the Tablets of Sumer: Twenty-five Firsts in Man's Recorded History*. Indian Springs, Colo.

Landsberger, B. 1937. *Materialien zum Sumerischen Lexikon*. 1 Die Serie ana ittišu. Rome

Larsen, M. T. 1967. *Old Assyrian Caravan Procedures*. Istanbul

1974. The Old Assyrian colonies in Anatolia. *Journal of the American Oriental Society* 94: 468–75

1976. *The Old Assyrian City State and its Colonies*. Copenhagen

Last, M. 1967. *The Sokoto Caliphate*. London

Leach, E. 1954. *The Political Systems of Highland Burma: A Study of Kachin Social Structure*. London

Le Brun, A. and Vallat, F. 1978. L'Origine de l'écriture à Suse. *Cahiers de la délégation archéologique française en Iran* 8: 15–18

Levtzion, N. 1966. Early nineteenth century Arabic manuscripts from Kumasi. *Transactions of the Historical Society of Ghana* (1965) 8: 99–119

Lieberman, S. J. 1980. Of clay pebbles, hollow clay balls, and writing: a Sumerian view. *American Journal of Archaeology* 84: 339–58

Llewellyn, K. N. and Hoebel, E. A. 1961. *The Cheyenne Way*. Norman, Oklahoma

Lloyd, A. B. 1983. The Late Period, 664–323 BC. In B. G. Trigger *et al.*, *Ancient Egypt: A Social History*. Cambridge

Lloyd, G. E. R. 1979. *Magic, Reason and Experience: Studies in the Origin and Development of Greek Science*. Cambridge

Lloyd, P. C. 1962. *Yoruba Land Law*. London

Lopez, R. S. 1952. The trade of medieval Europe: the South. In M. M. Postan and E. E. Rich (eds.), *The Cambridge Economic History of Europe*, vol. II, *Trade and Industry in the Middle Ages*. Cambridge

MacChapin, N. 1983. Curing among the San Blas Cuna. Ph.D. dissertation, University of Arizona

Maine, H. S. 1931. *Ancient Law*. London (first edn 1861)

Malamat, A. 1973. Tribal societies: biblical genealogies and African lineage systems. *Archives Européenes de Sociologie* 14: 126–36

Malinowski, B. 1938. Introductory essay on the anthropology of changing African cultures. *Methods of Study of Culture Contact in Africa* (International Institute of African Languages and Cultures, Memorandum 15). London

Marriott, M. 1955. Little communities in an indigenous civilization. In M. Marriot (ed.), *Village India*. Chicago

Matthiae, P. 1980. *Ebla: An Empire Rediscovered*. London (Italian edn 1979)

Mellaart, J. 1968. Anatolian trade with Europe and Anatolian geography and culture provinces in the late Bronze Age. *Anatolian Studies* 18: 187–202

Morley, S. G. and Brainerd, G. W. 1983. *The Ancient Maya*, rev. by R. J. Sharer. Stanford

Morris, H. S. 1953. *Report on a Melanau Sago Producing Community in Sarawak* (Colonial Research Studies, no. 9). London

Murdock, G. P. 1959. *Africa, its Peoples and their Culture History*. New York

Murra, J. V. 1980. *The Economic Organisation of the Inka State*. Greenwich, Conn.

Nadel, S. F. 1942. *A Black Byzantium*. London

Nash, M. 1968. Economic Anthropology. *International Encyclopaedia of the Social Sciences* (New York) 4: 359–65

Neugebauer, O. and Sachs, A. 1945. *Mathematical Cuneiform Texts* (American Oriental Series, 2). New Haven

Nordenskiöld, E. 1938. *An Historical and Ethnological Study of the Cuna Indians*. Göteborg

Obeyesekere, G. 1963. The great tradition and the little in the perspective of Sinhalese Buddhism. *Asian Studies* 22: 139–53

O'Connor, D. 1983. New Kingdom and Third Intermediate Period, 1552–664 BC. In B. G. Trigger *et al.*, *Ancient Egypt: A Social History*. Cambridge

Oppenheim, A. L. 1954. The seafaring merchants of Ur. *Journal of the American Oriental Society* 74: 6–17

1959. An operational device in Mesopotamian bureaucracy. *Journal of Near Eastern Studies* 18: 121–8

1964. *Ancient Mesopotamia: Portrait of a Dead Civilization*. Chicago

1978. Man and nature in Mesopotamian civilization. *Dictionary of Scientific Biography* (ed. C. C. Gillespie), vol. XV, suppl. 1. New York

Ordericus Vitalis 1854. *The Ecclesiastical History of England*, transl. T. Forster. London

Parsons, T. 1937. *The Structure of Social Action*. Glencoe, Ill.

1947. Introduction to M. Weber, *The Theory of Social and Economic Organization*, transl. A. R. Henderson and T. Parsons. Edinburgh

1951. *The Social System*. Glencoe, Ill.

1960. *Structure and Process in Modern Society*. Glencoe, Ill.

Pettinato, G. 1981. *The Archives of Ebla: An Empire Inscribed in Clay*. New York

Piggott, S. 1950. *Prehistoric India to 1000 BC*. Harmondsworth, Middlesex

Planiol, M. and Ripert, G. 1925–34. *Traité practique de droit civil frančais*. Paris

Polanyi, K. *et al.* 1957. *Trade and Markets in the Early Empires*. Glencoe, Ill.

Pospisil, L. J. 1958. *Kapauku Papuans and their Law*. New Haven

Postgate, J. N. 1974. *Taxation and Conscription in the Assyrian Empire* (Studia Pohl, series maior 3). Rome

Pound, R. 1942. *Social Control through Law*. New Haven

Powell, H. A. 1981. Three problems in the history of cuneiform writing: origins, direction of script, literacy. *Visible Language* 15: 419–40

Prebble, J. 1966. *Glencoe: The Story of the Massacre*. London

Pryor, F. L. 1977. *The Origins of the Economy: A Comparative Study of Distribution in Primitive and Peasant Economies*. New York

Radcliffe-Brown, A. R. 1933. Primitive law. *Encyclopaedia of the Social Sciences* (New York) 9: 202–6

1935. Patrilineal and matrilineal succession. *Iona Law Review* 20: 286–303

1940. Preface to M. Fortes and E. E. Evans-Pritchard (eds.), *African Political Systems*. London

Rattray, R. S. 1929. *Ashanti Law and Constitution*. London

Renger, J. 1979. Interaction of temple, palace and 'private enterprise' in the Old Babylonian economy. In E. Lipiński (ed.), *State and Temple Economy in the Ancient Near East* (Orientalia Lovaniensia analecta 5–6). Leuven

Robertson Smith, R. 1889. *The Religion of the Semites*. London

de Roover, R. 1963. The organization of trade. In M. M. Postan, E. E. Rich and E. Miller (eds.), *The Cambridge Economic History of Europe*, vol. III, *Economic Organization and Policies in the Middle Ages*. Cambridge

Sahlins, M. 1958. *Social Stratification in Polynesia*. Seattle

Schapera, I. 1938. *A Handbook of Tswana Law and Custom*. London (second edn 1955)

1955. The sin of Cain. *Journal of the Royal Anthropological Institute* 85: 33–43

Schmandt-Besserat, D. 1977. An archaic recording system and the origin of writing. *Syro-Mesopotamian Studies* 1/2: 1–32

1978. The earliest precursors of writing. *Scientific American* 238: 38–47

1980. The envelopes that bear the first writing. *Technological Culture* 21: 357–85

1981a. Decipherment of the earliest tablets. *Science* 211: 283–4

1981b. From tokens to tablets: a revaluation of the so-called 'numerical tablets'. *Visible Language* 15: 321–44

1982a. How writing came about. *Zeitschrift für Papyrologie und Epigraphik* 47: 1–5

1982b. The emergence of recording. *American Anthropologist* 84: 871–8

1983. Tokens and counting. *Biblical Archaeology* 46: 117–20

1984. Before numerals. *Visible Language* 18: 48–60

Schoske, S. and Wildung, D. 1984. *Nofret die Schöne: die Frau in alten Ägypten*. Cairo and Mainz

Schulz, F. H. 1936. *Principles of Roman Law*, transl. M. Wolff. Oxford

Seagle, W. 1937. Primitive law and Prof. Malinowski. *American Anthropologist* 39: 275–90

Semenov, Y. I. 1980. The theory of socio-economic formations and world history. In E. Gellner (ed.), *Soviet and Western Anthropology*. London

Shils, E. 1962. The theory of mass society. *Diogenes* 39: 45–66

Smith, M. G. 1960. *Government in Zazzau*. London

1968. Political anthropology: political organization. *International Encyclopaedia of the Social Sciences* (New York) 12: 193–202

Smith, R. S. 1985. Rule-by-record and rule-by-reports: complementary aspects of British imperial rule of law. *Contributions to Indian Sociology* N.S. 19: 153–76

Southall, A. W. 1953. *Alur Society*. Cambridge

Southwold, M. 1961. *Bureaucracy and Chiefship in Buganda* (East African Studies, No. 14). Kampala

Srinivas, M. N. 1956. A note of Sanscritization and Westernization. *Far Eastern Quarterly* 15: 481–96

Stock, B. 1983. *The Implications of Literacy: Written Languages and Models of Interpretation in the Eleventh and Twelfth Centuries*. Princeton

Stocking, G. W. 1979. *Anthropology at Chicago: Tradition, Discipline, Department* [exhibition catalogue for the Regenstein Library]. Chicago

Suret-Canale, J. 1961. *Afrique Noire*. Paris

Tambiah, S. J. 1970. *Buddhism and the Spirit Cults in North-east Thailand*. London

Thomas, K. V. 1978. *Religion and the Decline of Magic: Studies in Popular Beliefs in 16th-century and 17th-century England*. Harmondsworth, Middlesex (first edn 1971)

1983. *Man and the Natural World: Changing Attitudes in England 1500–1800*, London

Thompson, E. P. 1975. *Whigs and Hunters. The Origin of the Black Act*. Harmondsworth, Middlesex

Trigger, B. G. *et al.*, 1983. *Ancient Egypt: A Social History*. Cambridge

Turkle, S. 1984. *The Second Self: Computers and the Human Spirit*. New York

Tylor, E. B. 1871. *Primitive Culture*. London

Udovitch, A. 1985. Islamic law and the social context of exchange in the medieval Middle East. In S. Humphreys (ed.), The Discourse of Law. *History and Anthropology* 1: 445–65

Veenhof, K. 1972. *Aspects of Old Assyrian Trade and its Terminology* (Studia et Documenta ad Iura Orientis Antiqui Pertinentia, vol. 10). Leiden

Walton, L. 1984. Kinship, marriage and status in Song China: a study of the Lou lineage of Ningbo; *c.* 1050–1250. *Journal of Asian Studies* 8: 35–77

Weber, M. 1947a. *The Theory of Social and Economic Organization*, transl. A. R. Henderson and T. Parsons. Edinburgh

1947b. Religious rejections of the world and their directions. In H. H. Gerth and G. W. Mills (transls. and eds.), *From Max Weber*. London

1947c [1919]. Politics as vocation. In H. H. Gerth and C. W. Mills (transls. and eds.), *From Max Weber*. London, 1961

Weil, T. E. *et al.* 1972. *Area Handbook for Panama*. Washington

Wheatley, P. 1975. Sātyanṛta in Suvarṅadvīpa: From reciprocity to redistribution in ancient Southeast Asia. In J. A. Sabloff and C. C. Lamberg-Karlovsky (eds.), *Ancient Civilizations and Trade*. Albuquerque

White, L. 1940. Technology and invention in the Middle Ages. *Speculum* 15: 141–58

1962. *Medieval Technology and Social Change*. Oxford

Wilks, I. 1966. Aspects of bureaucratization in Ashanti in the nineteenth century. *Journal of African History* 7: 215–32

Wilson, J. N. 1945. The assembly of a Phoenician city. *Journal of Near Eastern Studies* 4: 245

Wittfogel, K. A. 1957. *Oriental Despotism: A Comparative Study of Total Power*. New Haven

Woolley, L. 1963. *Prehistory and the Beginnings of Civilization, History of*

Mankind: Cultural and Scientific Development, vol. 1 part 2 [UNESCO]. London

Yoffee, N. 1977. *The Economic Role of the Crown in the Old Babylonian Period* [Bibliotecha mesopotamica: primary sources and interpretive analyses for the study of Mesopotamian civilization and its influences from late prehistory to the end of the cuneiform tradition, ed. G. Buccellati, vol. 5]. Malibu

  1979. The decline and rise of Mesopotamian civilization: an ethno-archaeological perspective on the evolution of social complexity. *American Antiquity* 44: 5–35

Zuidema, T. 1982. Bureaucracy and systematic knowledge in Andean civilisation. In G. A. Collier, R. L. Rosaldo and J. D. Wirth (eds.), *The Inca and Aztec States, 1400–1800: Anthropology and History*. New York

Index

accounts, 45, 50, 54, 58–62, 65, 72, 76,
  83, 84, 93, 94, 102, 104, 115, 175,
  180, 181
  balancing of, 67–8, 76, 82, 93
  bills, 83
  language employed for, 94
  as non-syntactical language, 94
  palace, 67–8, 93
  see also book-keeping, records
administration, 26, 36, 45, 49, 51, 54,
  55, 57, 64–7, 70, 93–9, 105, 119,
  160, 169
  of food, in Egypt, 65, 66
  introduction of, in Ghana, 113–15
  administrative reforms of Gregorian
    papacy, 160
  administrative role of priests in
    Ancient Near East, 34
  administrative systems, 89
Africa, 3, 4, 7, 9, 43, 46, 68, 69, 83, 85,
  86, 87, 88, 90, 91, 93, 94, 95, 99,
  103, 106, 110, 111, 112, 116, 117,
  118, 125, 126, 130, 131, 136, 145,
  147, 150, 153, 162
  Alur, 89, 111
  Azande, 111
  communication and government,
    106, 107, 108, 109, 110, 111, 114,
    115
  East, 3, 82, 83, 91, 137, 167
  Ethiopia, 100, 146
  literacy, status of, 117–18
  Ngoni, 89, 111
  Nigeria, 20; Nupe of, 118
  North, 99
  Sokoto Caliphate, 112

Southern, 137; Tonga of, 149, 150
Tanzania, 167; Nyamwezi of, 111;
  Kamba chiefdom, 111
Uganda, 117; judicial system, 167
Vizier of Sokoto, 112
West, 22, 29, 53, 56, 65, 68, 95, 99,
  100; medicine shrines in, 173
writing and economy, 82–6
see also Ghana, Lozi, LoDagaa, Vai,
  Tiv, Dahomey, Busoga, Asante,
  Gonja
agendas, 122
agreements, 101, 102, 123; see also
  contracts, transactions
Akkad, 66, 96
  Sargon I of, 96
Akkadian, 36, 80, 99
America, 47, 126, 132
  Central, 94, 95, 156; Indians of, 157
  New Spain, 22
  Panama, 155; Kuna Indians of, 123–4
  Pre-Columbian, 94
  South, 58, 118; Peru, 69; Brazil, 159,
    180; fazienda clergy, 159; Incas, 66;
    quipu, 66, 94
Americas, the, 26, 91, 94; Spanish
  conquest of, 94, 156
Anatolia, 31, 71, 74
  Kanish, 74, 76
Anglo Saxon, 135, 169
  book-right, 149
  England, 155, 160
  'riht', 154, 155
  see also England
archives, 162, 169
Aristotle, 88, 119

1722

Please remember that this is a library book,
and that it belongs only temporarily to each
person who uses it. Be considerate. Do
not write in this, or any, library book.

DATE DUE

AP 8 05			
GAYLORD			PRINTED IN U.S.A.